ROI OTTLEY'S WORLD WAR II

Roi Ottley. Courtesy of the Photographs and Prints Division, Schomburg Center for Research in Black Culture, The New York Public Library, Astor, Lenox and Tilden Foundations.

ROI OTTLEY'S
WORLD WAR II

The Lost Diary of an
African American Journalist

Edited with an introduction by
Mark A. Huddle

 UNIVERSITY PRESS OF KANSAS

Published by the University Press of Kansas (Lawrence, Kansas 66045), which was
organized by the Kansas Board of Regents and is operated and funded by
Emporia State University, Fort Hays State University, Kansas State University,
Pittsburg State University, the University of Kansas, and Wichita State University

Library of Congress Cataloging-in-Publication Data

Ottley, Roi, 1906–1960.
  Roi Ottley's World War II : the lost diary of an African American journalist / edited
with an introduction by Mark A. Huddle.
    p. cm.
  Includes ISBN 978-0-7006-1769-2 (cloth : alk. paper) 1. Ottley, Roi, 1906–1960—Diaries.
2. World War, 1939–1945—Personal narratives, American. 3. World War, 1939–1945—
African Americans. 4. World War, 1939–1945—Journalists. 5. African American journalists—
United States—Diaries. 6. Journalists—United States—Diaries. 7. War correspondents—
United States—Diaries. 8. War correspondents—Europe—Diaries. 9. World War,
1939–1945—Social aspects. 10. African Americans—Civil rights—History—20th century.
I. Huddle, Mark A. II. Title. III. Title: Roi Ottley's World War 2. IV. Title: Roi Ottley's
World War Two.
  D811.5.O86 2011
    940.53′08996073—dc22
                        2010049536

British Library Cataloguing-in-Publication Data is available.

Printed in the United States of America
10 9 8 7 6 5 4 3 2 1

Contents

Acknowledgments

Many people have offered me advice, encouragement, and support as I struggled to bring this modest project to completion. At St. Bonaventure University, the fine staff at the University Archives of the Friedsam Library provided me access to their Ottley collection, answered countless questions, and tracked down photographs and citations. Archivist Dennis Frank and his staffers Ellen Winger and Alicia Lengvarsky were always patient no matter how crazy the request. This project would not exist at all if it were not for university librarian Paul Spaeth. It was Paul's phone call in the winter of 2004 informing me that he had some papers I might be interested in that set this *Roi Ottley's World War II* in motion. I am in his debt. Likewise, journalist Johanna Neumann was helpful in the early stages of this project. She shared her insights and interpretations of Ottley's work and took time away from her own Ottley project to talk me through a few rough spots.

I would be remiss if I did not also mention my colleagues at both St. Bonaventure and Georgia College and State University, who were always willing to lend an ear as I talked my way through this work of history. At Bonas, I would like to thank Joel Horowitz, Phillip Payne, Karen Robbins, and Tom Schaeper for their friendship and support during my time there. At Georgia College, many thanks to Craig Pascoe and Bob Wilson, who on more than one occasion listened while I rattled on incessantly about Ottley's world.

At the University Press of Kansas, I have incurred many debts. Thanks to Nancy Jackson who years ago recognized the potential of the project. During the middle stages of the project, Kalyani Fernando was my editor. Her kindnesses to me in that period are too many to list. Finally, Ranjit Arab brought this project across the finish line. His counsel was always sound and his patience much appreciated. I did not make it easy on him, but I hope he's proud of our final product. Thank you, Ranjit.

I have been very lucky during my brief time in this profession to have as mentors a group of historians who never cease to inspire me. John Inscoe, John David Smith, Joan Wallach Scott, and Bryant Simon have all at various times provided me with friendship and advice. More important, they have been role models for how to work and perform as a historian. I appreciate that more than I can express.

Finally, I would like to thank my family. My parents, Richard and Jeannine

Huddle, have supported me in myriad ways. Clarice, Macaela, Nicholas, Violet, and Iris, I love you all so much. To my wife, Beth, what a long, strange trip it has been. But I couldn't imagine the journey without you. This book is dedicated to you. Peace and much love.

✪ INTRODUCTION

Roi Ottley's War: Black Internationalism and the Long Freedom Struggle

In 1958, *Sepia*, a photojournalism magazine dedicated to chronicling the achievements of African Americans, presented its readers with a curious query: "What became of Roi Ottley?" The question must have struck Ottley as at least a little odd. At age fifty-two, he was a fixture in Chicago journalism, having been a columnist for both the *Chicago Defender* and the *Chicago Tribune*. His show on the Windy City's radio station WGN was wildly popular. He'd dabbled in African American history and biography. He was completing his first novel. *Sepia*'s implication that his celebrity was in eclipse must have stung the proud Ottley just a bit.[1]

In fact, Roi Ottley's career trajectory had been erratic. During the 1940s, he seemed to be everywhere. He burst onto the national literary scene in 1943 with his best-selling description of life in African America, *New World A-Coming*. Ottley parlayed that success into a military commission and a prolonged stint as a war correspondent, publishing regularly with the labor newspaper *PM* as well as the *Pittsburgh Courier*. After the war, he continued to cover international events for the *Courier*, and experiences from his travels provided the raw material for his book *No Green Pastures*, a comparative study of American and European race relations that was published in 1951.

Unfortunately, critics and readers alike rejected Ottley's controversial book, and work as a freelance writer was difficult to come by. To make matters worse, his personal life was in chaos. Those factors contributed to his decision to leave Harlem and relocate to Chicago in search of a new start. Ottley found success there but on a far more local basis than before. Rarely did he find himself in the national spotlight: hence *Sepia*'s curiosity as to his whereabouts.

1. "What Became of Roi Ottley?" *Sepia*, September 1960, 60.

[1]

Two years after the magazine piece was published, Ottley was dead of a heart attack at the age of fifty-four. Since then, his writing has receded from historical memory. To be sure, his most-cited work, *The Lonely Warrior,* a biography of *Chicago Defender* editor Robert Abbott, is still used by scholars in the field, and *New World A-Coming* garners the occasional footnote. In addition, some of his magazine pieces from the 1940s have been anthologized. But for the most part, Ottley and his work have been forgotten.[2]

Trends in the literature of American race relations and recent archival discoveries have made necessary a reevaluation of the man and his writing. Ottley was one of the great observers. As a reporter, columnist, and editor at the *Amsterdam News,* he was a ubiquitous figure in the Harlem of the 1930s. He was witness to the depths of the economic catastrophe there, and he documented and at times participated in the great political groundswell that swept through the community and much of Black America during the Great Depression. He covered the rise of his childhood friend, Adam Clayton Powell, Jr., and wrote about the "Don't Buy Where You Can't Work" campaign. He reported on the protests surrounding the Italian invasion of Ethiopia and on the Spanish civil war. He was involved in labor politics as well as the political organizing surrounding the National Negro Congress (NNC).

When his politicking cost him a position at the *Amsterdam News,* he went to work for the Harlem branch of the Federal Writers' Project (FWP), where he supervised a team that included Ralph Ellison, Richard Wright, Waring Cuney, Ellen Tarry, and Dorothy West. His employment with the Works Progress Administration (WPA) came to an end when the growing anticommunist hysteria cost his division precious funding. After World War II began, Ottley used his connections in organized labor to land a position as publicity director of the National CIO War Relief Committee. Commissioned as a captain in the U.S. Army in 1944, he spent the remaining war years covering events in Europe, North Africa, and the Middle East.

2. Accurate biographical material about Ottley is difficult to come by. Archival materials are scarce, and there is little extant correspondence in other collections. Information in interviews is often conflicting. The Roi Ottley Collection at St. Bonaventure University contains much of what is known about Ottley's early life. Also of use is Jenifer W. Gilbert, "Vincent Lushington Ottley," in *American National Biography,* ed. John A. Garraty and Mark C. Carnes (New York: Oxford University Press, 1999), 16:844–845; Luther P. Jackson, Jr., and John Garaty, eds., "Roi Ottley," *Dictionary of American Biography,* suppl. 6, 1956–1960 (New York: Charles Scribner's Sons, 1980); Dexter Teed, "Ottley Sees New World A-Coming," *New York Post Daily Magazine,* April 7, 1944, 1; and Obituary, "Roi Ottley Dies; Wrote on Negro," *New York Times,* October 2, 1960, 80. Also particularly useful is Alan Bernard Delozier, "An Examination of Racial Relations in Great Britain and the United States, 1942–1945, by Black American Journalist Roi Ottley" (master's thesis, Villanova University, 1998). Delozier was able to track down and interview Ottley's few living family members, mostly from his brother's family.

In recent years, historians of the civil rights movement have focused increasing attention on the decades immediately preceding the so-called classical period of the movement, which began ostensibly with the 1954 decision in *Brown v. Board of Education of Topeka*. They have attempted to break free of traditional periodization and geographical constraints that have rooted histories of the movement in the South.[3] We have also witnessed the emergence of an important literature that has "internationalized" the struggle and viewed it through a global lens of anticolonialism, anti-imperialism, and antifascism.[4] Top-down histories that begin with federal intervention no longer suffice. The role of organized labor and Left political parties and organizations, the energies unleashed by the New Deal, and the galvanizing effects of World War II are all seen as components in what historian Jacqueline Dowd Hall has termed the "long civil rights movement."[5]

In Hall's formulation, this preclassical period saw the development of a coalitional politics that fused civil rights agitation with radical demands for economic democracy and social justice. The period offered a window of opportunity when it appeared the politics of the Popular Front, energized during the war by the rhetoric of anti-Nazism and the "Double V" campaign (victory over fascism abroad and racism at home), as well as by FDR's prolabor policies, would bear fruit. It was also a moment when African Americans drew very public connections between American racism and the anti-Semitism of the Nazi Holocaust and tied their own struggles at home to national liberation movements around the globe. As Martha Biondi has noted, 500,000 African American troops deployed in Africa, the Pacific, and Europe had ringside seats to witness the crumbling of Euro-

---

3. See Glenda Elizabeth Gilmore, *Defying Dixie: The Radical Roots of Civil Rights, 1919–1950* (New York: W. W. Norton, 2008); Martha Biondi, *To Stand and Fight: The Struggle for Civil Rights in Postwar New York City* (Cambridge, MA: Harvard University Press, 2003); Robert O. Self, *American Babylon: Race and the Struggle for Postwar Oakland* (Princeton, NJ: Princeton University Press, 2005); Robert Korstad and Nelson Lichtenstein, "Opportunities Found and Lost: Labor, Radicals, and the Early Civil Rights Movement," *Journal of American History* 75 (December 1988): 786–811; Korstad, *Civil Rights Unionism: Tobacco Workers and the Struggle for Democracy in the Mid-Twentieth Century South* (Chapel Hill: University of North Carolina Press, 2003); and Steven F. Lawson, *Running for Freedom: Civil Rights and Black Politics in America since 1941* (New York: Wiley-Blackwell, 2008).

4. Brenda Gayle Plummer, *Rising Wind: Black Americans and US Foreign Affairs, 1936–1960* (Chapel Hill: University of North Carolina Press, 1996); Penny Von Eschen, *Race against Empire: Black Americans and Anticolonialism, 1937–1957* (Ithaca, NY: Cornell University Press, 1997); Thomas Borstelmann, *The Cold War and the Color Line: American Race Relations in the Global Arena* (Cambridge, MA: Harvard University Press, 2003); and Mary L. Dudziak, *Cold War Civil Rights: Race and the Image of American Democracy* (Princeton, NJ: Princeton University Press, 2000).

5. Jacquelyn Dowd Hall, "The Long Civil Rights Movement and the Political Uses of the Past," *Journal of American History* 91 (March 2005): 1233–1263.

pean colonialism.[6] Many thousands returned home believing that Jim Crow would be the next to go.

But ultimately, these "civil rights unionists" and "Black international-ists" went down to defeat. In the immediate postwar period, conservatives turned anticommunism into a "mass-based weapon" and bludgeoned the labor-Left coalitions. According to Glenda Gilmore, southern anticom-munism in particular "eviscerated postwar social justice movements and truncated the civil rights movement that emerged in the 1950s."[7] Southern conservatives painted the civil rights movement red and broke apart the Popular Front coalitions. The movement that did eventually emerge out of the Black church was stripped of its economic and public policy goals and had a far narrower political agenda.

This revision of the traditional civil rights narrative is built on a wildly diverse and often exciting literature, but it is a synthetic framework and not without its critics. Some have noted that in their zeal to roll back tem-poral restrictions, historians of the long movement have homogenized an often conflicted and paradoxical politics, subsuming it under the heading of the "Black freedom movement." The willingness of some to move the Communist Party to the center of the narrative rankles those scholars who would privilege other liberal and noncommunist radicals.[8] For me, the question can be boiled down to what constitutes a movement. To ar-gue that the racial politics of the 1920s and 1930s constituted a movement implies a political coherence that did not exist. Those early decades were marked by significant institution building in the Black community but also a politics of shifting coalitions that would coalesce around particular issues and then break apart. Everywhere, there was evidence of a rising political

6. Biondi, *To Stand and Fight*, 13–14.

7. Gilmore, *Defying Dixie*, 8.

8. The most far-reaching critique of the emerging literature of the "long movement" is Eric Arnes-en's "Reconsidering the Long Civil Rights Movement," *Historically Speaking: The Bulletin of the Historical Society* 10 (April 2009): 31–34. Arnesen takes note of the imprecision of the attempts to reperiodize the movement, worrying that by continually pushing back the genesis of the civil rights movement, scholars risk homogenizing an extremely "messy" and contentious politics. Unfortunately, however, much of Ar-nesen's criticism is ideologically motivated. He singles out Glenda Gilmore's *Defying Dixie* for particular criticism for its emphasis on the role of the Communist Party in this early movement politics. He claims that her focus excludes liberals and noncommunist radicals and cites A. Philip Randolph as a case in point. It is a curious choice, given that Gilmore dedicates long sections of her narrative to Randolph's efforts, and although she certainly privileges the Communist Party, she hardly shortchanges noncom-munist activists. Arnesen challenges the "celebratory" tone of what he clearly considers Left scholarship but implies that all might be well if historians of the long movement would just celebrate someone else. Regardless, Arnesen does highlight important epistemological questions that scholars wrestling with this framework are going to have to tackle.

consciousness. But African American leaders also struggled to find the issues and strategies that would serve as a catalyst to unity.

World War II provided that catalyst. The piecemeal assault on Jim Crow gave way to unified demands for the desegregation of American society as African Americans at the grass roots organized to end racial discrimination in employment, education, and the range of public accommodations. The global fight against fascism provided a dramatic counterpoint to the groundswell at home. Black leaders tied southern racism directly to Nazi ideology, and for a time, Jim Crow was thrown back on its heels. One of the major players in this muscular new politics was the African American press, which often chose advocacy over mere reporting and became the unofficial mouthpiece for an energized movement. Journalist Roi Ottley was an observer of and participant in many of the dramatic events of the interwar period. Then, in 1943, he went to Europe and North Africa to cover the deployment of African American troops. Ottley became more and more certain that the war would undermine Europe's colonial empires, and he was equally confident that the victory over white supremacy abroad would empower civil rights activists at home. This volume is the first collection of his work from this period.

Vincent Lushington "Roi" Ottley was born in Harlem on August 2, 1906. He was the son of Jerome Peter Ottley and Beatrice Maud Brisbane. Ottley's parents were members of the Caribbean diaspora that carried nearly 40,000 immigrants of African descent to Harlem between 1900 and 1930. His father, born in 1882 on the island of Grenada, and his mother, from St. Vincent, both migrated to the United States in 1904. Family lore held that they met on the ship that took them to their new lives.[9] In the early years of the twentieth century, the Caribbean basin was swept up in vast economic dislocations and labor unrest. That turmoil sparked considerable demographic upheaval as the immigrants sought out new employment opportunities. Many were drawn to labor in the burgeoning Panama Canal Zone and then moved on to the United States. Others skipped that Central American way station and directly pursued America's urban promise.[10]

West Indian immigrants had a powerful effect on Harlem race relations. Unlike many Europeans during this last great age of immigration, the Caribbean migrants tended not to be agriculturalists. They had higher educational attainments, and many were skilled workers. Historians have noted the

9. Delozier, "Examination of Race Relations," 15.

10. See Irma Watkins-Owens, *Blood Relations: Caribbean Immigrants and the Harlem Community, 1900–1930* (Bloomington: Indiana University Press, 1996), 11–29; Winston James, *Holding Aloft the Banner of Ethiopia: Caribbean Radicalism in Early Twentieth Century America* (London: Verso, 1998), 26–29.

seemingly ubiquitous presence of West Indians in the leadership of American radical organizations. Hubert Harrison, Richard B. Moore, Cyril V. Briggs, W. A. Domingo, Grace Campbell, and of course Marcus Garvey, just to name a few, rose quickly in Harlem's rough-and-tumble political world.

Most of the new arrivals, however, were not particularly political. They instead wanted only a better life for themselves and their families. Jerome and Beatrice Ottley fit most comfortably in this category. Jerome had an indomitable work ethic. He toiled as a handyman doing odd jobs, and when time permitted, he took business classes at a neighborhood high school. According to one source, by 1916 he had accumulated enough credits to graduate. Soon, he was making a living brokering real estate and selling insurance, while Beatrice worked as a domestic to supplement the family income.[11] By the early 1920s, after years of scrimping and saving, Jerome Ottley hung out his own shingle, opening a real estate brokerage in Harlem. He focused on the elite neighborhoods of Sugar Hill and Striver's Row. At the end of the decade, he could boast to his son that he was managing as many as 100 properties.[12]

By any measure, Roi Ottley was raised as a child of privilege. The family lived in a very comfortable brownstone on Striver's Row. And young Roi was pampered by his parents, especially his mother. Longtime friend Adam Clayton Powell, Jr., remembered that the first time he encountered Ottley as a small child, he turned and asked his buddy W. C. Handy, Jr., "My God, is that a boy or a girl?"[13]

Growing up, Ottley ran with a pack of friends whose names read like a who's who of Harlem society. Along with the future congressman Powell and Handy (the son of "Father of the Blues" W. C. Handy, Sr.), there was also Thomas "Fats" Waller and Frankie Steele, a future physician. The members of the group were nearly inseparable. A precocious and curious bunch, they formed themselves into a club called the Young Thinkers, which met frequently at Powell's father's church, the formidable Abyssinian Baptist. Ostensibly, they envisaged the organization as a discussion and debate society, and they competed against other debate teams in Harlem, including the prestigious Beaux Arts Club.[14] But according to Powell, the group had another preoccupation. In the den they set up underneath the

11. Delozier, "Examination of Race Relations," 15–16.

12. Jerome P. Ottley, Sr., to Roi Ottley, April 21, 1928, in Roi Ottley Collection, St. Bonaventure University Archives, Friedsam Library, St. Bonaventure University, Olean, NY.

13. Adam Clayton Powell, III, *Adam by Adam: The Autobiography of Adam Clayton Powell, Jr.* (New York: Kensington Publishing 1994), 17.

14. Wil Haygood, *The King of the Cats: The Life and Times of Adam Clayton Powell, Jr.* (New York: Amistad, 2006), 2–3.

porch at Ottley's home, they would discuss books pilfered from family elders and "read all the pornographic literature we could beg, borrow or trade. This was our club."[15] It is certainly no surprise that sex might capture the imagination of growing young boys, but it proved a particular temptation to Ottley and his friend Powell.

Ottley came of age in the 1920s, when the so-called Harlem Renaissance was at its peak and the "Negro," as Langston Hughes has written, "was in vogue."[16] The influx of migrants from the South, the Caribbean, and Africa swelled Harlem's already overcrowded neighborhoods. The African American population of New York City exploded during the first thirty years of the twentieth century. Between 1910 and 1920, it increased 66 percent to 152,467. From 1920 to 1930, that population increased 115 percent to 327,706.[17] And Harlem, as historian David Levering Lewis described it, "seemed to flash into being like a nova."[18] It was the sound of the "Black Mecca" that Ottley remembered: "From the windows of countless apartments, against the dull red lights, silhouetted figures rocked and rolled to mellow music. Harlem was dancing to the syncopations of Fletcher Henderson's band and listening to the moanin' low of Bessie Smith. Urchins were happily tricking dance steps on the sidewalks. Laughter was easy, loud."[19]

Harlem in the 1920s had a singular energy, but it also wrestled with the paradox that so often comes with the trappings of success. Yes, the arts, literature, and music flourished. The community was a political hothouse that spawned some of the greatest African American leaders of the century. But its uncontrollable growth laid the foundations for a great human tragedy when the economy collapsed and the high hopes of the decade gave way to futility and misery.

For young Ottley and friends, however, New York was an enormous playground. They attended elementary school at Harlem's P.S. 5. When they were not solving the world's problems as members of the Young Thinkers, they played church-league basketball for Abyssinian Baptist's championship team. In the early twenties, they matriculated at Textile High School. Ottley and Powell were extremely popular. They ran track together, and in 1926, Ottley earned local fame when he won the Citywide Sprinting Championships.

15. Powell, *Adam by Adam*, 26.

16. Langston Hughes, *The Big Sea: An Autobiography* (New York: Hill and Wang, 1993), 223.

17. Gilbert Osofsky, *Harlem: The Making of a Ghetto—Negro New York, 1890–1930*, 2nd ed. (New York: Harper Torchbooks, 1971), 128–129.

18. David Levering Lewis, *When Harlem Was in Vogue* (New York: Penguin Books, 1997), 27.

19. Roi Ottley, *New World A-Coming: Inside Black America* (Boston: Houghton Mifflin, 1943), 59.

But it was the social swirl of what Ottley termed Harlem's "era of noisy vitality" that really appealed to the boys. Ottley wrote in nearly ecstatic tones about that period in his life. From his vantage point, it was a time of great prosperity, when "money seemed to flow from everyone's pockets as easily as laughter from their lips."[20] The streets were filled with the sort of spectacle that was guaranteed to capture the imaginations of young teenage males. Ottley always had an eye for the day-to-day ephemera. He described the street-corner preachers and food vendors, the "policy kings" and prizefighters. He was drawn to the ostentatious living of the "theatrical people" and cultivated a lifelong passion for jazz and musical theater. He saw Charles Gilpin and Paul Robeson on the stage and went with his family to revel in the silky tenor of Roland Hayes.[21]

As he got older, he frequented the clubs and speakeasies—places such as Smalls' Paradise—to hear the jazz musicians "take a Boston" (improvisatory leads) and to dance the "bump" and the "mess around." And then there were the "house-rent parties" that were the entertainment of choice for the Black working class. A mere 15 cents earned a person entrée into a near-empty apartment with an old box-beater piano in one corner and pots of chitterlings and pigs' feet on the stove. "Shorties" (quarter pints) of corn whiskey were dispensed from a makeshift bar, and of course all proceeds went to pay the rent to the landlord the next day. The house-rent parties attracted a very different clientele than the clubs and theaters of the main Harlem thoroughfares. They attracted what Ottley called a "large transient trade" of Pullman porters, truck drivers, and domestics who wanted to take advantage of the short break in their workweek and dance until dawn on Sunday mornings whenever they could.[22]

It wasn't all Jazz Age revelry for the young Ottley. Although his political awakening would come later, at the trough of the Great Depression, Harlem was a political incubator in the 1920s. There were street-corner orators aplenty. Socialists and Black nationalists alike competed against jackleg preachers and assorted cult leaders for the souls of struggling Harlemites. But it was Marcus Garvey and his Universal Negro Improvement Association (UNIA) that made the biggest impression. Ottley was fourteen years old when he witnessed the massive procession of Garvey's 1920 Universal Negro Convention wind its way through the uptown streets. He and his

20. Ibid.
21. Ibid., 59–61.
22. Ibid., 63.

friends watched from the roof of the Abyssinian Baptist Church,[23] and the scene made a dramatic impression on him.

In his later writings, Ottley often adopted an easy, flowing style that moved deftly from the colloquial to the formal. When he wrote about politics, there was always a hint of sarcasm in his tone. Few were spared in his critiques, including his friend Powell, who, late in his life, was left wondering what exactly had happened to their close friendship.[24] Marcus Garvey, by contrast, received a grudging respect. Ottley did poke a little fun at the pomp and circumstance of the Garveyites, and he was critical of what he characterized as Garvey's "anti-mulatto campaign" against the National Association for the Advancement of Colored People (NAACP). But he recognized that for significant elements in Harlem and across the Black world, Garvey was immensely important. He gave people hope. "The cotton-picker of the South, bending over his basket, the poor ignorant worker of the Delta, crushed beneath a load of prejudice, the domestic of the city trudging wearily to white folks' kitchens, and even the peasant of the Caribbean islands, dispossessed of the land, lifted his head and cried, 'Let's go to Harlem and follow this Black Moses!'"[25] Ottley recognized that the kind of fanaticism that men such as Garvey inspired was nearly always their undoing. He himself was no militant and certainly not a nationalist; in fact, he was relatively conservative in his personal politics. But he understood that Garvey energized a grassroots following that would, by the 1940s, account "for much constructive belligerency today."[26]

In 1926, Roi Ottley parlayed his success on the athletic field into a full scholarship to St. Bonaventure University (SBU) in Olean, New York. The Franciscan institution, nestled in western New York's "Enchanted Mountains," seemed an odd choice for such an ardent and confirmed urbanite. Local universities had expressed interest in the young sprinting champion: St. John's, New York University (NYU), and Brooklyn College had offered scholarships.[27] However, two of Ottley's New York friends—Charlie Major and Gus Moore—had been contacted by St. Bonaventure's athletic director, Father Cyprian Mensing, and were headed west. When he, too, received a telegram from Mensing offering an "unconditional track scholarship,"

23. Ibid., 75–76.

24. Powell, *Adam by Adam,* 23.

25. Ottley, *New World A-Coming,* 75.

26. Ibid., 81.

27. Clipping, *New York Amsterdam News,* September 15, 1926, in "Vincent and Jerome Ottley's Memory Book," Roi Ottley Collection, St. Bonaventure University Archives, Friedsam Library, St. Bonaventure University, Olean, NY.

Ottley decided it was time to experience life beyond the confines of Harlem and New York City. Perhaps his decision to go to Bonaventure was influenced by his friend Powell's decision to travel upstate to Colgate University in Hamilton, New York. Regardless, from 1926 to 1928, Ottley was a proud St. Bonaventure man.

It is testimony to his athletic ability that he was sought out along with Major and Moore, both of whom were world-class athletes. Major was born in the Bahamas and moved to New York when he was thirteen. During his career on the track, he won two National Amateur Athletics Union (AAU) championships and a Melrose Games championship, as well as both New England and New York Metropolitan Games championships. He was also a national champion high jumper in 1928. Major won a coveted spot on the 1928 Olympic team but was unable to compete due to injury. Eventually, between 1933 and 1934, he coached the St. Bonaventure track team. Similarly, Gus Moore was a dominant runner and one of only a few nationally who could sometimes defeat Major. In 1926, he placed third at the national championships. He left St. Bonaventure in 1928 and for the next two years competed as a member of the U.S. National Cross Country team. Along with Ottley, Major and Moore were among the first African Americans to attend the university, and for the short time they were together, the triumvirate dominated the regional track and field world.[28]

St. Bonaventure might have been isolated in a rural part of the state, but it had a rich and varied social life—and it did not take Ottley long to find his place there. His scrapbooks are full of clippings, handbills, notices, and ticket stubs. He was a charter member of the school's University Club, which listed among its activities "entertaining pretty women." He also helped to charter the Dumas Club, a group ostensibly created in the service of the performing arts; the fact that the members listed their "club yell" as "booze, booze, booze!" would lead one to believe that perhaps they had other interests as well.[29] Although the African American community in New York State's western counties was comparatively small, Ottley wasted no time in finding female companionship. His scrapbooks feature photographs of young women in Olean and Ellicottville, New York, as well as friends in nearby Bradford, Pennsylvania. Powell was a frequent visitor at SBU, as was Frank Steele, who was going to school not far away, at Alfred

28. "The St. Bonaventure University Track Team," St. Bonaventure University Archives, St. Bonaventure University, http://web.sbu.edu/friedsam/archives/athletics/Track/Meet%20the%20Team.html (accessed January 23, 2010).

29. "Vincent and Jerome Ottley's Memory Book."

University.[30] So despite his rather obscure locale, Roi Ottley seems not to have had much difficulty in maintaining an impressive social schedule.

But Ottley's time at SBU was not simply spent engaging in undergraduate debauchery or in athletic competition. His years at Bonaventure also marked the beginnings of his intellectual awakening. Overall, Ottley was a solid B student. In the two years that he was at the school, he enrolled in a classic liberal arts curriculum. He excelled in geometry, biology, trigonometry, and Latin. He was a voracious reader, listing Rafael Sabatini, Nathanial Hawthorne, Booth Tarkington, Edith Wharton, Jack London, and Walter White as his favorites. He commented in his scrapbooks about how much he enjoyed Professor Enright's English courses. It appears that Enright and Father Gerald McMinn, academic vice president and dean of arts and sciences, were the first to encourage Ottley to write.[31]

The future journalist availed himself of multiple opportunities to learn his craft. He churned out articles, reviews, columns, and editorials for the campus newspaper. In one notable piece that was proudly displayed in his "Memory Book," Ottley assessed the cultural and intellectual life of the school and found it lacking. He urged the formation of debate teams and literary clubs. As an athlete, he argued that a true education had to develop mind, body, and spirit.[32] Along with his journalistic output, Ottley was a frequent contributor to SBU's literary journal, *The Laurel*. He also avidly drew cartoons and comic strips.

Ottley looked back fondly on his years at St. Bonaventure. He told interviewer Dexter Teed that he found no racial prejudices there but was accepted at all social gatherings. His success as an athlete gave him a certain prominence. According to Teed, "He forgot he was a Negro."[33] Unfortunately, that acceptance did not follow him when he transferred to the University of Michigan at the beginning of his junior year. Nothing in Ottley's papers or published writings explains the decision to leave Bonaventure, but he may have been lured by promises from the Michigan track coach because he did compete as a sprinter. He also roomed with future Big Ten and world 100-yard dash champion Eddie "Midnight Express" Tolan. Ottley majored in literature, with a concentration in journalism, and he pledged the Alpha Phi Alpha fraternity. But the overt racism he encountered at the University of Michigan was a rude awakening. He was forbidden to join any of the debating societies, and he was excluded from the drama

---

30. Ibid.
31. Ibid.
32. Ibid., "Track Athlete Asks: 'How about Culture?'"
33. Teed, "Ottley Sees New World A-Coming."

club.[34] Years later in an interview with historian Richard Bardolph, Ottley remembered always feeling like the odd man out. According to Bardolph, while at Michigan Ottley was "affably tolerated as an eccentric Negro who had yet to learn his station."[35] It is no surprise that his Michigan sojourn lasted only one year. He dropped out and returned to New York.

Upon his return, Ottley worked a series of jobs and took classes at schools across the city. He studied playwriting at Columbia and writing for magazines at City College. At NYU, he attended a lecture series by James Weldon Johnson entitled "Negro Contributions to American Culture," which surveyed African American poetry, literature, and folklore. Ottley was much influenced by Johnson's ideas, and eventually, he would produce two collections on Black history: *Black Odyssey: The Story of the Negro in America*, published in 1948, and the posthumous collection (published in 1967) entitled *The Negro in New York: An Informal Social History*, which he edited with William Weatherby.[36] Ottley even did a semester of law school at St. John's before realizing that writing was his one true passion.

Unfortunately, however, without a college degree and with little experience, professional writing jobs were difficult to come by. Ottley meandered through a series of day jobs. He worked variously as a bellhop, a soda jerk, and a railroad porter—and he was lucky to find those jobs. The Harlem he left when he went away to school was no more. The Great Depression exacerbated the economic and social problems already in play during the 1920s, and the results were disastrous. The community already suffered from overcrowding and poor housing conditions, high rents, high food prices, limited access to manufacturing jobs, and a heavy reliance on unskilled labor. As unemployment rose, wages declined. The economic collapse of the 1930s created a perfect storm of misery. Unemployment topped 25 percent. Applications for public assistance, already high, doubled between 1925 and 1930. Private relief agencies saw demand increase by as much as 75 percent. Harlem's churches stepped in to try to stem the tide by providing food and rudimentary health care, but they were overwhelmed by sheer numbers.[37] Of course, the economic turmoil was heightened by racism and ongoing discrimination.

Roi Ottley had a spectacular vantage point for observing the suffering.

34. Ibid.

35. Richard Bardolph, *The Negro Vanguard* (New York: Rinehart, 1959), 250.

36. Roi Ottley, *Black Odyssey: The Story of the Negro in America* (New York: Charles Scribner's Sons, 1948); Roi Ottley and William Weatherby, eds., *The Negro in New York: An Informal Social History* (New York: New York Public Library, 1967).

37. See Cheryl Lynn Greenberg, *"Or Does It Explode?" Black Harlem in the Great Depression* (New York: Oxford University Press, 1991), 18–21, 28–31, 39–47, 56–59.

In 1932, he went to work for the New York Welfare Department as a social worker. He spent his days processing relief applications and trying to find aid for the flood of poor surging through his office. He remained at the Welfare Department until 1937, and in the evenings and on weekends, he helped to administer the relief programs at the Abyssinian Baptist Church.[38] What he witnessed during these years both moved and enraged him. He described the members of the growing underclass as the "slum-shocked." Most of them, he believed, had come from the South as migrants, only to find a "new life . . . composed of greasy and rundown tenements in filthy and evil-smelling, littered, crowded streets." They came looking for hope. Instead, they "became the bulk of destitute slum dwellers." Their situation was beyond desperate.

> Those who came to Harlem lived in unheated railroad flats typical of thousands in the Negro communities of the nation, with dank, rat-infested toilets, footworn nondescript linoleum, dirty walls ripped and unpainted, and roaches creeping about the floors and woodwork. From dark unlit hallways came musty odors mingling with the smell of cooking. Ever present was the cacophony of grinding jukeboxes, squalling infants, and angry argument. For all this, white landlords had the effrontery to hang signs on the buildings specifying, "FOR SELECT COLORED TENANTS ONLY."[39]

To Ottley's thinking, it was no surprise that these conditions provided the dry tinder that exploded into violence on the morning of March 20, 1935, when the Harlem riot buffeted the city. Ten thousand people rampaged through the Harlem streets, destroying millions of dollars in white-owned commercial property. Three were killed, thirty were hospitalized, and over a hundred arrests were made. The violence rang a stark warning bell that was heard across the country.

Also in 1932, Ottley finally convinced the editors of Harlem's *Amsterdam News* to give him some newspaper assignments. As an avid theatergoer and former sportsman, he began by writing an occasional radio and theatrical review column called "Are You Listenin'?" as well as an athletics piece entitled "Sportopics." Slowly, he worked his way up the ladder, assuming greater editorial duties and eventually authoring the popular human interest column "Hectic Harlem"—the column that established Ottley as a celebrity and an influential commentator on local political affairs. His writing

38. Gilbert, "Vincent Lushington Ottley," 845; Delozier, "Examination of Racial Relations," 21.
39. For Ottley's descriptions of Depression-era Harlem, see Ottley, *New World A-Coming*, 153–157.

covered a wide range of political, social, cultural, and racial issues. The more he observed and reported on the political action welling up around him, the more often he became involved in that action.

If the Great Depression visited horrible suffering on the people of Harlem, it also created the crucible in which a new brand of activist politics was forged. There were significant resonances with the mass politics of the UNIA and Asa Philip Randolph's Brotherhood of Sleeping Car Porters. It was a brand of politics that historian Beth Tompkins Bates has termed "new-crowd protest politics," and it was contingent upon direct mass action.[40] This confrontational brand of politics emerged in the context of the widespread economic dislocations, New York City's liberal and antiracist political administration, the liberalizing impact of New Deal policies, and a powerful international impulse that saw the struggles of African America in the context of antifascist, anticolonial, and anti-imperialist movements around the world. It was also a political moment when radical and liberal organizations, trade unions, and civil rights groups joined together in a great "popular front" to drive the nation's political agenda decidedly to the left.[41]

This new brand of confrontational politics had wide appeal, especially among middle-class Harlemites who struggled to fend off the numerous threats to their quality of life. Many walked willingly into the warm embrace of radical organizations such as the Communist Party; others, including Roi Ottley, were never particularly radical but accepted the political agenda of the Popular Front. Jobs, housing, education, and health care were issues that resonated across a broad political spectrum. Whether it was the battle to increase the number of Black doctors, improve care, and end discriminatory practices at Harlem Hospital or the extended protests against area businesses that refused to hire Black labor, the 1930s was a time of political ferment. And Ottley was often in the middle of these campaigns. When the Citizens' League for Fair Play decided that its behind-the-scenes approach to persuading white-owned Harlem businesses to hire within the community was not having the desired effect, Harlem's citizenry took to the picket lines in mass protests. Ottley's columns on the "Don't

40. Beth Tompkins Bates, *Pullman Porters and the Rise of Protest Politics in Black America, 1925–1945* (Chapel Hill: University of North Carolina Press, 2001), 7.

41. Ibid., 15; Greenberg, *"Or Does It Explode?"* 6; Gilmore, *Defying Dixie*, 106–154; Mark Solomon, *The Cry Was Unity: Communists and African Americans* (Jackson: University Press of Mississippi, 1998), 258–284; and Mark Naison, *Communists in Harlem during the Depression* (Urbana: University of Illinois Press, 1983), 169–175.

Buy Where You Can't Work" boycotts were among his earliest pieces of substantive journalism.[42]

The 1930s were also a decade when labor and civil rights issues became increasingly entwined. Until the middle of the decade, unions were notoriously segregated. Twenty-four international unions—ten that were affiliated with the American Federation of Labor (AFL)—excluded African Americans from membership. That brand of labor politics received a considerable jolt in 1935 when the mass-production industries of the AFL bolted and formed the Congress of Industrial Organizations (CIO), welcoming thousands of Blacks into the labor movement for the first time.[43] Ottley not only approved of this dramatic sea change in union politics but also experienced it directly. Despite the fact that the *Amsterdam News* had thrown its editorial support behind much of the grassroots politics and agitation sweeping aross the Harlem landscape—including the "Don't Buy Where You Can't Work" campaign—attempts to unionize its own workforce were met with resistance.

In November 1933, members of the editorial staff applied for membership in the left-leaning American Newspaper Guild. In August 1935, guild members began negotiations with the paper for union recognition and a labor contract. In Ottley's rendering, this was the "first open dispute between organized Negro workers and Negro employers." In response to the union effort, management locked out seventeen members of the editorial board, including Ottley, and thereby touched off an eleven-week strike. The strikers took to the picket line and were soon joined by guild president Heywood Broun and other top African American political leaders, among them Adam Powell and the NAACP's Walter White.[44]

In the context of Harlem politics, Ottley believed the strike forced local leaders to take a position one way or another. Other labor organizations threw their support behind the walkout, including the powerful Harlem Labor Center and Negro Labor Committee. Soon, the strike was a cause célèbre as the representatives of Black and white civic groups sent their members to walk the line. But what made the most powerful impression on Ottley was the number of white guild members from newspapers across the region who flocked to Harlem to man the picket line with their soon-to-be union brothers and sisters. That experience drove home to him the

42. Ottley, *New World A-Coming*, 113–116.

43. For Ottley's positive assessment of this new labor politics, see Ottley, *Black Odyssey*, 264–265.

44. See Ottley, *New World A-Coming*, 281–282; Ottley and Weatherby, *Negro in New York*, 283–284; and Solomon, *Cry Was Unity*, 292.

potential of interracial cooperation. He believed that the *Amsterdam News* strike "dramatized the role of the trade union movement in Negro life."[45]

By October, with protests growing, Mayor Fiorello La Guardia decided to intervene. He asked the principals on both sides to meet with his representative Elinore Herrick, chair of the Regional Labor Board. The paper's majority stockholders, Sadie Warren Davis and her daughter, failed to show up, but guild president Broun and members of the *News* strike committee provided their side of the story. In the meantime, a boycott of the paper and a campaign to persuade advertisers to pull their ads were having the desired effect. Within weeks of the failed mediation effort, the paper agreed to rehire the strikers and negotiate with the guild for a new contract.[46] But the victory proved to be a double-edged sword. The prolonged battle had decimated the paper's finances, and in a move that was part revenge and part financial exigency, the owners claimed that the business was no longer solvent. They let go much of the staff, including many of the former strikers, and declared bankruptcy. Roi Ottley was among those released. In December, the Powell-Savory Corporation purchased the *Amsterdam News* at auction. The new ownership agreed to a union contract but was less kind to those who had been involved in the strike. Tensions grew, and eventually several of the strike leaders who were still on the payroll were terminated. According to Ottley, by 1940 only three of the original strikers were still employed by the *News*.[47]

In the short term, Ottley turned to freelance journalism to pay his bills. But in time, he found his way, as so many writers did in that period, into the Works Progress Administration's Federal Writers' Project. Due to his high public profile and local celebrity, he was made a project supervisor in the Harlem branch of the FWP. The WPA's arts projects provided a lifeline for thousands in the last half of the 1930s. The New Deal agency paid writers to collect folklore and oral histories and to research and write state guidebooks and histories. Ottley supervised a team of writers who researched and wrote about the African American experience in New York. The writers passing through the Harlem project constituted a literary movement all their own. They included Claude McKay, Richard Wright, Ralph Ellison, William Attaway, Dorothy West, Waring Cuney, Ted Poston, Ellen Tarry, and Abram Hill.[48]

45. Ottley and Weatherby, *Negro in New York*, 284.

46. Ibid., 285.

47. Ibid.

48. See Jerrold Hirsch, *Portrait of America: A Cultural History of the Federal Writers Project* (Chapel Hill: University of North Carolina Press, 2006), 141–159; Greenberg, *"Or Does It Explode?"* 112–113.

Ottley's tenure with the Harlem project was controversial. He had a brusque, even harsh, management style. One colleague resented the "secrecy" by which he made decisions. He tended to compartmentalize assignments so that the other writers never knew his "comprehensive vision." Another person called him a dictator. He refused to accept advice or criticism.[49] Ralph Ellison believed that Ottley only cared about "the bar, the bed, and the table" and that he lacked the sort of political consciousness needed to fully grasp the state of American race relations.[50] Worse yet was the accusation that Ottley was a womanizer who made inappropriate advances toward his female coworkers.

It is difficult to pinpoint the sources of these frictions. And the case against Ottley is decidedly one-sided, for he never wrote about his time with the FWP. Some of his colleagues—Dorothy West, for instance—were far more complimentary in their assessments of his leadership. As for his management style, Ottley was perceived as arrogant throughout his career, a charge that did not bother him in the least. As Richard Bardolph observed, even as a college student Ottley tended to offend white students due to his independence and his refusal to accept his place in their racial hierarchy. Reared in comfort, he was not often confronted by the hard realities of American racism. One writer has noted that Ottley's Caribbean-born parents consciously raised both their sons not to accept the racial status quo.[51] For many of his African American colleagues who had been brought up in more meager circumstances and who knew the sting of white supremacy, his abrupt haughtiness and his overt sense of privilege rubbed their sensibilities raw.

Ottley's reputation as a philanderer was, it seems, well earned. The memoirs of his friend Adam Clayton Powell, Jr., are replete with descriptions of their adventures with various chorus girls and others they met during long nights of carousing. In Ottley's own unpublished writings, wine, women, and song were among the favorite topics. When he was traveling in Europe to cover the war, he was a keen observer of the expressions of sexuality he encountered, and he wrote about them in long letters to his wife, Gladys. As might be expected, Ottley's proclivities conspired against a stable home life. A brief marriage to Mildred Peyton ended in the 1930s. He

49. The most extended description of Ottley's term with the Harlem branch is in Lawrence Jackson, *Ralph Ellison: Emergence of Genius* (New York: John Wiley and Sons, 2002), 200–201. Jackson's treatment is harsh, and his documentation is thin. Also see Arnold Rampersad, *Ralph Ellison: A Biography* (New York: Alfred A. Knopf, 2007), 111–112.

50. Ralph Ellison to Richard Wright, August 18, 1945, JWJ MSS 3, Box 97, Richard Wright Papers, Beinecke Rare Book and Manuscript Library, Yale University, New Haven, CT.

51. Delozier, "Examination of Race Relations," 27–29, 31–35.

married the white pianist Gladys Tarr in 1941. The failure of that marriage at the end of the decade was one of the catalysts for his move west to Chicago, where he met and married Alice Dungey, the librarian at the *Chicago Defender*.[52] His marriage to Alice was happy and solid. Nonetheless, having three marriages before the age of forty-five was certainly emblematic of the type of behavior that troubled critics and coworkers alike.

Apart from questions of temperament and personal behavior, another aspect of Ottley's working relationships in this period bears noting. He was an ardent, even obsessive, self-promoter. As the supervisor of the Harlem project, Ottley felt he had a proprietary interest in the materials compiled by the people who worked for him, and for whatever reason, he believed he could use those materials with impunity. In 1939, when the Harlem branch came under the scrutiny of Martin Dies and the House Un-American Activities Committee (HUAC) and Ottley suddenly found himself out of a job, he allegedly "borrowed" thirty-five boxes of project research and writing. That material provided fodder for both *New World A-Coming* and his 1948 foray into African American history, *Black Odyssey*. The fact that Ottley used the writing of others without attribution was particularly troubling to a number of his former colleagues. Thus, in his review of Ottley's book, Ralph Ellison lambasted the work, rejecting it as "neither scholarly nor responsible journalism." According to Ellison, Ottley's treatment of Black life was exploitive and "sensational," and the author was "guilty of stylistic clowning."[53] Regardless, the ethical questions involved were valid, and this was the sort of episode that contributed to some of the negative assessments of Ottley's character.

Much of the fire directed at Ottley came from Ellison and, to a lesser

52. Ibid., 31–35; Gilbert, "Vincent Lushington Ottley," *American National Biography*, 844–845.

53. Ralph Ellison, "New World A-Coming," *Tomorrow* 4 (September 4, 1943): 67–68. Ellison was not the only person to question Ottley's ethical standards. In his autobiography, *Mirror to America*, historian John Hope Franklin remembered his anger and frustration with a review that Ottley wrote of Franklin's history of African America, *From Slavery to Freedom*. At the time of its publication in September 1947, Ottley was working on his own history, *Black Odyssey: The Story of the Negro in America*. He used his considerable connections to wrangle an invitation to review Franklin's rival text in the "paper of record," the *New York Times*. Ottley took the opportunity to unscrupulously savage *From Slavery to Freedom* as a "bulky, unwieldy, conventional history, with the studied scholarship of a doctoral thesis. . . . There are neither the sharp, crisp, incisive observations expected of a first-rate journalist, nor the perspective, balance and interpretation expected of the historian." Franklin rightly felt as if he had been sandbagged by Ottley's treachery. Writing nearly sixty years later, he was still upset about the episode, and he gave three paragraphs to Ottley in his memoirs. See Franklin, *Mirror to America: The Autobiography of John Hope Franklin* (New York: Farrar, Straus and Giroux, 2005), 134. Many thanks go to Joel Horowitz for drawing my attention to those pages.

degree, Richard Wright. Questions about Ottley's commitment to the freedom struggle spoke to ideological differences between the three men. Ellison (in this period) and Wright were clearly further to the political left than the often elitist Ottley. Yet Ottley was at his most politically active at the time, so it is curious that he was accused of lacking the appropriate political consciousness. He had made significant connections to the labor movement as a result of the *Amsterdam News* strike. He was also present at the creation of the National Negro Congress, a national coalition of civil rights, labor, and church organizations that was charged with coordinating mass action in the face of a worsening economic situation.[54] The NNC was initially chaired by A. Philip Randolph, and for a short time, it was considered one of the spectacular successes of the Popular Front. Ultimately, ideological conflicts and differences over strategy hamstrung the organization. The signing of the infamous Nazi-Soviet Non-aggression Pact in 1939 shattered the unity of the Popular Front coalitions and split the Congress. It also unleashed a wave of anticommunist hysteria that energized the Dies committee and led to the investigations of the federal arts programs that cost Ottley his job.[55] His politics were at least "subversive" enough to draw the ire of federal investigators.

In many ways, the rough-and-tumble politics of the 1930s was but a prelude for the energies unleashed by World War II. The often chaotic political groundswells of the Depression decade, with their shifting political coalitions, created the conditions for a full-fledged civil rights movement. World War II was the crucible in which that unified movement was forged. The red scare that destroyed the Popular Front and threatened the growing ties between labor and civil rights activists ended when the Nazi armies rolled into the Soviet Union. The Popular Front was, to some degree, restored. More important, there was a new political context for understanding the oppression of African Americans. Antifascism, anticolonialism, and antiracism meshed into a political program that picked up momentum

54. Mark Naison places Ottley at the initial planning sessions of the New York Sponsoring Committee in January 1936. Along with Ottley were Lester Granger of the National Urban League, Benjamin McLaurin of the Brotherhood of Sleeping Car Porters, and Roy Wilkins and Charles Houston of the NAACP. See Naison, *Communists in Harlem*, 179; also see Bates, *Pullman Porters*, 135–138; Solomon, *Cry Was Unity*, 285–289; Raymond Wolters, *Negroes and the Great Depression: The Problem of Economic Recovery* (Westport, CT: Greenwood Publishing, 1970), 353–382; John B. Kirby, *Black Americans in the Roosevelt Era: Liberalism and Race* (Knoxville: University of Tennessee Press, 1980), 152–186; and Harvard Sitkoff, *A New Deal for Blacks: The Emergence of Civil Rights as a National Issue: The Depression Decade* (New York: Oxford University Press, 1978), 169–189.

55. See Rampersad, *Ralph Ellison*, 116–117.

throughout the war. A window of opportunity appeared to have opened. The broad internationalism engendered by the conflict created the conditions for systemic change at home.

Black internationalism did not just magically appear at the start of the conflict. African America was always influenced by events abroad. Intellectuals such as W. E. B. DuBois had long situated American race relations in the context of a global struggle against colonial domination. In the twentieth century, significant international events energized the African American community, fueled this internationalist impulse, and redefined the relationship between peoples of color around the world, especially in Africa.[56] In the 1930s, African American newspapers were full of stories about labor unrest from Lagos to Kingston to Delhi. Pan-African activists such as George Padmore, C. L. R. James, Jomo Kenyatta, and Kwame Nkrumah made enormous impressions on Americans such as Ralph Bunche and Paul Robeson. In 1937, Robeson was a prime mover behind the new Council of African Affairs (CAA), which became an important clearinghouse for journalism on African issues.[57] The Marxist Left and the nationalists found common ground in their confrontation with colonialism, imperialism, fascism, and Jim Crow.

Roi Ottley believed that internationalism's contemporary roots were to be found in Marcus Garvey's Black nationalism and the centrality of a mythic Africa to Garvey's ideology. The success of Garveyism could be measured, he argued, "by a growing *world* consciousness, expressed in feelings of kinship with colored peoples elsewhere in the world." When the UNIA collapsed and Garvey was deported, the organization splintered into warring factions. This "world consciousness" receded as the economic crisis forced African America to turn inward and as various nationalist organizations battled for supremacy. Ottley was decidedly negative in his assessments of these "race missionaries" and "race apostles," whom he dismissed as "loud-mouthed charlatans." He blamed them for everything from street crime to anti-Semitism. But international events forged a new nationalist consensus that captured the imagination of communities across the country.[58]

In March 1935, Italian armies invaded Ethiopia. Fascism was on the

---

56. See, for instance, W. E. B. DuBois, "The African Roots of War," *Atlantic Monthly* 115 (May 1915): 707–714; also for DuBois's role in the organization of the early Pan-African Congresses, see David Levering Lewis, *W. E. B. Du Bois: Biography of a Race, 1868–1919* (New York: Henry Holt, 1993), 248–251, 574–578.

57. Von Eschen, *Race against Empire*, 14–18.

58. Ottley, *New World A-Coming*, 103–104.

march, and an independent African nation was threatened. The war drove home the connections between African Americans and other oppressed peoples. A new attitude toward Africa in general emerged that shifted interest away from discourses of uplift and civilization toward an emphasis on mutual interests. The Black press and churches were relentless in drawing attention to the issue. New organizations were created to raise money and gather relief supplies.[59] As Ottley remarked, "From the beginning the Ethiopian crisis became a fundamental question in Negro life." It was a litmus test for politicians and the subject of angry debate in "poolrooms, barber shops, and taverns" in cities across America.[60] More important, it set African Americans against their Italian American neighbors. Boycotts and picket lines were started, and street violence occasionally flared. "I know of no event in recent times," Ottley commented, "that stirred the rank-and-file of Negroes more than the Italo-Ethiopian War. . . . Clearly, Negroes in America had cast their lot with colored peoples elsewhere in the world!"[61]

Much of Ottley's writing during the war mixed hopefulness with words of warning about the mind-set of African Americans. Many, he argued, remembered the promises made during World War I when leaders such as W. E. B. DuBois had urged the community to close ranks around the American war effort. They also remembered what that support had earned them: violence and degradation. When *New World A-Coming* was published in 1943, some of its best writing concerned the growing frustration in Black communities across the country. Ottley lashed out at the recurring incidents of violence against Black servicemen in the South, arguing that they had significant consequences for national security as African American citizens questioned why they should be loyal to a government that ignored their oppression. He quoted NAACP executive secretary Walter White as attributing "this countrywide apathy of Negroes to discrimination in the

---

59. The fullest account of the impact of the Italo-Ethiopian War is William R. Scott, *The Sons of Sheba's Race: African-Americans and the Italo-Ethiopian War, 1935–1941* (Bloomington: Indiana University Press, 1992); see, as well, Scott, "Black Nationalism and the Italo-Ethiopian Conflict, 1934–1936," *Journal of Negro History* 63 (April 1978): 118–134. Also see James H. Meriwether, *Proudly We Can Be Africans: Black Americans and Africa, 1935–1961* (Chapel Hill: University of North Carolina Press), 27–56; Plummer, *Rising Wind*, 37–57; and John Henrik Clarke, *Marcus Garvey and the Vision of Africa* (New York: Vintage, 1974), 326–327. Also quite important for the assessment of the Ethiopian war's impact on Black America is the excellent work by Robin D. G. Kelley, "'This Ain't Ethiopia, but It'll Do': African Americans and the Spanish Civil War," in Kelley, *Race Rebels: Culture, Politics, and the Black Working Class* (New York: Free Press, 1994), 123–158.

60. Ottley, *New World A-Coming*, 109.

61. Ibid., 111–112.

Army, Navy, and Air Corps, and especially in the war industries."[62] Worse yet, discrimination created the conditions in which Black communities were increasingly susceptible to Japanese propaganda, not to mention the inordinate value of American racism to the enemies' efforts in the inevitable battle for hearts and minds. He noted, for instance, that the British unwillingness to discuss independence in India or any of its other colonies was front-page news in Black newspapers. "What this all adds up to in the minds of Negroes," Ottley argued, "is a pattern of continued white domination of colored peoples. Therefore conflicts between the races are regarded as inevitable."[63]

If Ottley's reporting was news to white Americans, it came as no surprise to the American government, which was becoming more and more anxious about militancy in Black communities. Events had their own relentless momentum. The threatened march on Washington in July 1941 culminated in Franklin Roosevelt's Executive Order 8802, which allegedly ended employment discrimination in the defense industries and created the Fair Employment Practices Committee to oversee that effort. In December, the Japanese demolished Pearl Harbor, drew the United States into the global conflict, and touched off the calculated hysteria that led to the forced relocation of Japanese and Japanese Americans on the West Coast. And it was not only the Japanese who drew government scrutiny. The director of the Federal Bureau of Investigation (FBI), J. Edgar Hoover, and Postmaster General Frank Walker demanded that the increasingly militant African American press be punished for its perceived provocations. An intense internal debate ensued about whether the World War I–era sedition statutes should be applied against select editors in hopes of silencing the Black media. More reactionary voices in the administration wondered if the Black press should be shuttered for the duration of the war. Only the fierce resistance of Attorney General Francis Biddle and the Justice Department averted a nationwide crackdown on civil liberties.[64]

Undeterred, Hoover launched a massive internal security investigation into "foreign-inspired agitation among the American Negroes." Commissioned in June 1942 and completed in August 1943, the findings of the investigation were published as the FBI's *Survey of Racial Conditions in the*

---

62. Ibid., 314–315.

63. Ibid., 326. For a lengthy digression of the influence of Japanese propaganda among Black nationalist groups across the country, see 327–342.

64. See Patrick S. Washburn, *A Question of Sedition: The Federal Government's Investigation of the Black Press during World War II* (New York: Oxford University Press, 1986), 8.

United States during World War II.[65] The report singled out the Black press as a powerful shaper of African American opinion and a "strong provocateur of discontent of among Negroes."[66] In fact, as many as seven federal agencies launched investigations of the Black press, including the FBI, the Post Office Department, the Office of Facts and Figures, the Office of War Information, the Office of Censorship, and the U.S. Army.[67]

The actual response of the African American media to the war was mixed. Newspapers were attracting an unprecedented readership. In 1940, conservative estimates placed the circulation of African American newspapers across the country at 1,276,000 readers. In 1945, the number was 1,809,000. The Office of War Information estimated that Black newspapers had 4 million readers per week out of a total population of 13 million. Other observers estimated that as many as 6 million African Americans read these newspapers weekly, including one-third of the urban Black population.[68] It is logical that in certain instances, such as the "Double V" campaign, the press fueled expressions of militancy, which was often the position of many white Americans and the federal government as well. But Roi Ottley, for one, noted that this causal relationship was far more complicated. In reality, there were no calls for noninvolvement in the war effort. Ottley pointed out that even though linking international fascism to America's system of racial oppression and calling attention to racist excesses at home exhibited a new militant spirit, the "Double V" campaign also urged African Americans to buy war bonds, contribute to blood banks, and participate in civilian defense initiatives and conservation efforts.[69] Historian Lee Finkle has argued that observers of the Black press have often confused militant rhetoric with action. Rather than being a revolutionary force, according to Finkle, African American editors and journalists "[sought] to avoid a direct assault on segregation" and "[embraced] traditional avenues for change."[70] In this formulation, the Black press was a clearinghouse for information; it set and advocated a political agenda that attacked segregation at home; and

65. Robert A. Hill, comp. and ed., *The FBI's RACON: Racial Conditions in the United States during World War II* (Boston: Northeastern University Press, 1995), 4.

66. Ibid., 419.

67. Washburn, *Question of Sedition*, 8.

68. Lee Finkle, "The Conservative Aims of Militant Rhetoric: Black Protest during World War II," *Journal of American History* 60 (December 1973): 693–694.

69. Ottley, *New World A-Coming*, 287.

70. Finkle, "Conservative Aims of Militant Rhetoric," 693. Also see Finkle, *Forum for Protest: The Black Press during World War II* (Rutherford, NJ: Fairleigh Dickinson University Press, 1975), and Harvard Sitkoff, "Racial Militancy and Interracial Violence in the Second World War," *Journal of American History* 58 (December 1971): 661–681.

it served as a "safety valve" and "moderating force" on a grass roots that was growing more restive. African Americans demanded that the realities of the American national life live up to national ideals, and Black newspapers reflected their desires.

In 1943, Ottley published his first book, *New World A-Coming: Inside Black America,* and its success earned him national recognition. He had struggled to find a publisher who believed the text would be marketable to the white readers necessary to ensure the book would succeed. Finally, with the help of his wife, he secured a contract with Houghton Mifflin. But even then, the book might have gone largely unnoticed were it not for the impeccable timing of its publication. Ottley's text was prereleased to the media for review on August 1, 1943, the same day the Harlem riot exploded into the national headlines.[71] Racial tensions built steadily throughout the war. In 1943, forty-seven cities reported "racial incidents." Los Angeles, Detroit, Mobile, and Beaumont, Texas, had full-blown race riots. In Harlem, rumors that a white policeman had gunned down a black soldier touched off a spasm of violence as hundreds rampaged through the streets burning and looting.[72] Suddenly, here was Roi Ottley poised to explain Black America to uncomprehending whites. During its first print run, *New World A-Coming* sold 50,000 copies and garnered generally positive critical reviews. Ottley was given Houghton Mifflin's Life in America Prize, and he won the Ainsworth Award in 1944. Many of the book's vignettes were adapted for the radio, and in 1945 those adaptations earned Ottley a coveted Peabody Award. To cap this impressive string of successes, he received a $2,500 grant from the prestigious Rosenwald Foundation. That money provided the financial cushion necessary for him to embark on his extended wartime tour of Europe, Africa, and the Middle East.[73]

New World A-Coming is a maddeningly uneven work. Two-thirds of the text was drawn from previously published *Amsterdam News* columns, the WPA materials that he had absconded with, and reminiscences about his Harlem experiences. This approach would prove to be Ottley's template. He often recycled older work. And though his subtitle claimed to offer a glimpse "Inside Black America," *New World A-Coming* was actually firmly rooted in its Harlem milieu. Some African American reviewers noted Ottley's use of anecdote in place of deep analysis and his penchant for dwelling on some of the seamier or more exotic elements of Black life, presumably to titillate white readers. They also argued that Ottley's claim that his book

71. Sitkoff, "Racial Militancy," 668–671; Delozier, "Examination of Racial Relations," 25.
72. Gilmore, *Defying Dixie,* 374.
73. Gilbert, "Vincent Lushington Ottley," 844–845; Jackson, "Roi Ottley," 490.

was "a study in black nationalism (and indeed black chauvinism)" was over-blown and his use of the phrase *black nationalism* imprecise.[74]

However, the sections of the book that dealt with more contemporary personages and events—such as Roosevelt's "Black cabinet," the Black press, the threatened march on Washington and "Double V" campaign, and the impact of World War II on the African American community—demonstrated keen insight. Ottley knew all the key players. His writing may not have been particularly artful, but his relaxed and fluid style connected well with a general readership. Again, the timing of publication was immensely important and not just because of the racial unrest sweeping the country. Almost exactly one year later, the Swedish sociologist Gunnar Myrdal published his magisterial *American Dilemma: The Negro Problem and Modern Democracy.* Myrdal's study offered the depth of research and analysis that *New World A-Coming* lacked, and with its publication, Ottley's book slowly receded from public view. Many of the human interest–oriented vignettes found their way to the radio, but Ottley's more perceptive writing was more often than not forgotten.

That did not, of course, keep the journalist from capitalizing on his newfound fame and fortune. After he lost his job at the Federal Writers' Project, Ottley freelanced for a couple of years and then in 1943 was able to parlay his long-standing connections to the labor movement into a position as publicity director of the CIO's National War Relief Committee, a group that raised over $20 million for relief efforts around the globe. With the success of *New World A-Coming* and the financial independence that brought, Ottley began to broaden his horizons. He convinced the editors at the labor newspaper *PM* and its sister publication *Liberty Magazine* to take him on as a war correspondent. He also wrote for the *Pittsburgh Courier* and the Overseas News Service. In 1944, he was commissioned as a captain in the U.S. Army and set off on a two-year, 60,000-mile journey through Europe, the Middle East, and Africa. Much of Ottley's writing from this period comprises the body of this volume.[75]

Ottley's employment with *PM* and *Liberty* is especially notable. *PM* was founded in 1940 by Ralph Ingersoll, who made his reputation when he helped turn around the *New Yorker* and then salvaged Henry Luce's

74. Ellison, "New World A-Coming," 67–68. Ellison, somewhat unfairly, rejects Ottley's descriptions of Garvey, Father Divine, Joe Louis, and Adam Clayton Powell, Jr., as representing "opportunities for Ottley to exploit the sensational—a blight upon books about Harlem since Van Vechten's *Nigger Heaven.*" But despite Ellison's obvious distaste for the author, even he admits that the reporting on the impact of the war, the Black press, the pro-Japanese movements, and so on is sound and "most reliable."

75. Gilbert, "Vincent Lushington Ottley," 844–845; "Roi (Vincent) Ottley," *Current Biography 1943* (New York: H. W. Wilson, 1944), 566–567.

struggling ventures *Fortune* and *Life*. Ingersoll was far more liberal in his politics than Luce, with whom he ideologically butted heads. He loathed Luce's continual assaults on FDR and the New Deal, his strident criticisms of the CIO and labor movement, and above all his support of Francisco Franco and the fascists in Spain. Ingersoll envisioned a new kind of newspaper that embraced the aesthetic innovations of magazines such as *Life* but that also embodied his liberal-Left politics. *PM* was a product of the politics of the Popular Front. It reflected Ingersoll's political commitments to the liberal wing of the Democratic Party, the labor movement, and antifascism. He reached out to a stable of like-minded reporters that included the Pulitzer Prize winner George Lyon, Penn Kimball, James Wechsler, and I. F. Stone. Ingersoll also decided that in order to guarantee the editorial independence of the new venture as well as signal that this was a new kind of paper, *PM* would eschew any form of advertising. It was a fateful decision. *PM* proved to be an innovative journalistic experiment but a financial debacle.[76]

It was extremely rare for an African American journalist to write for a white publication in that period. It is a testament to Ottley's celebrity and political connections, as well as *PM*'s antiracist editorial position, that he was hired for such a high-profile job. The novelty of his position might also help us comprehend the unique reporting he did during his time as a war correspondent. Given the often extreme conditions facing African American soldiers in the Jim Crow military, the Black press had to play an advocacy role as well as simply report the war. The relegation of African American troops to menial labor, their stereotyping by way of "intelligence testing," and the terrible violence inflicted on Black troops as they trained at bases in the South politicized the war coverage of African American correspondents.[77] When they deployed to all corners of the globe, they continued to focus on inequality and ill treatment, and their reports often ran afoul of military censors. Black correspondents were forbidden to take battlefield photographs, especially when they depicted the second-class status of Black troops. Ottley's close friend Ed Toles was chastised by army censors when he filed a report stating that Black nurses were only allowed to

76. For an excellent history of *PM*, see Paul Milkman, *"PM": A New Deal in Journalism, 1940–1948* (New Brunswick, NJ: Rutgers University Press, 1997), esp. 6–59.

77. For an excellent study of Black war correspondents in World War II, see John D. Stevens, "From the Back of the Foxhole: Black Correspondents in World War II," *Journalism Monographs*, no. 27 (February 1973). Stevens compiled information on twenty-seven correspondents deployed for Black newspapers and interviewed many of them. Unfortunately, he did not include Ottley in his study because he had worked as a "special writer" for a white publication. Regardless, this work is an impressive bit of research.

tend German prisoners. Stories about simmering tensions and occasional violence between white and Black troops were especially embarrassing to the military establishment.[78] Throughout the war, African American war correspondents were dogged in their advocacy of the men and women they covered, and they often found themselves on the front lines of some of the most vicious fighting.

Ottley had quite close relationships with some of his African American peers, including Ollie Stewart of the *Baltimore Afro-American,* Ollie Harrington and Randy Dixon of the *Pittsburgh Courier,* and Toles of the *Chicago Defender.* He traveled with them and occasionally shared housing. However, he often refused to bend to the racial mores of the segregated military, and he used his affiliation with *PM* to break free of the restrictions that race thrust upon him. He did spend time with the troops at the front and of course filed his share of human interest stories about Black GIs. More often, though, Ottley broke away from the pool of African American correspondents and followed his own muse. He had a particular interest in understanding American race relations in a global context. He saw that the war was obliterating the old colonial order, and he was dogged in tracking down interviews with public officials across Europe who could speak with authority about colonial peoples. Ottley also connected to the network of young African intellectuals who would lead the fight for decolonization in their home countries. For nearly four years, he was witness to the revolutionary changes that swept across the international community.

The first selection in this collection of Roi Ottley's World War II writing is an unpublished manuscript entitled "Notes, Observations and Memoranda Concerning Travels in Scotland, Ireland, Wales, England, France, Belgium, Italy, and North Africa." Although the document claims to cover the period "June to December 1944," the last entry is dated November 3, 1944. This was Ottley's workbook for the first swing of his international tour. It contains diary entries, copies of correspondence, and drafts of articles—some of which were censored by military authorities. There are descriptions of fellow journalists and encounters with celebrities such as Ernest Hemingway, Edward R. Murrow, and Joe Louis. More important, this text introduced themes that preoccupied the journalist for years. He commented frequently on conflicts between white and Black troops, on the efforts by white southern officers to transplant Jim Crow to European soil, and on the similarities between fascism and southern racism.

Ottley expressed resentment whenever he felt he was being pigeonholed

78. Ibid., 9–17.

as just an African American journalist. When asked by the captain of the troop transport carrying him to England if he would offer a lecture on the "Negro problem" in America, Ottley declined. And while traveling, he was adamant about breaking away from the journalistic pack. Partly, his desire to travel alone was driven by competition. "Too many Negro newspapermen in one spot," he argued, "clutters up the outlets for stories." However, it also gave him the opportunity to observe race relations in a variety of European locales as well as to focus on the treatment of colonial peoples. Roi Ottley enjoyed the freedom of movement and general lack of discrimination that he experienced in Europe, but he also recognized that for all of the political correctness of his European hosts and their criticisms of American racism, they had their own colonial systems of racial and ethnic domination. His own burgeoning internationalism meshed well with *PM*'s editorial position. The best of his *PM* journalism appears in this document.

It is unclear whether the African American press would have been as interested in the nuances of European colonial policy while covering an ongoing war: at that point, correspondents were far more intent on writing about the contributions and travails of Black GIs. Yet in the immediate aftermath of the war, as Europe struggled to stabilize and begin the long and painful process of reconstruction, there was a pronounced upswing in the number of stories about the fluid international situation. The old colonial empires crumbled, and the chartering of the new United Nations seemed a hopeful signal for the future. Ottley had traveled for most of 1944 and 1945 for *PM*. Toward the end of 1945, he began submitting articles as the foreign correspondent for the *Pittsburgh Courier*. He continued to travel abroad off and on through 1947 and into 1948.

After the war, there was a significant shift in the tone and substance of Ottley's writing. From the unpublished materials, it is clear that he planned on writing about his World War II experiences. Given the internal evidence, the envisioned monograph would have mirrored *New World A-Coming* in style and structure. Ottley was constantly comparing race relations at home and abroad. He built an impressive network of contacts among government officials as well as individuals involved in anticolonial politics. Though he was always one to cast a skeptical eye on the politics of the day, there was also a sense of hopefulness in his diary scribblings and his articles. He knew that Europe's former colonies would be independent nations, and the prospect, especially as it might impact race relations in the United States, thrilled him. Regardless, his book on his war experiences did not appear immediately. Instead, in 1948 he published his history text, *Black Odyssey,* which received generally positive reviews and sold modestly.

Meanwhile, he was going through a period of instability in his personal life, including his divorce from Gladys Tarr, and except for an occasional freelance piece, he did not catch on with any of his hometown newspapers. In 1950, deciding that greener pastures lay to the west, he relocated to Chicago.

There, Ottley made a fresh start. He became a frequent contributor to the *Chicago Defender*, and in 1953, he achieved another journalistic coup when he was invited to write a weekly human interest column for the *Chicago Tribune*. Once again, he was one of the few African American journalists in the country writing for a predominantly white newspaper. But it was in the offices of the *Defender* that Ottley met the woman who would become his third wife, Alice Dungey. Dungey was working as the newspaper's archivist and librarian. She would provide Ottley with the love, encouragement, and stability that had been impossible for him to attain with his peripatetic lifestyle. They married in February 1951 and were together until his death from a heart attack in 1960.

It was Dungey who pushed Ottley to return to his comparative study of American and European race relations. The result was the publication of *No Green Pastures* at the end of 1951. This was by far his most controversial work. Gone from his analysis was the idealism of the Popular Front. He force-marched through the text from England to France, Italy, Germany, the Balkans, Greece, Egypt, and Israel, and with each chapter, he railed at what he considered the hypocrisy of those nations. At a moment when many African American artists and intellectuals sought solace in Europe away from the noxious racism and politics of the United States, Ottley issued a stinging indictment of what he argued was only the facade of freedom. The positive treatment that many African Americans received, he claimed, masked far more negative realities for indigenous people of color, who were discriminated against in jobs and education. In fact, the possibilities for material gain fueled his increasingly positive assessment of American race relations. Yes, racial violence and segregation continued to mar the democratic experiment, but the rising living standards for Blacks made the United States superior to Europe. For Ottley, standard of living and quality of life were one and the same thing.[79]

Although some white reviewers were quite pleased with Ottley's conclusions, many of his peers were not. Marvel Cooke, for instance, a colleague at the *Amsterdam News* who had stood shoulder to shoulder with him on the picket line during the Newspaper Guild strike, was enraged by

79. Roi Ottley, *No Green Pastures* (New York: Charles Scribner's Sons, 1951), 1–8, 11–13.

the book, which she called an "empty mockery and a slap in the face to the countless thousands of black and white men and women who battle conscientiously for freedom for black men in America." According to Cooke, Ottley's depictions of "Negroes in other countries . . . [were] stereotypes. They have ugly cuts across their cheeks, they are illiterate and frayed, they live, for the most part, on the edge of culture." Just in case the reader was unclear about where she stood on the book, Cooke's review appeared with a photograph of its author bearing the caption "Roi Ottley: Prisoner of White Supremacy."[80]

A more nuanced, but no less eviscerating, engagement with the book was offered by James Baldwin. Baldwin began by noting that Ottley's journalistic style was not appropriate for taking on a subject of such complexity: the piling up of anecdotes did not an argument make. His "journalistic method" was "capable of description but rarely of penetration." More significant still, in his zeal to prove his thesis that "American Negroes are better off than Negroes anywhere else in the world, and that Europe ought to clean house before trumpeting our lynchings," Ottley described a Black America that was a sanitized cartoon version of itself. Baldwin assailed Ottley for claiming "our heritage is great" while at the same time removing "its more troubling aspects." *No Green Pastures* denied "past humiliation and present trouble" in order to reduce "black-white history to a kind of tableau of material progress." Baldwin mocked its author's style of argument. "It is not . . . enough to suggest that . . . 'the bulk of blacks in Europe are abysmally poor,' American Negroes are better off because some are able to drive a Cadillac. The history of the Negro in America is a heavier weight than this celebrated vehicle is able to carry."[81]

There was one notable exception to the generally angry reaction of Black reviewers. Roy Wilkins of the NAACP found Ottley's text "interesting reading with no forbidding profundity, moving along easily in the hands of a competent reporter and storyteller." He, too, noted that Ottley's argument rang hollow in light of continued oppression in this country. At the same time, though, he believed Ottley's analysis was a vital corrective at a moment when "Communists and their friends [exploited] America's treatment of its Negro minority." It was important to remind the country's nominal friends in other parts of the world that these problems often tran-

80. Marvel Cooke, "*No Green Pastures* Is No Favor to Negroes," *New York Daily Compass*, November 16, 1951.

81. James Baldwin, "The Negro at Home and Abroad," *The Reporter*, November 27, 1951, 36–37.

scended national boundaries.[82] Wilkins recognized the political utility of Ottley's book.

The wartime Popular Front coalition of Left political organizations, labor unions, and civil rights activists was demolished when Cold War tensions between the United States and the Soviet Union were transformed into a full-blown anticommunist witch hunt. In response, so-called mainstream civil rights organizations such as the NAACP fell all over themselves to be the first to shear off any militant appendages.[83] Meanwhile, one of the most dramatic examples of the witch hunt's effect was the treatment accorded W. E. B. DuBois. Within just a few weeks of the publication of *No Green Pastures*, DuBois was indicted for allegedly serving as an "agent of a foreign principal" for his work with the Peace Information Center. This episode was just the latest phase in the Truman administration's calculated effort to isolate and silence the more militant voices in the freedom movement. The eighty-two-year-old DuBois was threatened with five years in prison and a $100,000 fine. The case was eventually thrown out, but the federal harassment continued. DuBois was routinely hauled into court on specious charges, and his passport was seized by the State Department. All the while, Walter White directed NAACP Legal Defense lawyers to stay away from the beleaguered dissident, claiming that the federal government had overwhelming evidence to convict DuBois.[84] The organization that DuBois had helped to found forty years before not only sat on the sidelines during his time of need, it also helped spread the rumors that nearly destroyed him.

Roi Ottley certainly had nothing to do with DuBois's troubles, but the rightward swing of his politics mirrored what was happening in liberal civil rights circles. Ottley was never a radical. As a young, aspiring journalist, he was swept up in the political tides of the 1930s. The internationalism of the war years provided the context for some of his best writing. But Ottley's was a solidly middle-class sensibility that was born of his privileged upbringing. It was easy for him to turn his back on the political allies of

82. Roy Wilkins, "Lot of the Negro in Europe," *New York Herald Tribune*, November 4, 1951.

83. There is a rapidly expanding literature on the impact of Cold War anticommunism on the civil rights activism of the Popular Front years. See Gilmore, *Defying Dixie*, 400–444; Biondi, *To Stand and Fight*, 137–163; Manning Marable, *Race, Reform, and Rebellion: The Second Black Reconstruction and beyond in Black America, 1945–2006*, 3rd ed. (Jackson: University Press of Mississippi, 2007), 12–31; Borstelmann, *Cold War and the Color Line*, 45–84; Plummer, *Rising Wind*, 167–216; and Jeff Woods, *Black Struggle, Red Scare: Segregation and Anti-communism in the South* (Baton Rouge: Louisiana State University Press, 2003).

84. See David Levering Lewis, *W. E. B. Du Bois: The Fight for Equality and the American Century, 1919– 1963* (New York: Henry Holt, 2000), 496–553; Marable, *Race, Reform, and Rebellion*, 26–28.

his youth. And like his politics, his writing also turned, becoming more mainstream and less controversial. Roi and Alice Ottley settled into a very comfortable life in Chicago. Although he never again achieved the national notice he'd enjoyed with *New World A-Coming,* he continued to be a prolific writer. He churned out columns for the *Defender* and the *Tribune.* He published occasional freelance pieces with *Ebony* and other periodicals. He also undertook a quite well received biography of *Chicago Defender* founder and editor Robert Abbott. And he tried his hand at writing fiction as well: his novel, *The White Marble Lady,* was published posthumously.[85] Finally, he hosted a successful radio show on Chicago's WGN that could be heard through much of the Midwest. In the context of the peak of his fame in the 1940s, *Sepia's* 1960 query — "What became of Roi Ottley?" — might make a certain amount of sense. But by just about any other measure, the man lived a full and successful life.

Historians will continue to wrestle with the ways that we conceptualize the so-called long civil rights movement. Our sense of the periodization and our definitions of "movement politics" will become sharper, and the people and events of the civil rights struggles in the interwar years will come into brighter relief. Of course, no one life story can provide the perfect context for understanding an era. And it is certainly true that Roi Ottley has never appeared in the histories as anything more than an occasional footnote. Yet by piecing together his experiences in this critical period in American race relations and trying to understand the trajectory of his life and career against the backdrop of historical events, we have a unique means for engaging his writing. Likewise, the writing that comprises this volume offers a fascinating opportunity to think about the political awakening that took place in the 1930s and 1940s and the vital international impulse that drove it.

85. Roi Ottley, *The White Marble Lady* (New York: Farrar, Straus and Giroux, 1965).

A NOTE ON TRANSCRIPTIONS, ANNOTATIONS, AND SELECTED JOURNALISM

Roi Ottley's unpublished manuscript is transcribed here just as it was originally typed: the occasionally strange wording and punctuation were his alone. The original manuscript was also incomplete. Consequently, there are a number of pages missing, and where there were incomplete entries, those have been eliminated. In each case, no information central to the unfolding narrative has been excluded. The annotations in the un-published manuscript were chosen very carefully. My goal was to enhance certain sections of Ottley's narrative and provide readers with important context, without allowing those notes to become a distraction. In many instances, evidence internal to the document was sufficient to identify peo-ple, places, and events. I did not feel that it was necessary to identify celeb-rities such as Ernest Hemingway or Edward R. Murrow, except where an annotation could highlight some special significance in the text. Likewise, I did not offer long annotated digressions on minor government function-aries. Ultimately, my goal was to find a balance in the annotated text that would appeal to both scholars and students alike.

The articles in this volume were chosen with an eye toward coherence and with attention to the themes explored in those pieces. This project was never intended to offer Roi Ottley's "complete works." Instead, it was designed to focus specifically on his experiences during World War II. At war's end, Ottley returned to the United States and immediately began an-gling to return to Europe as a foreign correspondent. He eventually landed a position with the *Pittsburgh Courier* and spent an extended period traveling in Europe and the Middle East. But that was a different chapter in his life, a chapter that had no bearing on his experiences as "an African American newspaperman in World War II." The newspaper stories in this volume cover the period from Ottley's commissioning and deployment through his work on the Nuremberg trials, and as such, they offer the most coherent record of his experiences in the war.

The second criterion for choosing these articles was thematic. Roi Ottley was deeply concerned with the paradoxes of America's war effort — the nation's desire to serve as the bulwark of democracy in the face of fascist aggression abroad even as oppression continued to be practiced at home. In that context, Ottley was also fixated on the treatment of African American servicemen in the Jim Crow military as well as the way they were treated by their European hosts. Obviously, he had a keen interest in the conditions of communities of color abroad, together with the impact of the war on European colonialism. Many of the articles chosen for this volume emphasize those interests and concerns.

This volume was crafted to reinsert Ottley's work into discussions of wartime race relations. *Roi Ottley's World War II* is meant to appeal to scholars and students interested in World War II, the segregated military, the civil rights struggle, and the broader issues of American race relations.

✪ THE DIARY

Notes, Observations and Memoranda Concerning Travels in Scotland, Ireland, Wales, England, France, Belgium, Italy, and North Africa

By
Roi Ottley
PM-Liberty War Correspondent

Period: June to December 1944

July 1, 1944

Well, the great adventure began today—around 8 P.M. to be exact. My world tour! Everyone of the dock officials have been cooperative in aiding me clear baggage, get aboard, etc. Negro soldiers are aboard, too. As we started up the gang plank I noticed that the Negro soldiers entered a different hole in the ship from the white troops and few passengers.

I was placed in a room with a group—seemingly representative of American life: there are six of us in one cabin—Lewis Gannett (Herald-Tribune), Kaplan (radio technician), Harold Kulick (photographer), Richard Meyer and Burke Miller (Office of Strategic Services).[1] All were very cordial.

We are aboard an English ship—S.S. Scythia—manned by an English crew. Ship pulled out some time around 3 A.M. As we stood on the deck and watched the skyline fade into obscurity, Kaplan confessed to me that he has a great—very great—fear of death!

Tonight found me very restless, wondering what was to come. The feeling that preying subs are in the Atlantic Ocean seems to be a very tangible thing aboard ship.

July 2, 1944

As yet nobody seems to have gotten sick—seasick. So far, a very smooth voyage.

---

1. As a wartime correspondent, Roi Ottley, much to his chagrin, often found himself in the company of other scribes. Lewis Gannett (1891–1966) was a longtime book critic and columnist for the *New York Herald-Tribune.* Information about Gannett's life can be found in his personal papers: Lewis Gannett, 1891–1966: Correspondence and Compositions, Houghton Library, Harvard College Library, Harvard University, Cambridge, MA. Although W. Burke Miller is identified as an officer in the Office of Strategic Services, the forerunner to the Central Intelligence Agency, he was also a journalist. In fact, he was the recipient of one of the earliest Pulitzer Prizes for reporting, for a story he did for the *Louisville Courier-Journal* about the attempted rescue of caver Floyd Collins in 1926. After the war, Miller continued his journalistic career both in print and on the radio. See Karen Rothmyer, *Winning Pulitzers: The Stories behind Some of the Best News Coverage of Our Time* (New York: Columbia University Press, 1991). Harold Kulick was a young photographer for *Popular Science Monthly.* Kulick was killed when the airplane he was on crashed on its return flight from a bombing raid. See "Commander Pays Tribute to Photographer Harold Kulick," *Popular Science Monthly* 145 (November 1945): 30.

Among the instructions given us for our own safety today brought this remark from the transport commander: "Any man who falls overboard is on his own."

I learned today that there are Jamaican Negro troops aboard ship, members of the British Army.

I talked with the American Negro troops for the first time today—they seemed quite happy about making the trip. All of them are seeing the ocean for the first time. They are all very simple fellows with little education. They are members of a service division and quartermaster corps. They were showing photographs around. One of the American Negroes remarked that the Jamaican Negroes "certainly have some pretty wimmins," meaning wives [or] sweethearts.

Most of the white soldiers and officers seem to have come from the South. My presence—and the privileges I have as a W.[ar] C.[orrespondent]—seems to bewilder them.

July 3, 1944

Today I was invited to help write a show for the entertainment of the enlisted men aboard. I accepted but it was all very simple continuity for a master of ceremonies. Gannett asked me if I thought anyone would object to the singing of "That's why Darkies are Born." What do you answer in such a case—here in the middle of the Atlantic Ocean? I told him that perhaps a gentle hint would prevent it being sung.

Today a Negro soldier told me about another Negro soldier who, stationed at Camp Kilmer, deliberately took his gun and shot himself in the foot so he wouldn't have to go overseas. He will be courtmartialed for this, my informant told me.

I'm beginning to know my cabin-mates better—for example, Harold Kulick—the photographer for Popular Science Mag. who has been abroad before,—is quite a lover. He has a wife in New York, but seems very concerned about a girl he left behind in London. Richard Meyer smokes his cigarettes through his teeth. He is affable, well-travelled, intelligent, but fussy as an old woman about his personal effects. Miller—the former NBC executive—is very methodical. Gannett is still somewhat of a puzzle.

Food has been good—so far.

July 4, 1944

Just completed reading a story of the French Underground, "Army of Shadows," by Joseph Kessel. After reading the newspaper accounts of Nazi brutality—this book comes off second-best. Yet it has an authentic ring to it.

Sea was very rough today. Nobody seasick yet.

During the night, while the ship tossed, a G. I. was successfully operated on for appendicitis. The attending nurse was very seasick, but she carried on nicely nevertheless. A Chinese army surgeon assisted in the operation.

The Southern soldiers have just begun to get used to seeing me about. They now are beginning to talk with me. They never ask me what I do. And I never volunteer any information. War has imposed a silence on everyone. It is considered bad form to inquire about what a man is doing.

The English crew discovered musical instruments in the hole of the ship. Now the Negro troops are entertaining everyone with a "Dixie Land Band." Pretty good, too.

July 5, 1944

This morning at breakfast our waiter, who is very very English, was very very critical of American women. He said they didn't seem to understand that a war was on. He said English women were going without new clothes.

Finished reading a rather nostalgic book, "Lost Island" by Norman Hall. Threw a new light on the extent to which the war has reached into the furthest ends of the earth—even to the South Sea Islands—and disrupted normal living.

There are few women aboard—returning wives of English diplomats. They are having the time of their lives with the men, though they are none too prepossessing.

Today I was asked to lecture on "racial problems" for orientation course for soldiers. Don't know whether or not I shall do it. No, I don't think I will.

Sea is calm today. No one seasick.

Richard Meyer, it turns out, lost a son in the war. He was a member of the RAF. He never bellyaches about his loss though.

A beautiful moonlight night. One of the fellows remarked that it was light enough to knock us off with a torpedo. Morbid, I say.

July 6, 1944

My cabin mates and I had pictures taken with Colonel Dennis—troop transport commander—He chatted with us afterwards very amiably. Harold Kulick, the photographer, took the pictures.

Gannett remarked at dinner today that he talked with Colonel Dennis later. He was told that the Nazi prisoners when taken never once concede the defeat of Germany. No logic can persuade them that they are not the superior people of the earth.

This seems to be a great puzzle to my friends. Yet, they do not seem to recognize the inherent Fascist character of the anti-Negro Southerners, and his refusal to admit the truth about the Negroes in the face of facts.

The Chinese army surgeon aboard mingles very freely with the men, though somewhat ill at ease. He avoids me. [But] maybe that's my imagination.

There is also an American Indian aboard—a Comanchee—who sings in a quintet with white troops. He seems well adjusted and happy.

Talked with an officer from Iowa today. Soon we were discussing the "race question"—but he did it as though we were conspirators planning something subversive, being conscious all the time that he was being watched by the Southerners aboard.

July 7, 1944

Today a Negro soldier drew a knife in an attack upon one of the English crew members. There has been much hush-hush about it. Colonel Dennis—transport commander—immediately took charge and settled the affair without further incident. He spent four hours talking with the Negro soldiers and was successful in bringing the whole business to a close. I am attempting to get the back-of-the-scenes facts. But I must go slowly.

There has been much drilling to prepare us for boarding life boats in the event there is a submarine attack. Richard Meyer remarked, quite humorously, that he bemoaned the fact that if we do have to take the lifeboat, Tallulah Bankhead won't be with us. "Think of it," he said, "a lifeboat without Tallulah!"[2]

Finished reading, "Sword of Fate" by Dennis Wheatley, a love story against a background of war. Strictly cops-and-robbers stuff, but entertaining.

I can't help being amused by Miller—one of my cabin mates. He is a reddish blond chap with a Chaplin mustache which he is constantly smoothing down. He is most inoffensive, but his little minching [sic] mannerisms seem

2. Meyer refers to screen actor Tallulah Bankhead's breakthrough performance in Alfred Hitchcock's 1944 film *Lifeboat*. Bankhead (1902–1968) won a New York Film Critics Circle Award for that performance, which many thought was the best of her career. She began her career on the London stage in 1918 and moved to Hollywood in the early 1930s. She continued making films into the 1950s and was a mainstay on the television screen in the 1950s and 1960s. The most complete biography of Bankhead is Joel Lobenthal, *Tallulah! The Life and Times of a Leading Lady* (New York: HarperCollins, 2004). Also see Tallulah Bankhead, *Tallulah: My Autobiography* (Jackson: University Press of Mississippi, 2004), 267–269.

to give him a poppycock appearance. My cabin mates have pronounced him an "old maid." His full name: "W. Burke Miller."

July 8, 1944

Last night an ordinary Negro soldier surprised everyone by entertaining the troops with competent piano solos of Debussy's "Clair de Lune" and Beethoven's "Moonlight Sonata." Everyone expected boogie woogie! The G. I.'s name was Sgt. Abner White. Incidentally, I met an English diplomat aboard named "White."

Finished an abridged book, "The Lost Weekend" by Charles Jackson. An excellent psychological tale of an alcoholic. Now I am reading "Green-Mantle" by John Buchan, author of "The 39 Steps" who was Lord Tweedsmuir, governor of Canada. It is spy story of the first world war, but it contained this curious passage, through one of his characters:

"You are an intelligent fellow, and you will ask how a Polish adventurer . . . and a collection of Jews and gypsies, should have got control of a proud race (Turks.)"

And again — reinforcing popular mis-conceptions about Jews:

"He (the German) has no gift for laying himself alongside different types of men. He is such a hard-shell being that he cannot put out feelers to his kind. He may have plenty of brains . . . but he has the poorest notion of psychology of any of God's creatures. In Germany only the Jew can get outside himself, and that is why, if you look into the matter, you will find that the Jew is at the back of most German enterprises."

John Buchan, I understand, was a prominent member of the British diplomatic service. Richard Meyer assures me he is a very fine man.

Today I met a rather interesting fellow. He was Edwin Beal, a Lieutenant, who was formerly a union organizer with United Electrical Workers — CIO. Parents were formerly missionaries in India. He speaks Arabic. He confesses to having a tough time in the Army because of his labor background.

Today, I chatted with the Jamaican soldiers. They seemed quite happy, though they had been at sea for six weeks, traveling from Jamaica to Norfolk, then to New York, and now on to England.

July 9, 1944

One thing that is reassuring about the West Indian contingent aboard is that they include without distinction — Negroes, Caucasians, East Indians and Chinese. They all bunk and mess together. They are, however, a little disturbed at the attitude [of] the American troops from the South!

Gannett told us today something about George Sokolsky, the New York Sun columnist.[3] It seems that he was once in love with a very wealthy gentile girl. He is an Orthodox Jew. Her family did everything to break up the affair, even to forming a fake news syndicate and having it employ him and then sending him to Russia and China as a foreign correspondent.

This eventually broke up the affair. He finally married a Westernized-Chinese girl. She is dead now, but she had one son before her death. Sokolsky made her go through the rites of becoming a Jew before he would marry her. Today, according to Gannett, Sokolsky is on the payroll of the N. A. M. He regards him as the "most venal man" he knows, believing that he came to be as he is because of his abortive love affair. He quotes Sokolsky as once saying that the U. S. government was the only big nation in the world that had never given money for propaganda.

"Indigo," a book about life in India, was recommended to me for reading as an excellent book about life in this country.

Today I met the first Negro from Harlem. He is Clarence Davis, a schoolmate of mine at P. S. 5.

The voyage is beginning to pall on me—too long.

July 10, 1944

Richard Meyer told me a tale today about Adolph Berle, who is with the American State Department. It seems that he is an egotist and feels his importance in the Department. Gannett says he is fiercely anti–De Gaullist. Anyway, soon after the U. S. entered the war, a woman said to Berle—knowing of his vanity—"It seems, Mr. Secretary, that this is a war of 'Adolph vs. Adolph,'" to which he smiled agreement.[4]

Today I saw a man—a lieutenant—who I believe is passing for white. More power to him! But he seems to avoid my eyes. He is in command of

---

3. George Sokolsky (1893–1962) was a columnist for the *New York Herald-Tribune* and the Hearst newspaper chain for many years. He was also affiliated with the National Association of Manufacturers and was a bitter critic of the New Deal and organized labor. In the 1950s, Sokolsky championed the anticommunist crusades of Senator Joseph McCarthy. See Richard Gid Powers, *Not without Honor: The History of American Anti-communism* (New York: Free Press, 1994), 182, 231–232, and Louis Pizzitola, *Hearst over Hollywood: Power, Passion and Propaganda in the Movies* (New York: Columbia University Press, 2002), 369–360.

4. Adolf A. Berle, Jr. (1895–1971), was a professor of corporate law at Columbia University Law School and an esteemed member of Franklin Roosevelt's brain trust, an informal council of public policy advisers. Berle also served as an assistant secretary of state for Latin American affairs and as ambassador to Brazil. See Jordan Schwarz, *Liberal: Adolf A. Berle and the Vision of an American Era* (New York: Free Press, 1987), and Adam Cohen, *Nothing to Fear: FDR's Inner Circle and the Hundred Days That Created Modern America* (New York: Penguin Books, 2009), 70–75.

a white unit. Gannett talked with him—found him quite hesitant about his ancestry. He avoids me.

What has been an uneventful voyage so far turned out to be quite a surprise last night. Word was passed to us that a menacing sub was in the vicinity of our ship. Everybody scrambled about to get on warm clothing, etc. Nothing was said to the troops below deck to avoid possible panic. After an hour or so everything turned out O.K. Rather anti-climax, but certainly preferable to the real thing.

Today I talked with a Negro corporal who made this observation: "You can't make a first class soldier out of a second class citizen."

It seems that I am one of the few men aboard who didn't bring along a stock of women's stocking, candy and lipstick for romantic activities in London! These are the pay-off, I am told.

July 11, 1944

I can't help noticing that Negro soldiers are much more sturdy and physically developed than the Jamaican boys—some of whom weigh as little as 90 pounds. Perhaps lack of proper diet in the tropics has stunted their growth.

Now reading Sumner Welles' book, "The Time for Decision."[5] Rather naïve in spots, though he may be concealing the truth. Interesting passage on Nazi (Goering) reaction to U.S. race situation (p. 117) and French attitude toward Jews (pp. 130–131).

Today the sea looked like a great greenish-blue blanket with white tufts over its entire expanse. Illness seems to have overtaken my cabin-mates—first Kulick, Kaplan, then Miller and Meyer. And now Gannett. Nothing serious though.

It was announced today that we will debark at Liverpool. Then from there to London by train.

Gannett confided to me—that with the men on board being almost 80% from the South, there still had been no off-the-record comments about the privileges I enjoy—which of course I should enjoy! Certainly no one has offered any word or gesture to indicate animosity.

The English women aboard have finally broken the ice and started chatting with me. They seem anxious that I like England.

---

5. Sumner Welles (1892–1961) was a longtime member of the American diplomatic corps, serving as Franklin Roosevelt's undersecretary of state from 1937 to 1943. He was one of FDR's most-trusted foreign policy advisers. See Benjamin Welles, *Sumner Welles: FDR's Global Strategist* (New York: St. Martin's Press, 1997), 313–374.

July 12, 1944

According to schedule, today was the day we were to debark, but the tide went out before we arrived so we must wait until tonight or tomorrow. Which means back to reading. Ran across this interesting line in Sumner Wells' "The Time for Decision:"

"... one of the objectives in the battle being waged by the United Nations is to make it safe and possible for all peoples to return to the land of their origin and to be treated without discrimination and upon a basis of full equality with their fellow citizens."

One can't help wondering how this high-minded objective squares with the treatment of Negroes in the U.S.!

Negro soldiers told me about a conflict between white and Negro troops in a Georgia camp, caused by the raping by a white soldier of a Negro Wac: One boy admitted that it may have been a rumor. But an armed battle followed in which 38 white MP's, 2 Negro and 20 white officers were killed. They say 300 Negro soldiers were sentenced to Leavenworth for periods ranging from 10 to 24 years. The rest of the division was broken up and sent to different parts of the country.

The facts of this story have been repeated to me by five different fellows on three different occasions.

Today is the second day we have been standing outside Liverpool waiting to disembark. The time drags horribly. Everyone is swiftly becoming demoralized. As we went on deck today, a great flock of seagulls came out to greet the ship. Nice sight.

July 13, 1944

Yesterday an English officer lectured to the Negro troops concerning life in England. The thing which seemed to be uppermost in the minds of Negroes was: How will we be treated? In particular, they asked if English women would associate with them—to use their language—"would the women perform?" The Englishman answered that women in England were like women everywhere, "Some do. Some don't." and this was entirely up to the individual soldier and the girl. However, he admonished them that Negro troops should observe the American standards, meaning they should observe the amenities of Jim Crow.

It seems rather significant that the problem of race relations can be a topic for Negro troops, and absolutely taboo for white troops—who, I would imagine, need more information. Indeed, it is a low estimate—in this connection—of the American intelligence that Richard Meyer, in his lecture to the white American soldiers about the French people, felt called upon to warn the soldiers that "Every French woman was not a whore!"

Another day idling in the harbor. What a drag.

One Negro corporal told me today that he had been in the Army for almost a year and had only shot his carbine four times. He is a member of a service group, but feels he should have had more training with firearms before being sent abroad.

I talked with a white major—from the South—who was amazed that there was no Jim Crow in England. He said the white Southern troops will be very disturbed when they find out. They assume that Jim Crow exists everywhere.

July 14, 1944

Last night I spent two hours talking with two Russian engineers and a Czecho-Slovakian who works for BBC. The Czech interpreted. The Russians expressed amazement at the separation between Negroes and whites aboard. So did the Czech, who, however, understood it better since he had spent some time in the U.S. The Russians were quick to say that all peoples in the Soviet were equal. They wanted to know why—in the face of inequalities—Negroes still loved their country. I explained they love the U.S. for the same reasons that Russians loved Russia during the Czarist regime. Negroes obviously hate the unfair treatment that they receive by certain elements in the government—but for three hundred years they have put their blood, sweat and tears into building the nation, so they have the love one has for a possession. This statement seemed to make sense to them. However, I found myself at something of a disadvantage trying to explain the American race problem to a foreigner without any background for the subject. Its implications and subtl[e]ties are so unique and the problem so vast that I almost found myself speechless. The Czech felt that the Negro problem in the U.S. was increasingly being recognized as fundamental by a growing number of white Americans. The Russian commented on the paradox of American[s] fighting for "democracy" and at the same time denying it to their Negro citizens. They felt it was a luxury that any nation could ill-afford in a total war against Fascism.

Tomorrow positively we have been assured we will got off this tub! Thank heaven!

July 15, 1944

Gannett told us a story about Theodore Roosevelt, Jr.[6] We just heard by radio he died of wounds. Gannett attended Harvard with him. It seems an issue came up at Harvard over a Negro student living in the dormitories. Gannett and others protested that the Negro should be admitted on a basis of equality with others. They appealed to Roosevelt to support the petition. He was indifferent. Soon afterwards Heywood Broun wrote a blistering newspaper column castigating Harvard for its intolerance.[7] Promptly thereafter Roosevelt came out with a "beautiful" statement supporting the Negro's right to live in the dormitory.

Today we finally pushed into Liverpool. The ship was unloading all night. The whole business of waiting had become pretty tedious. Tonight — London! And the beginning!

Liverpool finally! Looks very much like Scranton, Pa., a sprawling, dirty industrial city. The trip to London was enjoyable — and the first real chance to see the English countryside. Every inch of land seems cultivated. The soldiers aboard seemed amused by the little "dinky" railroad freight cars which are half the size of American cars. The car in which we rode was filthy, showing how England has run down because of the lack of manpower. All along the route people waved to the troops in the most friendly fashion. The welcome seems utterly genuine.

Arrived in London at 9 P.M. Took one hour to secure a taxi to take us to the hotel. The U.S. Billeting Service reserved rooms for us at the Russell Hotel.

July 16, 1944

Today is my first day in London. And what a day. I arrived late last night. I am staying at the swank Russell Hotel, but I expect to be moving Monday since I ran into another correspondent who has a flat and says I can share it with him. It will be much cheaper.

I am writing this from the Public Relations office of the War Department, where they provide all sorts of services for the correspondents. Everyone said they knew I was coming and were quite cordial.

---

6. Theodore Roosevelt, Jr., was the son of former president Theodore Roosevelt. He served in many capacities in the military, in the government, and in the private sector. He was awarded the Medal of Honor for his valor on D-day. See H. P. Jeffers, *Theodore Roosevelt, Jr.: The Life of a War Hero* (Novato, CA: Presidio Press, 2002).

7. Heywood Broun (1888–1939) was a newspaper reporter, columnist, editor, and founder of the left-leaning Newspaper Guild union. See "Obituary: 3000 Mourn Broun at St. Patrick's Mass," *New York Times*, December 21, 1939.

The brief taste I have of this city convinces me that living can be mighty grand. The service, for example, at the Russell Hotel is impeccable. This morning the maid brought tea to my bed—as an eye opener. Everyone is very friendly. As you know, there is no Jim Crow, so the city is open to me to get my fill.

To flash back to my ship experiences: I was assigned to a first class cabin aboard ship. My cabin mates were Kulick, the photographer; Miller, Office of Strategic Services; Myer, Office of Strategic Services; Rube Kaplan, radio technician; and Gannett. What a gang! They were, of course, friendly and cordial, but such drips. Miller was a shorty-george with a general's complex. He was constantly upbraiding the gang of us because we didn't show enough deference to Army officers aboard. Myer, who isn't Jewish, lived abroad for 16 years before the war. He was a fussy somebody who played solitaire throughout the whole trip. He had a big belly, a bald head with a little fuzz on the back and talked with the high soprano of a queen in drag. His big belly made me self-conscious about mine—so I began watching my diet. Rube Kaplan, a Jew, and very conscious of it, was the swellest of the lot. He is from Brooklyn! Kulick, a Jew, but not conscious of it, was a complete show-off—a little on the Bronx wiseguy side. He knocked himself out flashing his camera around and taking a lot of senseless pictures. Gannett turned out to be the complete drip I expected. He never lost a moment to demonstrate his "liberality" when there was no occasion for it.

Among the troops aboard was a Negro contingent. I spent little time with them as they could add nothing to my knowledge about the problem. They were quite charming, friendly, and without malice. I played cards with them a few times. With my captain's rank—which all correspondents have—I had the run of the ship. The Southern boys aboard were a little bewildered at first to see me—e[s]pecially with all the privileges I was entitled to. After they got over their bewilderment, they started chatting and soon bored me with their woofing. I was the only Negro aboard who ate in the grand dining room. This of course surprised the Negroes aboard!—as it did the white boys from the South.

The most interesting part of the trip was talking with two Russian engineers aboard and a Czech working for the BBC. He translated. They were anxious to know about the U.S. as they had not spent any time there. They had passed through on their way to England from Russia. Incidentally, they had their secretaries with them. They bunked in the same cabin together—the four of them! Nice going!

The first thing that they were amazed about was the separation of the Negro troops from the white troops. They had heard of the problem in the

U.S. but did not know it took that form. One of them asked me why it was Negroes still loved America in spite of the way they were treated. I tried to explain that the answer to that question was the same as why the Russian peasants loved Russia during the Czarist regime. They don't love the treatment but they love the country. This seemed to make sense to them.

The Czech was quite convinced that the "problem" would eventually become a world-wide issue. He had spent some time in the U.S., and met a number of white people who felt that the issue was coming to a head and would have to be settled.

Back to Gannett—he was—all during the trip—the "what-ever-happened-to-Joe-Doakes in Chipmonk" type. He constantly was asking soldiers if they knew old Joe Doakes back in Tougaloo—to which the soldiers always said no! For they are drawn from a different background than he, and would hardly know the same type of people. He's an old gossip too—he told stories about a number of people.

★ ★ ★

Last night I went to Picadilly Circus. I went alone—thus ending my relationship with the gang from the ship. Good riddance!

Picadilly Circus today is a cheap edition of Broadway, but much more on the Coney Island side in some respects. The streets swarm with American soldiers. Here are found the theatres, restaurants and night clubs. Prostitution abounds. Haggling is heard above the din of street noises, and often under the very noses of the Bobbies! Average price: 5 pounds!

Many of the whores are working girls who earn so little they must seek supplementation. Others are "spree girls." And still others seek a little adventure for otherwise drab lives. However, money seems the chief incentive for the Americans are spending like drunken sailors. The streets are darkened so the area almost looks menacing. I came much too late to see anything, as everything closes down at 11 P.M. Imagine! Incidentally, a quart of Scotch whiskey costs $20!

Back to Hotel, which is on the Victorian side in appointments, but very snooty. Only officers and fancy people stay here. Down the street at the Hotel Royal the enlisted men are billeted, along with the hoi po[l]loi. Ran into two R.A.F. fliers and chatted about life. Met them in the cocktail lounge. We chewed the fat until 2 A.M. They seemed worried about what the folks back home were doing. I was strangely not tired when it came time to go to bed.

This morning the chambermaid came in and woke me. She is a prostitute I learned after she indicated her pleasure. After my refusal, she then offered to supply me with the telephone operator! What a joint! Below the fancy tinsel of hotel, life is pretty sordid here—but supplies a vital need for the soldiers who need relaxation when they have their furloughs.

July 17, 1944

London's face is strong and sturdy—but pockmarked in places. The air attacks have torn up the city. Everyone here says the "robot" bombs are more menacing [than] the blitzkrieg, though the latter did more physical damage. America has no idea what day-to-day living in London is, with constant threat of these "robots" flying over head. There seems no way to stop them from coming in. You have the most hopeless feeling.

Today I was in a building that was partly shattered by a robot yesterday. The walls are cracked and gutted. Every window was shattered though the bomb exploded more than four blocks away. While I was in one of the offices being processed for my accreditation, a "robot" came over. Everyone stopped what they were doing and stood still. Fear was plainly visible on every face. I frankly was frightened.

There it came, coming with a loud hum. No one knows where it will land. Everyone prays that it won't hit the building in which he stands. The bomb flies overhead in a straight line, suddenly stops humming, and equally suddenly makes an abrupt dive. When this one came over the building I was in, I thought "Roi, what the hell are you doing here?" For one snatch of a second my heart stopped. It finally dived about a half mile from the building. Then the explosion. The concussion threw everyone to the floor.

And so it goes, day in and day out, every hour of the day and night. Under such conditions you can hardly concentrate.

Today I took a flat with Ed Toles, W.C. for the Chicago Defender.[8] He seems like a good guy and has been very helpful.

London! The old city is sturdy but a little frayed around the edges. Last night I went briefly to Piccadilly Circus—the Broadway of London. I traveled on the "underground" (subway). If you really want to know what war is, you should see women, children and old men sleeping on the staircases and platforms. Their pinched faces and startled eyes showed fear, despair, even wonder. But—at the same time—a bottle of whiskey costs $40!—and the Americans are spending money like it was water. Girls who

8. Edward B. Toles (1909–1998) graduated from the University of Illinois in 1932 and the Loyola University of Chicago Law School in 1936. He reported on the war for the *Chicago Defender* from 1943 to 1945. In 1961, he became the president of the Cook County Bar Association, and in 1968, he was appointed a U.S. bankruptcy judge for the Northern District of Illinois. He was the first African American to serve on the federal bankruptcy bench in Chicago. See "Just the Beginning Foundation: Edward Bernard Toles," Just the Beginning Foundation, http://jtbf.com/index.php?src=directory&view=biographies&srctype=detail&refno=137, (accessed May 1, 2010).

work in war plants often take their vacations as prostitutes — I am told. Yet there still seems to be a class of women in this town who look like glamor girls — and, if you ask me, don't look much different in dress and hair-do than American girls.

The lower classes, however, look mighty seedy and unkempt. Englishmen do not pay as much attention to their appearance as American men. Incidentally, I have only seen two Negroes walking the streets since I've arrived.

Back to London — it certainly is a fine mellowed looking city — but with tremendous pock-marks across its face. English authors have not overstated the case for old England — that is, physically looking. Picadilly Circus is, of course, the street where all the theatres and night clubs are located a little on the side. Prostitution is as open as all outdoors. Haggling is seen and heard. American soldiers swarm all over the place.

I arrived at 11 o'clock, which was much too late to see much. All night spots — that is, almost all — close at 11. So I returned to the hotel, where I had a whiskey and soda in the cocktail lounge. There I fell in with two R.A.F. fliers. We chatted until two in the morning. And that closed my first night in London. Today, I haven't been around yet. Only to the business places I must go to. The place I was to go to, I have just discovered was bombed out last night. So, I must wait until tomorrow. Incidentally, I heard my first robot bomb this morning. It fell two blocks from the hotel where I was staying. It nearly knocked all the windows out. The night before we arrived, the hotel was bombed and half the place was knocked away. I hope it doesn't get bombed again until I get out! Yet, somehow, people are not particularly nervous about the bombing and everything seems to go on normally — so am I.

July 18, 1944

I talked to a girl last night, who was very unhappy. She unburdened herself to me. She is about to be drafted for labor service. She is a clerical, but is being assigned a job peeling vegetables at 35 shillings a week! She says she doesn't understand why anyone would want to leave free America.

"The English people are so oppressed," she remarked.

Met Joe Louis today and talked with him briefly.[9] He is on his way to Africa on a morale tour. Few people seem to recognize him.

9. Joe Louis (1914–1981) was the heavyweight boxing champion of the world from 1937 to 1949. His prewar slugfests with the German champion Max Schmeling electrified the sporting world and made Louis a national hero. One of the finest histories of those events is David Margolick, *Beyond Glory: Joe Louis vs. Max Schmeling, and a World on the Brink* (New York: Vintage, 2006). During World War II, Louis served in the Special Services Division of the army, working to raise the morale of the GIs, especially African American troops.

Saw Carleton Moss, who is filming Negro troop activity for the War Department, briefly today.[10] Have a supper date with him. He was in uniform and seems, as always, like the cat that swallowed the mouse. He is in General Davis' party, which is going to France to take pictures of Negro combat troops.[11]

I have received word that I am going to France tomorrow—at 11 o'clock.

Met Ernest Hemingway yesterday. Had a long talk with him. He introduced me to an English couple as "one of the outstanding Negro writers of America." He's going away for three weeks. Says he wants to help me get around London when he returns. He has shaved off his famous beard. Told me he's busted—had to borrow $12,000 from his publisher. Says taxes took most of the money he has earned. Thinks "For Whom the Bell Tolls" was a lousy picture. I asked him why he had never written about a positive Negro character. He felt Negro writers could do it better. Expressed great admiration for Richard Wright as a writer.

Met "Frisco"—an American Negro who has lived in France since the last war. He runs a night club called "Frisco's." He opened London's first night club of the black-and-tan variety in 1934. Speaks French and German fluently. He is ink black and solidly built with bright gold teeth.

July 19, 1944

Met Frederick Kuh, United Press and Field Publications correspondent yesterday.[12] He has been very helpful in introducing me around. Some people at the British Ministry of Information have read my book. They are cooperative.

10. Carlton Moss (1909–1997) was a writer, filmmaker, and educator. During World War II, Moss worked for Frank Capra's military film unit, where he wrote the important documentary *The Negro Soldier* (1944), a propaganda film that was meant to encourage racial healing and African American participation in the war effort. See Thomas Cripps and David Culbert, "*The Negro Soldier* (1944): Film Propaganda in Black and White," *American Quarterly* 31 (Winter 1979): 616–640, and Erik Barnouw, *Documentary: A History of the Non-fiction Film*, 2nd rev. ed. (New York: Oxford University Press, 1993), 161–162.

11. Brigadier General Benjamin O. Davis, Sr. (1880–1970) was the first African American general in the U. S. Army. During the war, Davis served in the Office of the Inspector General and on the Advisory Committee on Negro Troop Problems. He also conducted multiple inspection tours of the African American soldiers serving in the army. The most complete biographical study of Davis is Marvin E. Fletcher, *America's First Black General: Benjamin O. Davis, 1880–1970*, Modern War Studies (Lawrence: University Press of Kansas, 1999).

12. Frederick Kuh (1895–1978) was a news reporter for United Press and International Press; for Roi Ottley's own employer, *PM*; and for the *Chicago Sun-Times*. He was also a frequent contributor to left-wing political journals such as *The Nation* and *The Liberator*. Although no one has yet produced a biography of Kuh, his papers are housed at George Washington University and remain the most reliable source of information about his life. See Frederick Kuh Papers, Special Collections Research Center, George Washington University, Washington, DC.

A radio man told me yesterday that he was up to a Negro camp, where he heard that 150 English girls were pregnant by the boys. Wondered what could be done about it, since Army discourages marriages between whites and American Negroes.

Last night I spent the most miserable and frightening night of my life. The "Buzz bombs" were coming over London at the rate of one every ten minutes. The Nazis started sending them over at midnight continuously until about 10 A.M. Next morning I lay in bed unable to sleep all night listening to the crash, crash, crash—wondering! At least three of them hit within two blocks of our flat and shook the house until the building seemed as though it would fall apart. I frankly was never so scared. I thought my time was up. Unless one has experienced these raids, he has no idea how demoralizing they can be. Every woman I have met in London is nervous, [al]most on the verge of hysteria. Ed Toles is a wreck.

Before going home last night, I stopped at "Frisco's" and met a red-headed German woman, who had just been released as a Nazi spy. She told me of her experiences while interned for three years. Food could be bought at prohibitive prices. Women turned to Lesbianism for sex. Work only source of maintaining morale. She is now a prostitute.

July 20, 1944

Today we are off for an advance section of the front in France. Left London for Southampton. Arrived in afternoon. Made a tour of the city. Negro troops quartered here. We—Randy Dixon, Ed Toles and me—had to travel by freight car to Southampton. We were in very aristocratic company—as today—first come, first served.

The ship taking us over is filled to twice its normal capacity. There are Negro and white troops aboard, as well as Englishmen and Canadians. Conditions are horrible, resembling the slave ships of old. We were assigned to the hatch [sic]—which is the hold of the ship. There are only a handful of bunks, so most of the men are sleeping on the floor. We slept on the deck wrapped in blankets. Late last night it rained. It poured into the hatch soaking every man below. So tired were some that they continued to sleep.

The Negro troops are full of injustices done them by various army officers, even of threatened lynching by officers when they meet in pubs. Americans deeply resent what little freedom Negroes enjoy here. The chief complaint by Negroes is the stories told the English people. Example: All Negroes have tails! Children, in very friendly fashion, meet Negro troops on the streets of English towns and ask very innocently to be shown their tails.

Judging by the troops on board—the English are very docile about miserable living conditions aboard ship. They do not complain.

Arrived! But cannot debark because sea is too rough. France stands firmly—about a mile away. Maybe tomorrow.

July 21, 1944

Today, the sea is tossing the ship as if it were a leaf in a hurricane. We all feel wet and miserable. We haven't had a cooked meal aboard. Eating "K" rations. Improvised toilet is so filthy that we have been unable to relieve our bowels. I welcome constipation at this point! We were told that when the sea is rough the ships remain outside sometime[s] for as long as nine days. There are, of course, no ports. The ships are unloaded by other boats which come alongside. Heavy military equipment aboard can't be moved while the sea is tossing.

The correspondents had a run-in with Colonel Cooper, transport commander. He has failed to extend any privileges or courtesies, normally extended to correspondents. We voiced our protest vigorously. But I can't help recognizing the difficult spot we are in, since our rank of "captain" is an assimilated one, and we are protesting against the absence of privileges which we are entitled to by no law or military order. We requested transportation ashore.

Another day aboard ship.

Negro troops get along excellently with English soldiers—boys from Wales, Scotland, England and Canada. They play a lot of stud poker together and exchange stories. There is not much fraternizing among the Negro and white troops. White Americans don't fraternize with the English soldiers. English soldiers don't like the Americans because of their overbearing manner.

One Negro aboard stands out: He is black, a 300-pounder, a technical sergeant, who says he has been busted of his rank seven times in a year. He runs the crap game aboard ship. He was the man white GIs wanted to hang. He is 21 years old and comes from Cleveland, Ohio. His name is Samuel Jackson.

July 22, 1944

Night holds a terror for the soldier that cannot possibly be understood or felt unless one actually lives with them under battle conditions. Aboard the transport, last night, I realized this. The clouds hung heavy and low. The thumping hum of Nazi planes could be heard overhead. Rockets were sent up from the beach, while co[a]stal batteries went off. The men down in the hatch—forbidden to leave—were trying to sleep. The stark terror of the situation came to me as I lay awake—just listening. Not to the activity above, but to the uneasy breathing of sleeping men. They shouted and groaned in their sleep—"Help me mother!" "Peggy, don't leave me!" "Get the guns!" They tossed and muttered all night conscious that they would be meeting the foe in a matter of hours. This hatch the men unimaginatively call "The Black Hole of Calcutta." It more resembles the fierce woodcuts of olden slave times of the slave ships transporting blacks from Africa.

July 23, 1944

Another day of waiting to get over to France. Nothing much to do but look at the sea. But this is hardly a pretty sight for all day long arms, legs and torsos of men, who had been blown up, drift by. The patch, white leg of a Nazi—bits of clothing hung to the leg—turn the stomach of all aboard. The frayed meat of the upper part gave me goose pimples.

Talked with a careerist soldier—a white captain of the paratroopers. He sought conversation with Negro correspondents because the "Negro question" in England was bothering him. He wondered what would happen when the American Negroes return to the U.S. after having had intimate relations with white women. He said the situation had reached the proportions of a scandal among the high command. He was quick to say that he believed in the equality of Negroes but he was opposed to giving them privileges of equality before they had received education.

Tonight Jerry is overhead raining bombs on the ships in the harbor. One plane came down in a swoop and strafed the ship. We all rushed for cover, diving for our helmets. The night is lighted up like an Xmas tree, as tracer bullets are sent up by our forces on the mainland to locate the planes in the sky. People at home may talk about peace and the end of the Luftwaffe, but here the war and Nazi planes are a stunning reality!

[*Page 33 of the manuscript has a leaflet "Dropped by Nazi Planes 7/23/44 over Negro troops at St. Laurent-sur-Mer." The leaflet reads "Why die for Stalin?"*]

July 24, 1944

Today we arrived on the beachheads of Normandy. Against a background—resembling the Palisades of the Hudson River—could be seen the wreckage of some 200 ships. The French coast was torn up, with big red splotches of earth—torn holes in the silent green mass of hills. As our barge brought us in the first sight of human being was a group of U.S. sailors playing football on the beach. A handfull of French children were watching curiously.

Once on shore we climbed the hills to the top where we ran into a barrage balloon outfit of Negroes. They were very cordial and happy to see new faces. They fed us — a regular G.I. meal, but given a special hand — rice, coffee, and a sort of sausage meat of pork.

From there we took off for the front, going by jeep supplied to us by the beach headquarters of the Army. Driving to the front, we met devastation on every hand. Our naval guns from the Channel played havoc with the German fortifications but also with the homes of the French people.

These are some of my initial observations of Normandy:

1. Nearly two out of every three American soldiers is a Negro. They seem to be everywhere.
2. In the small town of Isigny I saw a funeral parlor displaying a coffin with a baby. The showcase was windowless.
3. Making a swift turn around one of Isigny's narrow streets, I caught a glimpse of a 12-year old boy in a barber shop (coiffeur) in white uniform shaving a man who looked to be five times his age.
4. Castles of old Norman lords.

July 25, 1944

Today we went on a tour of the front at St. Lo. We visited the Negro troops — Signal Corp. and Trucking Co. They are a hardy band, who are making the best of a bad situation. On our way back we visited the war prisoners — just captured. They certainly didn't look or act like supermen! They were in barbed wire pens. With the aid of an interpreter I interviewed six men — a druggist, a restaurateur, a paratrooper (Luftwaffe) and the rest were a pretty average group. They are from Essen, German. I asked them if they had heard about the blacks in America. Yes. But they knew nothing about their condition. They showed no animosity toward me, but were polite and cooperative. They had no knowledge of the fact that American Negroes were in Normandy or fighting. When asked how the felt, they said they felt nothing. Asked if they thought it unusual, they said No! and added that Negroes were human beings just like themselves. Their average age was 29. Their average education: public school. Two owned their own small businesses in Germany. They manifested a deep fear of the Russians, particularly the sort of peace terms they thought the Soviets would exact. Told that the Russians might want German labor to rebuild their country, they showed astonishment, and said, "But war will be over!" Told that Germany had enslaved French labor, they explained this as conscription, "and therefore Russia had no right to conscript them." Germany's act was a wartime measure, they explained. Asked whether or not they thought Germany would win the war, they showed considerable doubt. They express the hope—if Germany lost—that England and the U.S. would occupy Germany. They are definitely afraid of Russia!

* * *

We correspondents—Ed Toles (Defender), Randy Dixon (Courier) and myself—left London July 20th for an advance section of the front. From there we went to Southampton, where in peace time ships dock for people going to London. We spent the day there sightseeing. We had to travel in freight cars to Southampton. We were in very fancy company as trains operate on the first-come-first-serve plan. There are no Pullman cars. Southampton looked much like main street in any American city. The people, however, were very civil and helpful about giving directions. I saw only one Negro here! Others were American soldiers, who swarmed everywhere.

That night we boarded a transport for France—rigged out in full battle equipment of American soldiers. Nothing in one's imagination could describe the horrible conditions aboard these transports. We were assigned to a hatch, or hole of the ship—there is, of course, no first-class travel. In space about the size of a two-room apartment in a tenement hundreds of men slept in their clothes. Me too! For it rained and we were unable to sleep on deck. The rain nevertheless poured down on us in the holes. Jim Crow could not operate here—so Negro and white troops slept side by side.

Next morning we arrived. But were unable to debark. It was a nice feeling seeing France for the first time—standing there hilly but firmly. You may get an idea of things to know that we spent five days a mere half mile from shore aboard ship. The sea was extra rough and tossed the ship about like it was a leaf in the breeze. Many men got seasick. I didn't though. Food was cold and from cans—K rations—for the entire five days. Improvised toilets were so filthy that I had enforced constipation for three days—finally I had to break down and do my number!

Night holds a terror that no civilian can possibly imagine. For from midnight to morning the Germans bombed relentlessly the ships lying outside France. Often their dive-bombers would come down with a roar sufficient to drive a man crazy and then strafed the boats. I make no bones about it—I was scared as hell. On the whole, though, our planes and shore batteries protected us from any serious harm. One night I stood on the deck with others—German planes were roaring overhead—and wished with all my heart that I was home. It's a hell of a miserable feeling. For each bomb that comes down you wonder whether it has your number on it. Moreover, you feel so damned helpless—unable to defend yourself or even run.

Though France's coastline is a beautiful sight to see, we had a number of intrusions. Hanging over the deck rails looking at the sea, every once in a while a man's leg, or arm, torso, would float by, mute evidence of the horrors of war. One such leg almost fascinated us—it was a well formed limb frayed at the top where the leg was torn away from the body and was full of bullets and blanched white.

But there is a beauty of a sort in war—One night Jerry's planes were overhead. One came down with a mighty swoop and strafed the deck. We all dashed for cover, diving for our helmets in order not to be hit by flak, and peeked out to see what was going on. The night was lit up like a Xmas tree. Tracer bullets from the shore batteries poured out a great rainbow. This showed brilliantly against the dark skies. Across the scene would travel a Nazi plane. Then ack ack of our guns. And soon the plane would come down in burst of fire—blazing yellow, red, and swishes of white.

To flash back—Monday we finally arrived on the beachheads of Normandy. From there we took off for the front, after being processed by the Army officials, traveling by jeep. Driving along toward the front, we saw devastation everywhere. Our naval guns played havoc with German fortifications, some ingeniously hidden in the hills and in the homes of the French people. Here is a brief sample of some of the things I saw:

1. Nearly two out of every three American soldiers was a Negro soldier. They seem to be everywhere working like dogs.
2. In one small town, I saw a funeral parlor displaying an open coffin with the body on view. It stood in the show window—which incidentally was windowless.
3. In making a swift turn around one of the small narrow streets I caught a glimpse of a 12-year-old boy in a barber shop in white uniform shaving a man who looked to be six times his age.
4. The architecture is built along feudal lines. They have the cold Norman outlines of Norman personality.

Arriving at our destination, we were given a tent to live in. There is a continuous burst of shells, planes overhead, and thousands of trucks jogging along. Troops everywhere. The French people are little in evidence. You may be interested to know they do not appear to be filled with any great hatred for the Germans.

They say the Germans paid for everything they received and were very courteous. Imagine! Well, you must understand something about Normandy. Actually, it is more English than French. For the Normans belong to the same racial stock as the English. Indeed, William the Conqueror, a Norman, was the first English king—or so I believe if I remember my history correctly. The people live on the land and have all the conservatism inherent in people who work the land. Ever since German occupation this section was the most prosperous in France. The resistance movement never reach[ed] any great heights here. Personally, they treat me exceptionally well. Many of the Negro soldiers have French girls. And until just before I arrived the French conducted a brothel for the exclusive use of Negro soldiers—a gesture of friendship and comradeship I suppose. Actually, race is no issue here. Either between Negroes and white or French and Americans. American soldiers have definitely relaxed and are according Negro soldiers their due, as all recognize the importance of each to the other. Death stares them all in the face!

Yesterday I visited the Nazi prisoners. It was quite an experience. Those people who talk about reeducating the Germans should first look to our own Southerners. This is not to say the German Nazi should be dealt with lightly. Most certainly they should feel the heavy hand of retribution—as a matter of fact, I'm all for the Russians drafting them for the rebuilding of devastated Russia.

They seem definitely without prejudice for Negroes, but this may have been a pose. The interpreter assured me, however, that he had been in Germany two years before the war on a special mission and Germany at that time had no crystallized feelings against Negroes. The Jews. Well, that's another matter. On that subject, they sounded like crackers talking about Negroes!

From here I am on my way to Cherbourg. I think there is better material there. I want to do a story for PM on the Army's civil administration of Cherbourg. And for Liberty, a story about a Negro who was leader of the Underground Movement in Cherbourg. There is much talk about him here.

July 26, 1944

A second thought came to me about my interview with the Nazi prisoners yesterday. They seem to have no fanaticism about color, so, in my view, they would be easily more re-educated than the Southerner on the Negro problem. Asked about the "Master race," theory (Herrenvolk) they honestly seemed bewildered and seem not to know its meaning at all.

Today we move on to Cherbourg. But the trip has been delayed until tomorrow. In any event, we are going for the day — only 65 miles.

Yes, we went to Cherbourg! What a city. The first thing that struck us was the smell of decaying bodies. Entering the city from the main road is a thrilling ride. There is a winding road down a steep hill walled by upright walls. A magnificent fortress — standing like a feudal castle — buttresses the entrance to Cherbourg. Devastation everywhere.

Our party was Allan Morrison, who used to be editor of the Negro Digest and now a U.S. Army war correspondent for "Stars and Stripes," and Randy Dixon.[13] A Negro sergeant drove us in a jeep. On our way here, we toured towns of Montebourg, St. Marie Eglise and Carentan, where some of the bitterest and fiercest fighting of the war took place.

Made a brief tour of the city of Cherbourg. Met Antoine Montbrun, a member of of the Resistance Movement (Underground). He now is a jailor at the Maison D'Arret. He is a handsome chap with a wonderful smile.

We returned for a "briefing" at Front Headquarters, where the movement, tactics and strategy of the new offensive was explained to us.

July 27, 1944

Cherbourg at last! We arrived today and were provided with headquarters at the American Press Club, 21 rue du Mont Belle. All the fellows are very cordial. An appointment was made for us to have lunch at the Hotel L'Estroille, most fashionable of the hotels in Cherbourg. The girls who waited on us admitted they had done the same job during the German occupation. These French are certainly realistic! Our party of correspondents included Ed Toles, Randy Dixon, Ollie Stewart and Rudolph Dunbar.[14] They all remarked that there was something historic in this meeting

13. Allan Morrison (1916–1968) was a journalist, music critic, and for a short time the publisher/editor of the *Negro Digest*. The *Digest* was a compilation of important journalism about African American life. It was purchased by Johnson Publishing Company, which also published *Ebony* and *Jet* magazines. Morrison was the first black correspondent for the U.S. military's newspaper, *Stars and Stripes*. See "*Jet/Ebony* Editor Allan Morrison Dies in NY," *Jet Magazine*, June 6, 1968, 51.

14. Ollie Stewart (1906–1977) was one of the correspondents for the *Baltimore Afro-American* during the war. After the war, Stewart briefly returned to the United States but then, bristling at the state of race relations, returned to Paris, where he spent the rest of his life. See John D. Stevens, "From the Back of the Foxhole: Black Correspondents in World War II," *Journalism Monographs*, no. 27 (February 1973): 10, 19, 21. Rudolph Dunbar (1907–1988) was a journalist from British Guiana who also happened to be an internationally recognized symphony conductor. He contributed articles to a number of news services, most notably the Associated Negro Press. In 1942, he conducted the London Philharmonic, and in 1945, he accepted an invitation to conduct the Berlin Philharmonic. See Stevens, "From the Back of the Foxhole," 10.

in France of Negro Correspondents—especially since we were all only partially acquainted before. This trip was arranged by the PRO [Public Relations Office] of the Army.

One thing that struck me was the caste system of the army—which holds in the face of race! For example, our chauffeur was a sergeant named Mark Barron.[15] In civilian life he was one of the editors of the Associated Press and former manager of the Guild Theatre in New York. He was decidedly a cultivated man. Yet, when we went to eat he had to mess with the enlisted men and we messed with the officers! I felt somewhat embarrassed for this superior man, for we all enjoyed his company and intelligent conversation. Furthermore, in the matter of sleeping, the race question has gone by the boards. No one here seems to have time for Jim Crow, nor do they seem to care. But the American Red Cross is now preparing to open a Jim Crow club. Upon inquiry why, they claimed the Army command forces them to do it.

★ ★ ★

When I first arrived in London I took quarters at the Russell Square Hotel. It was swanky and comfortable, but prohibitive in price. Five dollars a day! Finally I took a flat with Ed Toles—Chicago Defender correspondent—and I am paying 2 (pounds) a week, or eight dollars, which is considered extremely cheap. I eat most of my meals at the Officers' mess, which averages 50 cents a meal. I brought along ample things to get along with, except that there is such difficulty getting laundry done that often you must wear dirty shirts and underwear. Shower baths are a luxury few have here, though I get a sprinkling at the Red Cross club. Normally it costs about 100 dollars a week to live here, if you don't cut corners.

You might be interested to know that I am getting excellent cooperation from everyone here—so far, which of course enables me to get about and see many things. I'll be on the move again very soon. I am trying to get to Paris for a few climax stories, then to Africa and Italy. I had arrangements all set to leave last Saturday. I was going in General B. O. Davis' plane to Italy and Africa, but was granted interviews with the Belgian, Dutch, and English ministers of colonies. I thought these sufficiently important to delay my leaving.

My room mate aboard ship coming over to England, Harold Kulick was killed in an airplane crash. He was married. I have the unhappy task of

15. Before and after his stint in the military, Mark Barron (1905–1960) spent many years as a reporter for the Associated Press. He was also very well connected to the theater world in New York City. He managed the Guild Theatre and was married to the actor Erin O'Brien Moore. See John F. Barlow, "Mark Barron," Internet Movie Database, http://www.imdb.com/name/nm3175714/ (accessed May 2, 2010).

sending his things back to his wife. I know that while he was a gay sort of fellow with the ladies, he loved his wife profoundly. His whole reason for coming abroad, was pretty much like mine. He was trying to gain experience, knowledge, status, and prestige in his field, so that he could make a better life for himself and his wife. All this went to smash — I wonder about his wife, though I never met her. I've written her a nice letter. I guess being a war correspondent is a great gamble — for all or nothing.

July 28, 1944

Cherbourg! What a city! It must have been very beautiful before the war. It is nestled in a valley — one side has tremendous cliffs on which the French built huge fortresses and the other side opens to the sea. The streets themselves are hilly, narrow and a bit quaint. As a matter of fact, Cherbourg is little different in appearance from the French motion pictures we have seen, except — here in reality!

The war obviously has done things to the city and its people. Devastation is everywhere. Great architecture in churches, which had been standing for three and four centuries, have been leveled. Remains still contain great beauty and suggest that their building were labors of love. Ordinary houses are very small, the average room being the size of a tenement back room. Life here is primitive — though it is a large city — as compared with New York. Only the more expensive homes have modern plumbing. The country folk, or peasants, still use horse-drawn plows.

By and large the people are well-fed and healthy. These are the most realistic of the French people. They explain — for example — that they worked for the Germans! After all, the Germans paid high wages and big prices for merchandise. Imagine! The average unskilled laborer earning the equivalent of 8 dollars a day during Nazi occupation.

The vaunted political development of the French people is certainly not apparent here. Actually, I am told, hundreds of the healthiest and prettiest women of Cherbourg left with the retreating Germans. The four-year occupation obviously produced alliances, romances, and marriages, which these women apparently wished to continue — war or no war. Many a blond baby walks the streets. Every pregnant woman is referred to as carrying a "teuton."

The other side of the picture is this: The Nazis shipped all the healthy men — between the ages of 16 and 50 — to Germany to work in the war factories and on the farms. So, for four years, these women have been without Frenchmen. Obviously they needed men! So, they did the best under the circumstances even to doing the manual labor. It is an ordinary sight to see women here driving wagons, plowing fields, carrying tremendously large sacks on their backs, even working with pick and shovel. You should see the way these women swing a large ashcan over their shoulders.

Women who were not prepared to work in this manner had to turn to prostitution—unless they were independently wealthy. Prostitution flourishes openly in this city—as it does in all civilized cities of the world. But these houses here are filthy, seedy and haunting with disease. The women are a sight! Certainly no glamour girls here.

The American Army officials decided to solve the sex problem in a practical way. They allowed brothels to operate for a while. Negro soldiers were assigned their *own*. Imagine! But the large incidence of venereal disease caused them to finally declare all houses of prostitution "out of bounds." The Frenchmen, however, are allowed to visit the brothels. This certainly hasn't solved the problem of sex for the Americans.

I have finally discovered a character who should make a swell story. He is Antoine Montbrun, a Negro who was a leader of the underground movement here in Cherbourg. He is a handsome chap of six feet, with laughing eyes and a soft dark brown complexion. He was born in Martinique, but is a Frenchman to the core. He has a hatred for the Nazis so withering that it scares you to hear him talk about it.

Before the war he was a navigator in the French Merchant Marine. When the war began he became a member of the French Navy. When the French fleet—that is, the one anchored at the fort outside Cherbourg—decided to surrender, he protested so vehemently that Frenchmen told him that they would shoot him if he made a move against the invading Nazis. He was finally sent to a concentration camp at St. Lo, which is about 65 miles east of Cherbourg.

The Germans made distinctions between Negroes and whites in the concentration camps:

Most of the Negroes were Senegalese, and they were put in a section of the camp by themselves. It was here that Antoine was quartered. He told me that periodically the Germans would have sport at the expense of the prisoners. This was it: They would bring the prisoners—white and black—out into the open fields and tell them to run to a certain barrier. Then they would train a machine gun on the whole pack. The prisoners were to race for the barrier in a certain length of time—those who couldn't make it would be shot.

Well, at the crack of a gun the whole pack started running for their lives—you can imagine the fear that must have been in their faces! But the Nazis, instead of waiting for them to reach the barrier, would start shooting over their heads and at their feet to make them speed along. At everyone of these sporting events at least fifteen to twenty prisoners would be killed!

The Germans often sent for a prisoner on whim. When he had arrived and inquired what was wanted of him, the German would say, "Oh, nothing," and then tell the prisoner to return to his cell. As soon as he turned his back, the German shot him. Sometimes—if the German felt "humane"—he would merely shoot off an ear.

In this connection I cannot help recalling the most fantastic experience I have had here to date:

Yesterday I went out to tour the fortresses and underground forts the Germans had built to stave off invasion. Here was one of the most ingenious plans man has conceived. Words are inadequate to describe them. Anyway, I met an American officer who was in charge of this area since the day of liberation. He owns a German police dog, which he got during the invasion. This awful beast, looking like a huge wolf, had been trained by the Germans to hate the French: So today, whenever a Frenchman passes the dog, he snarls and growls and leaps for his throat. The officer told me that to his personal knowledge the dog had destroyed two French civilians since he had owned him! This is the enemy!

Before arrival in France, I was inclined not to believe all the horrible stories I had heard about Nazi brutality, but this eye-witness view has vastly changed my attitude. The propaganda didn't begin to tell the story about these German beasts. Theirs is not a brutality and cruelty of passion or of the moment—say like the lynching-bent Southerner. Theirs is a cold, ingeniously conceived method of torture—both of the mind and the body. Indeed, their control of the mind has even corrupted otherwise impeccable French people. Their "buzz bomb," for example, is another instance. For it destroys morale, though actually in terms of bombing destruction it achieves little.

Well, back to Antoine. Two years in a concentration camp did not break him. But he was declared insane by the Nazis and released. As it turns out, he too had a carefully conceived plan. He played the fool and thereby fooled the Nazis. Upon his release, he joined the Resistance Movement.

The Nazis allowed him a lot of freedom—after all, he was "enfeebled!" This freedom permitted him to become one of the couriers of Cherbourg's movement. Here the Resistance Movement did not have the wholehearted support of the French people, so it took considerable daring to operate. Interestingly enough, it was he who was the guide for the American forces when they landed for the invasion of Cherbourg.

There is a footnote to this story: Yesterday Antoine was assaulted on the streets by American soldiers! Why? Because he was talking to three French girls and the soldiers resented it. Not only did they attack and knock him to the ground, adding a few well placed kicks, but they dragged the girls off!

By no means do the French people welcome the Americans — we are not the vaunted liberators we hoped we'd be. Instead, many of them look at us as new oppressors — a change of masters so to speak. This, however, must be viewed against the background of four years of German occupation. Much of what went on in concentration camps, the average Frenchman has little knowledge of. But he does know of his day-to-day contacts with the German troops. Everyone says their conduct was impeccable. Whereas, the conduct of the American soldiers is disorderly, crude and domineering. They walk the streets with an arrogance that is offensive to right-thinking Americans here as it is to the French.

Wherever you go, one is apt to find divisions among the people. The group that is at the bottom of the social ladder in Cherbourg is the Algerians. They are mostly Mohammedans. They look like very dark Italians, indeed they both come from the same stock. For some reason, which I am unable to discover yet, they are discriminated against by the French. To hear a group of Algerians beefing about their condition, you'd think you were back in Harlem listening to Negroes air their grievances.

How did the Algerians get here and why? They tell me that they were in Paris and heard that the Germans were paying high wages in Normandy, so they came and worked on the fortifications! They resent being called Frenchmen — they are "Algerians."

Last night I spent a few hours at one of their cafes — "Buvette," was the name. It was the stinkiest hole I have ever been in, resembling much the joints on Beale Street during Prohibition. I drank a liquor called "calvados" — which is actually apple cider but tastes like bad corn. It costs 15 francs a drink, which is about 30 cents in American money.

The air of Cherbourg is putrid with the smell of decaying bodies — still buried under the debris of bombed buildings. Yet, the French people do not seem to mind much. They go about their daily chores as if there were no war. The merchants are having a holiday charging the Americans high prices.

Example: Antoine took me to a wine-merchant he knew to buy a bottle of calvados. He was a racketeer operating on the black market in liquor. He looked like the pictures of Al Capone, except that he was paunchy and had a red nose that stuck in your face when you talked with him. He charged 150 francs for a bottle. But the Americans buying along the avenue, legitimately, must pay 600 francs for a worse brand of the same thing. I bought a bottle for the boys which was 50 years old. It was good, nothing like that which I drank with the Algerians. Perhaps I got a buy because Antoine was along.

Incidentally, he seems very popular with the French people, for he has a very nice manner and a cute way of pouting his lips when he speaks. The women love it! But he doesn't seem particularly interested in women and is not conscious of being handsome and attractive to them.

I am staying at the U.S. Press Club operated by the Navy and situated—just for the record—along the Rue du Bello. I eat my meals here as the American cuisine is the best cooking in France today. As you might guess, the Americans have the lush brought over from the States. We don't even drink French water or milk and have been carefully warned against them. We even do not drink English milk, for neither the French nor the English have advanced dairy methods. Their cows still have T.B., and nothing the American authorities can do will persuade them to change.

I came to Cherbourg in company with four other Negro correspondents: Ollie Stewart, Ed Toles, Randy Dixon and Rudolph Dunbar, who, incidentally, is a very fine musician. He has conducted the London Symphony Orchestra and is well known in London. He represents the Negro Associated Press, but he is a bad writer. The boys left today, so now I am on my own, which I prefer. For they clutter the way to good stories and make it impossible for me to get cooperation from the Army authorities. I plan to stay here about a week to complete a story on Antoine and do a piece on civil affairs for PM. Then back to London.

French women are wearing scarfs made of parachute cloth—very chic! It is the most prized thing a woman can wear in France today, commemorating "D" Day. It is a prized possession. Women here, who can get a piece, wear it as a scarf, or bandana.

★ ★ ★

Today we went on a tour of the German fortifications. They have been destroyed beyond all reclaim. The man who planned the demolition job is said to have been decorated by Hitler. The American engineers say he deserved it! They show great admiration for the perfection with which he did his job. What remains is beyond the imagination. The fortifications were built six feet thick, reinforced with steel lacing. One fort is six miles long! In these subterran[e]an passages a whole army could live for months. There is an arsenal so big that few can imagine it without being an eyewitness.

Met a Lt. Rice, who owns a dog that hates French people. The dog was trained by the Nazis.

A wonderful story is going the rounds about the women correspondents:

They asked to have a beauty parlor opened so that they could have their hair finger-waved. I met them. Two stood out as characters: Proud Sonia Tomara, of the Herald Tribune, and Dopey Molly Maghoe, of the News Chronicle.[16] The men didn't like the idea of having women correspondents around — they get in the way.

Mark Barron told me the true story about Hubert Julian, the black ace, and his affair in Ethiopia.[17] He helped Julian to escape the wrath of Selassie, who threatened to have Julian shot for taking up his personal plane and demolishing it. He did this without permission and was thrown in jail. The American correspondents in Addis Abba got him out of jail and smuggled him into Djoubiti, which was then out of Selassies's control.

July 29, 1944

Just returned from an evening of new experiences. Ed Toles, Allan Morrison and myself went strolling about the city after dinner. We happened into a café, run by an Algerian. The place was called "Buette." It was a low-ceilinged affair about the size of a box car. In one corner was a bar, nasty and dirty, with the dirt of previous customers still on the bar. We drank "calvados" which looks like gin, made of apple cider, but tastes like bad corn. The Algerians are at the bottom of the social scale in Cherbourg, and they make a loud beef about it. They hate the French Catholics. They are Mohammedans! The proprietor had a slanting forehead, thick black hair, and looked much like a Sicilian. He wore German army boots and a yellow summer suit that had never seen a tailor since it was bought. His friends told me that they had come to Cherbourg from Paris two years ago, because they heard the Germans were paying high wages for labor on the fortifications. I have, as yet, to discover the real reason for their beef.

On our way home we stopped at the Hotel L'Etroille, to keep an appointment we had almost forgotten with a Major Holstein. Before entering the Army, he had conducted an investigation for government into adminis-

16. Sonia Tomara (1897–1982) was a war correspondent on the foreign staff of the *New York Herald-Tribune*. She covered the war in India, China, North Africa, and Europe. See "Obituary: Sonia Tomara Clark," *New York Times*, September 9, 1982, http://www.nytimes.com/1982/09/09/obituaries/sonia-tomara-clark.html (accessed May 2, 2010). I was unable to locate any additional information about Molly Maghoe.

17. Known as the "Black Eagle," Hubert Julian (1897–1983) was one of the first African Americans to earn a pilot's license. He was a notorious self-promoter and earned his celebrity by doing flyovers during Garveyite parades in Harlem. When the Italians invaded Ethiopia in 1935, Julian volunteered his services and was given command of Haile Selassie's air force, which consisted of three planes. See Brenda Gayle Plummer, *Rising Wind: Black Americans and US Foreign Affairs, 1935–1960* (Chapel Hill: University of North Carolina Press, 1996), 41, 43, 306.

tration in Puerto Rico. He said Puerto Rico's plight represented "American imperialism" at its worst. While there we also met a Mayor Lonsbury, Provost Marshal of the M.P.s. He was a lusty fellow, with a foul mouth, who was drunk and spoke loudly about his love for Negroes, but he was anti-Semitic! I suspect [he] did not know his host was Jew[ish]. He said he knew Paul Robeson and believed that racial equality was the thing. I didn't believe him though.

July 30, 1944

Today the boys returned to St. Lo. I am now alone for the first time this trip. I will stay awhile and do some stories before returning to London. Too many Negro newspapermen in one spot clutters up the outlets for stories. Nevertheless, I'll miss them for in the evenings they were a lot of fun. Ollie Stewart was pretty much of a lone wolf, hunting down cognac and French whores.

After lunch at Stars & Stripes mess, I returned to the Maison D'Arret to talk with Antoine Montbrun, a Negro. Today he asked me how he could get in the American Army. I never met anyone in my life with a greater hatred for the Nazis than he. However, it is not of the political variety sort. Having known the cruelties of a Nazi concentration camp, he has no illusions about the Nazis. Something happened today involving Antoine that made me sad. While I was talking with the chief (called chef), Antoine took bullets that I had picked up at the German fortifications, took the powder out and lit a match to it. The powder blazed in his face and burned him. He revealed his personality to me clearly: he dashed about like a wounded animal, with fear clearly written on his face. I took him to an American base hospital, after commandeering a jeep, and he was treated. Nothing serious, the doctor said, though he received second degree burns. I was very much relieved. The doctor, of all things, asked him if he could sing! He didn't understand, instead Antoine took out a picture of himself, autographed it, and gave it to the doctor as an indication of his appreciation for the treatment of his burns! What a man!

* * *

Observations:

1. American Red Cross club here—for Negroes—have a mixed staff, mostly white, though the executive jobs are held by Negroes.
2. The Normandy French seemed to have been accommodating to the Nazis, who were careful to make their conduct impeccable.

3. Practically every woman of working class in London sells her body! Before the war it cost 10 shillings. Now the women demand and get L 7 or 28 dollars! The Yanks are here!
4. The "doodle" bombs have affected the social pattern in a curious way: Few women today want to sleep by themselves, and will do most anything to have a man take them home. Actually it's not sex—they fear death alone!

July 31, 1944

Sgt. Mark Barron continues to amaze me. He was in Ethiopia covering the war between Italy and the Ethiopians for the Associated Press. He was a major in the Loyalist vs. Fascist war as a Loyalist, and is married to Erin O'Brien Moore, the actress who played Nana opposite Paul Muni in the motion picture, "Zola."

Had a grand time today interviewing various people. Wonderful material! Talked with the Mayor of Cherbourg, M. Paul Renault, who resembles Marshall Petain in more ways than one. He expressed the hope that there would be no President Wilsons at the peace table. Asked him to explain. He said Wilson had promised many things which the American people repudiated. His first assistant, called adjutant, M. Simon, was quite a character. He had thin white hair, prominent forehead, black bushy eyebrows and a pink complexion. He wore a frayed, wrinkled black suit, celluloid collar, ready made black tie, a black hombourg hat and a cane—and athletic sneakers, which, he admitted, his son bought twelve years ago in the U.S. He said he never knew anyone who was a member of the Resistance Movement (Underground) during German occupation. Not until the Americans came in did he discover who they were. His son was a member! His son is now in Savoie with the Maquis. The Mayor told of supporting 400 chambermaids to clean German quarters only to discover that they were the mistresses of German officers. Cost: 150,000 francs monthly.

Met Abbe Loile, who the Catholic Church assigned to work among the Todt workers, the mobile laborers of the Germans.

August 1, 1944

Today I continued my job of interviewing. Saw M. Charles, who documented Antoine's activities in the underground. He has a case history on him which he promised to allow me to see tomorrow. He was a short, intense, slight man of impeccable manners.

Saw Antoine again today. First went to see him at the Army Hospital, only to discover that he was transferred to Hospital Pasteur for French civilians. If Negroes had to go to such a filthy, run down, broken down place, they would howl their heads off — and they would be right. Antoine was not there. He had been discharged. Found him at Maison D'Arret.

Cherbourg was beginning to return to normal activity. Seven thousand were here when the Americans arrived. Now the population has jumped to twenty thousand. Before the invasion the population was thirty-eight thousand. The wealthy people have gone to their country places, or left the country before the war. The poor are compelled to stay here and take it. But nearly everyone seems to have at least one relative living in the country.

Interviewed a M. Valgones at the jail. He is being detained as a Nazi sympathizer. He spoke English well. He claims his enemies put him behind bars. He is a contractor who did work building fortifications for the Nazis. After talking—which, incidentally, is the third time—I am convinced he has Fascist leanings. He is wealthy. Almost daily his lawyer comes to see him. He doesn't seem to like Antoine.

August 2, 1944

Talked with M. Charles Raymond. He was Antoine's chief during the Nazi occupation in the Resistance Movement. He was full of applause for Antoine's bravery, but said that Antoine was a bit irresponsible. During my talk with M. Charles I discovered a lot of political activity is going on in Cherbourg.

The American Red Cross is preparing for a grand opening of a Jim Crow Club for Negro soldiers. The correspondents protested but without much effect. The decision came from above. Yet, to be honest about the matter, the Negro soldiers from the South seem to prefer their own club. They are somewhat ill-at-ease at the "white" club. But in the long run, it still would be better to have a club for *all* the soldiers.

I picked up the body lice which seems prev[alent] in this town. They itch like hell. The doctor told me that many of the soldiers have picked it up. It comes from the dust and dirt flying around—plus the wrecked buildings—which stir up all sorts of disease. Nothing serious though.

Allan Morrison, who is a reporter for Stars & Stripes and former editor of Negro Digest, has been very helpful in traveling around with me.

Ed Toles—on second thought is a good egg.

Incidentally, today's my birthday.

August 3, 1944

Had a hell of a time today getting a story through censor that reflected on American civil affairs in Cherbourg. I asked Sonia Tomara (Herald

Tribune) to support my protest—but she felt the issue wasn't big enough. I felt she was somewhat supercilious about it.

I wrote a story—which I got from the head of the Resistance Movement here. He showed me a list, compiled by the Movement, of men whose heads are slated to roll when the democratic forces come to power in Cherbourg. When I started to cable this story to PM, the military censors stopped it. They said C. D. Jackson, head of Psychological Warfare had ordered it killed.[18] I went to see him—a former Luce high-pressure executive on Fortune Magazine. He said at first my story was not accurate—and that it tended to start strife between our allies. I told him that this was clearly political censorship and that I would cable PM that such was the case in Cherbourg. After three full hours of argument he finally cleared the story but made me delete any reference to the American army and its civil affairs outfit. It took exactly twelve hours to get that story through. I hope PM recognizes its importance, because it indicates the Army is dealing with collaborationist elements in France. Should be front page stuff.

August 4, 1944

Left Cherbourg today—after what seemed to me a profitable trip. Sorry I didn't see Antoine before I left. No time. Had to make an appointment in Isigny to appear at General B. O. Davis' press conference.

Davis is a tremendous flop. He didn't have a thing to say that was important. Talked with a woman reporter from United Press who, wanted to know what could be done about the race problem. Carlton Moss was in the General's party, though he wasn't present at the press conference. When I saw him, I asked him about doodle bombs in London. He was staying at the Claridge Hotel—where the King of Greece lives. He said he asked one of the chamber-maids why the building had escaped bombing and she said because Hitler had his spies living there. This was, of course, a jocular comment on the fact that most of the bombing has hit the poor people hardest.

Talked with a G.I. who said the Negro soldiers were salty with the Negro correspondents because they failed to give them publicity. They want the Joe Doakes approach—so their home town folks can see their name in the papers. Can't blame them though.

18. General Charles Douglas Jackson (1902–1964) was an expert in psychological warfare who served in the Office of Strategic Services. After the war, Jackson moved back and forth between the media industry and the government. He was a speechwriter for Dwight Eisenhower and served as a liaison between the Central Intelligence Agency and the White House. See George P. Hunt, "Editor's Note: C. D. Jackson, 1902–1964," *Life Magazine*, October 2, 1964, 3.

Played a little poker with the boys tonight—to pass the time away. We played for Francs. You certainly learn fast how to count foreign money when you gamble with it.

Imagine. Officers are given a quota of two quarts of whiskey a month while at the front.

August 5, 1944

Well, my trip is here at an end. Leaving for London—then to Africa. But going to London has little charm. Those "doodle" bombs get everyone down.[19] I'll sleep at the Ministry of Information—which seems to be the sturdiest building in London.

Coming across the Channel from France by bomber, I saw an Army General who would lend himself to an excellent pen portrait. He fumbled with his pencil, then he took out a cigarette and lit it, then stamped it out. Stood up and stretched. Then looked out the window at nothingness. Yawned a little and drew a cup of water. He drank it screwing up his face as he got the after taste. He squeezed the paper cup into a ball, then looked for a receptacle to put it in. There was none. He hunted around awhile looking for some place to put it—finally he tucked it away in a corner beside him.

London looked pretty battered on return. Got dressed and went to Frisco's for a drink. Met a member of the Diplomatic Service from the South, who was said to be slated for the ambassadorship to Madrid. He is another of Frisco's admirers.

Decided to sleep at the Ministry of Information to escape the buzz bombs. When I arrived I met Gannett who hasn't gotten to France as yet. We talked until late. Sleeping here wasn't so bad—at least it was fairly safe.

August 6, 1944

Sunday in London is pretty dull but I had a chance to talk with Hedda Self, a notorious figure who might be called "Whore to His Majesty"—for she seems to have been mistress to everyone of consequence in British royalty. Indeed, a cousin of King George committed suicide over her. She has a number of interesting things to say about race and sex—they are grouped together in her view. Her explanation for the hatred of whites for Negroes—is that the white fears the Negro as a sexual competitor. They feel inferior to him. She says—from her experience—there is a vast difference between Negroes and whites sexually. Negro men, according to her,

19. The doodle bomb Ottley referred to was the German V-1 rocket, which was known colloquially as the "doodlebug" or "buzz bomb."

have greater staying power. They are, as a group, less inhibited. And more important, less perverted. From her experiences, extending from 1930, she found practically every Englishman perverted. She told me of a well-known author who could only have an orgasm by being made a clown of. He would visit her flat and dress up in woman's clothes and play the fool. When she thought up the idea of pushing a jar of cold cream in his face, he looked so foolish that she laughed uproariously, it was then he had his orgasm! Other Englishmen get their sexual kicks by being whipped, seeing her wear black gloves, silk stockings, etc.

Her life has been a Freudian holiday!

She is saving the money she earns to open a barroom after the war. She has a Negro boy friend who is now in France.

August 7, 1944

Today is a holiday in London — Bank Holiday. Everything shuts up tight — which greatly hampered my progress for work. The English — war or no war — take time for their tea morning and afternoon — as well as time for holidays.

With an introduction Rudolph Dunbar gave me, I went to see Una Marston [sic], who has a fairly important job at BBC.[20] She is from Jamaica and is in charge of West Indian broadcasts. She is a Negro, distinctly so. I had a pleasant conversation with her and then tea at the building's canteen. She asked me to do two broadcasts.

August 8, 1944

Got started today on my interviews. Saw Cruikshank, top man in M.O.I. [Ministry of Information] We talked at length about colonial problems and those in the U.S. He felt rather gloomy about the prospects of change in America. Yet, he said, the American criticizes the English. Talked with two other well-informed Britishers — Ursell and Marshall — two observations they made remain with me: Epstein, the sculptor, is indebted to Africans for his large conceptions of figures; and the Africans have a highly developed craft art. By and large, the cultivated Englishman is a smooth article.

Went to B.B.C. and witnessed an English broadcast. The band was a mixed one. Una Marston, a Negro woman, was the narrator. Nothing of the fierceness that characterizes American productions was apparent here. Everything was conducted on a casual level.

20. Una Marson (1905–1965) was a Jamaican journalist, feminist, political activist, and poet. She was one of the first women of color to produce programs for the BBC Empire Service. See Delia Jarrett-Macaulay, *The Life of Una Marson* (Manchester, UK: Manchester University Press, 1998).

Met Alexander Uhl at Russell Hotel.[21] He is foreign editor of PM. He gave me some good tips about filing my stories. We talked about political developments in Europe. He felt that the U.S. was supporting Fascists in Italy—he had just left Italy. He observed that Fascists were foolish to run away when we came in; for we usually work with them.

A personal observation: The English do not have the cold stares toward Negroes that characterize Americans. When they meet a Negro in a darkened hallway, none of the fear that Americans often show is apparent even in English women. The English are more civilized.

August 10, 1944

Today I visited the York Clinic, of the famous Guy's Hospital, to interview Dr. Alastair W. MacLeod. He is a psychiatrist. I was preparing to write a story on the psychological effects of the robot bombs on the English population. He was most cooperative. He told me, among other things, that psychiatry had not taken hold in England. He explained that the natural disinclination of the English people not to talk of their business to strangers was one of the main reasons. He took me on a tour of the most bombed sections of Southern England. He said a remarkable thing—only two patients had come to the clinic asking for treatment because of the buzz bombs. Suicides had decreased as well.

Somewhere along the line we got to discussing the English sex life. He explained that sex was essentially a biological function and that English women generally expected no pleasure or satisfaction from the act. From other quarters, though, I've heard much complaint about the coldness of Englishmen. American soldiers also complain about the coldness of English women. As a matter of fact, the Americans tell the English, in cracking about cold English women, that in America "we bury our dead!" The doctor seemed quite convinced that sex should be only a biological function. I have heard that it's an Englishman's Saturday night function! Altogether, my visit with the doctor and his colleagues was quite revealing as to the English personality and outlook.

---

21. Alexander Uhl (1899–1976) was a native of New York City and a graduate of City College. He studied for a time at the Columbia Journalism School before accepting a position in Madrid, Spain, with the Associated Press. There, Uhl covered the Spanish civil war from the side of the Loyalists. He was the foreign editor for PM from 1940 to 1948. His war reporting won him the French Legion of Honor. Uhl was one of the first journalists to speak out about Nazi treatment of the Jews. See "Literary Remains . . . by Alexander Uhl," Antiquarian Booksellers Association of America, http://www.abaa.org/books/244936205.html (accessed May 3, 2010). Also see Deborah E. Lipstadt, Beyond Belief: The American Press and the Coming of the Holocaust, 1933–1945 (New York: Touchstone Books, 1993), 221, 214–215.

August 11, 1944

Today I went to see Jack Beddington, a friend of Ted Kauffer's. He was very, very British and very, very charming. He had a special showing of a motion picture made by his department. He is film director of M.O.I. He invited me out to his country estate. I may go, if I can find time.

Dashed over to see John Carter, a Negro from the West Indies, who is secretary of an organization here similar to the N.A.A.C.P.[22] But there are only about a thousand Negroes in London! He is a very intense fellow, with considerable quiet passion about the race problem. He gave me some very valuable material on the race problem in England particularly as it [a]ffects Negro soldiers and whites. His assistant was an African, a graduate of Oxford and a member of the Ashanti tribe of Africa. I must go back soon and talk with them. Their efforts, though sincerely idealistic, are somewhat pathetic. They have not yet learned the techniques of protest and agitation. They are no match for the very smooth English officials, with centuries of tradition behind them in placating native demands. The trouble with all the protest activity here is that the natives seek to operate within a framework created by the British. There is no rough-and-tumble in the activity. Everyone maintains an air of good breeding, which is hardly the technique necessary for squeezing concessions from the British.

August 12, 1944

Today spent at George Padmore's place.[23] He arranged for me to meet a few Indian writers. One was from Ceylon. We discussed the "race problem." There is one thing they do have in common with American

22. Sir John Carter (1919–2005) was a lawyer, politician, and diplomat. Born in British Guiana, Carter went to England to study law in 1939. During the war years, he served as the secretary of the League of Coloured Peoples (LCP) and was active in Pan-African and anticolonialist circles. He was knighted in 1962 when British Guiana became independent (and was thereafter known as Guyana). See Peter Fraser, "Obituary: Sir John Carter," *Guardian*, June 4, 2005.

23. George Padmore (1903–1959) was a Trinidadian journalist and Pan-African intellectual and activist. Educated at Fisk University, New York University, and Howard University, Padmore became involved in the international communist movement as a student. He broke with the Comintern in 1934 and dedicated himself to the Pan-African struggle. He moved to London in the same year and began a fruitful collaboration with the Marxist revolutionary intellectual C. L. R. James. In response to the outbreak of the Italo-Ethiopian War, Padmore and James started the International African Services Bureau to disseminate news to media outlets around the world. Padmore's journalism appeared regularly in the *Chicago Defender, Pittsburgh Courier,* and *The Crisis.* In the immediate aftermath of the war, Padmore was instrumental in organizing the Manchester Pan-African Congress. See Penny M. Von Eschen, *Race against Empire: Black Americans and Anti-colonialism, 1937–1957* (Ithaca, NY: Cornell University Press, 1997), 11–15, 55; P. Olisanwuche Esedebe, *Pan-Africanism: The Idea and the Movement, 1776–1991* (Washington, DC: Howard University Press, 1994), 136–160; and Fitzroy Baptiste and Rupert Lewis, *Caribbean Reasonings: George Padmore—Pan-African Revolutionary* (Kingston, Jamaica: Ian Randle Publishers, 2009).

Negroes—color prejudice of whites. They feel prejudice keenly, though they were inclined to view it as an aspect of imperialism. They were fiercely anti-British. Curiously enough, they discussed the Indian problem much like Negroes discuss the race problem in America, by presuming everyone is ill-informed about their problems. They felt it necessary to give me the ABCs of the problem. Most of what they said I already knew from reading American papers.

One thing is certainly apparent: the treatment of Negroes in America is being widely known in the most isolated spots. White Americans definitely are not popular with colored peoples the world over. Such affairs as the Detroit riots and the more recent Philadelphia strike against the employment of Negroes, is given great publicity throughout the world. After our discussion, one of the Indians prepared a curry dinner that was some of the best eating I have had in England.

From here I dashed over to the CBS studio for my broadcast to America. In the midst of my talk a buzz bomb came over and exploded nearby. It shook me up terribly and affected my delivery. We all were quite nervous. I managed to complete my talk.

August 13, 1944

The trip to France was real blood and thunder adventure and excitement. Certainly more than I had planned or even expected. For example, I was on the front when General McNair was killed by bombs dropped by our own aviators. I was in a foxhole no more than fifty yards away. You don't write that sort of thing because people get the impression that you are laying it on thick. I don't suppose I will be going back, however. If the army enters Paris before I get to Africa, I will return—just to see Paris and report what goes.

The News Chronicle—one of the big dailies here—is flirting with the idea of taking a weekly newsletter from me—both about my trip and when I return to the States. I don't know what will come of it but it looks promising. The great difficulty is the fact that English newspapers are only two pages because of the shortage of new[s]print. Incidentally, the editor took me to lunch at the New Liberal Club—which is a liberal edition of the Union League. Such swank and formality you never saw. The English, as you suspect, make quite a fuss over people who they feel have accomplished something.

I could never detail in a letter all the things that happen day-to-day. It overwhelms me sometimes. It will take days for me to tell you what has happened just up to now. Incidentally, if the war is over it may be possible for you to come over. Murrow has his wife here. I asked him about it and he said there were angles that could be worked. He has invited me to meet his wife and have dinner at their home. He's quite handsome and in addition quite a guy. He respects me *not* as a Negro — it seems — but as a competent newspaper man. As a matter of fact, I am beginning to get recognition among the London corps of American newspapermen. Because I first broke the story here that the Resistance Movement opposed Mayor Renault, whom the Americans have supported. I don't know what PM did with the story but everyone here — from Army officials to reporters — thought it a front-page story.

George Padmore and I went to High Barnet today to visit some friends of his. We were guests at the home of a Dr. Clark, who is a successful physician with a white wife. He was charming. His friends were also quite nice. We had a lively discussion of the race problem. A fellow from Barbados, named Springer, made the comment that it was better to have "dignity" than economic advantages of the American Negro. He felt that the West Indian was treated with dignity by the Englishman. The American Negro was not treated with any dignity by the white American. I found myself, curiously enough, defending the condition of Negroes in the United States. Especially when everyone jumped on me and wanted to know what, if any, advances the American Negro had made. Altogether it was an enjoyable day.

George Padmore, incidentally, is quite a chap. He was once a prominent communist. He dropped out of the Party in 1933 when Russia decided to soft pedal the colonial question in the interest of making alliances with England, the U.S. and France. He is one of the brightest Negro minds I have met. He has written extensively both books and pamphlets. He is by no means anti-Red. He was one of the few writers in England to predict that Russia would stem the Nazi tide. He is a black fellow, who wears spectacles, and looks very much like a college professor. He earns his living writing for the Negro press of America.

August 14, 1944

There is of course sharp food rationing here in London. But everyone seems to get adequate food. No variety though. I talked with a fellow last night who hadn't seen an orange, pineapple or any other fruit in four years! I usually eat at the Officers' Club, which is located in a hotel and quite swank. It is the best eating in England — for it is the best from America.

The English troops, naturally enough, envy us. Needless to say, all the expert advice on dietary meals is shown in the balanced meals we get. Some interesting food combinations of food is gotten up — which we never think about in the States. The English have little milk. We are forbidden to drink English milk for much of it comes from cows who have T.B. England is behind America in pasteurization.

I have been adventuring about restaurants. The foreign eateries are located in Soho—a sort of combination Harlem-Greenwich Village place. The French cooking is the best; though I have eaten some good meals at Turkish, Greek, and Kosher restaurants. There are no American restaurants, curiously enough, or at least I haven't seen any. At one French restaurant I had a wonderful steak. Later I was told it was horse meat—in any case, it was delicious, and with fine wines too.

George Padmore, a Negro fellow who writes for the Crisis magazine and Pittsburgh Courier, invited me to his home. There I had a wonderful dinner prepared by a native of Ceylon. Incidentally, all the colored folks here—Hindus, Indians, Africans, etc.—are making quite a fuss over me and laying the ground work for my trip to other places.

The life in London is civilized. The people are civilized. Americans—even intellectuals—come off second best here. They seem to acknowledge their inferiority in their behavior. Generally speaking, Americans are not liked by the English—because they are crude, loud, pompous, and display very bad manners. They walk the streets and enter restaurants with the feeling, "We've come to save your country."

The English do everything in a leisured manner. The Americans are always in a hurry. Negro troops are very popular here. I think mainly because they generally have good manners—though, they too are loud. But they do not come here to "take over"—instead, they adjust themselves to the customs and do well for themselves.

Fights between Negro and white troops are common—though mainly when whiskey and white women are about. Like in the States, the whites resent Negroes having social equality. The English are frankly bewildered. Their newspapers are constantly raising the question. And it's my guess that in the post-war period the Americans will hear more from the English about this matter, especially when the Americans raise the question about freedom for India.

There is little fraternizing between American troops and English troops. Not even do the Generals have social relationships beyond what's necessary for waging war.

I do not think I would like to live here permanently. Life is lived like one would like it. People are respectful of each other—naturally and without great effort. I think the thing about England that is chiefly misunderstood by Negroes is that the class lines are sharp.

For example: I heard stories about discrimination against Cab Calloway. He said he was refused accommodations in a swank hotel. I believe it's true, but there is this difference. Cab is considered here only an entertainer, not an artist. Whereas that could happen to Cab, Louis Armstrong and rank-and-file of musicians and tap dancers, it would not happen to Marian Anderson.

Creative people are considered the aristocracy of civilization. They draw sharp lines against whites who have no status—and indeed refuse them accommodations in the better hostelries.

To give a concrete idea: Though we didn't hear much about it in the States, former Ambassador Kennedy's daughter married a "Cavendish." She came here early in the war, doing some sort of Red Cross work. The marriage caused both a sensation and a scandal—she has been ostracized. Now, the Kennedys are among the wealthiest people in America—the English know it too. But they say that the Kennedys are shanty Irish, without culture or manners. Moreover, the Cavendish family ruled Ireland back three, four, and five centuries ago.

Now, if a Roosevelt married a Cavendish, this would be okay here. Not because Roosevelt is president—but because he is a cultivated man, belongs to America's aristocracy, and has given his life to public service, like a gentleman should.

All this of course is a form of snobbery. Somehow my American background rebels against this sort of thing, but it is a formidable reality—supported both by the aristocracy and the working class—and if you hope to move about without incident in this country, you just adjust yourself to these things.

The Englishmen—those I have met—have considerable suavity and polish. But below the surface the Englishmen is a smooth article. Though they are not effusive, their greetings are always warm and friendly. Most Englishmen speak of the English as a "race." I was surprised, for example, to discover that no one here talks about freedom of India, etc. The empire, in the minds of every English, is secure. Even during elections there is a gentleman's agreement—acknowledged even by the communists—not to discuss in public the colonial questions. So, the people never have an opportunity to evaluate colonial policy.

When India was discussed in Parliament—and this is a burning question in America—only 27 members were present out of 650! The average Englishman knows so little about the Empire—and its colonies—that the average Englishman—including members of Parliament—do not know where Kingston, Jamaica is!

★ ★ ★

Flew to Glasgow, Scotland, today. Took rooms at the ornate Central Hotel. In the states this place would be considered a third-rate joint, but here it's swank. Our party includes Brigadier General B. O. Davis, Major Homer Roberts and Captain Toomey. Lewis Gannett, Herald Tribune correspondent, was supposed to make the trip but couldn't after all.

....

Glasgow is an interesting city, but dismal in appearance. The people, though, are much more friendly than the British. The girls all seem to have big legs. Few brunettes are seen about. Many redheads though. This is the one place where there are few American soldiers. It seems to make for better relations for Negroes with the natives. The few American soldiers I did see were cluttering up the main street of Glasgow. They hung around corners, ogling girls, much as they do on Main Street in the States.

Went on a short sightseeing tour. Visited the Castle of Mary, Queen of Scots. The ruins are on an island standing in the Clyde River. Somehow, to visit these places gives real meaning to literature and history.

After tramping about the city until 10 P.M. I returned to the hotel and had drinks with Major Roberts. In the cocktail lounge I saw about ten very vulgar Jewish refugees, who were drinking heavily, shouting, and generally acting up. They reminded me of vulgar Negroes! Met Elizabeth Welch, the American actress, in lobby.[24] She is doing a theater engagement here.

August 15, 1944

Up early to meet the Negro nurses arriving here in Glasgow, the first to be assigned duty in the European theater. Drove out to the port of embarkation with General Davis, Major Roberts, and a white public relations officer. A battery of Scottish correspondents were on hand. The girls seemed quite bewildered by the welcome they received. The first question they asked me was how would they be treated by the English people. I assured them everything was okay. They seemed relieved. Most of them were quite salty about having had to come abroad.

That evening we flew back to London. There were two white girls with us. They were members of the Army's public relations staff. Both quite good-looking and very pleasant to talk with.

---

24. Elisabeth Welch (1904–2003) was a fixture on the stages of London's West End and one of the most popular entertainers living and working in Britain. She lived in London for seventy years, working with everyone from Cole Porter to Bob Fosse. See Stephen Bourne, "Obituaries: Elisabeth Welch," *The Independent,* http://www.independent.co.uk/news/obituaries/elisabeth-welch-548425.html (accessed May 3, 2010.)

The trip gave me a chance to observe General Davis at close hand. He is really a nice guy, who has no conception of what his role in Negro affairs is. He seems to think he is divorced from the Negro community because he is an Army man. But he does give me the impression of being a man of real integrity. His adjutant, Major Homer Roberts, is something of a city slicker. In civilian life he was an insurance salesman.

During the flight we had something of a real scare — the plane ran out of gasoline. The motor began to sputter and then went dead. The plane dropped suddenly. Luckily for us, we were over a military airfield, so the pilot merely had to coast down and land. After refueling, he continued our journey without incident.

August 16, 1944

One thing about the English, I am learning fast, is that they never talk directly on any issue. They talk a lot about the non-essentials — in fact, they are masters of the non-essential. When you try to pin them down they look at you as though you are being offensive in manners. This is an excellent technique for ducking crucial issues!

Today I visited the office of the Belgian Minister of Colonies. I talked with M. P. de Brig, an attaché. He seemed quite nervous when I got around to asking questions about the Congo. He felt that the Belgians had been quite paternal in their treatment of the blacks. The Congo, incidentally, is half the size of Europe, has a black population of 13 million and a white population of 30 thousand. M. de Brig objected to the term "white." He preferred the use of "European" to describe the whites living in the Congo. He admitted that only one child in twelve even got a primary schooling! Beyond this he yielded little information.

★ ★ ★

Had a good trip. Flew up and back. When I returned I found your letter waiting. It certainly was a welcome sight. Try not to be too disturbed by what I write. For much of what I say is of course true, but I'm trying as well to record my feelings at the time these things occur. If too much time passes one can't always recapture the feelings of the moment. Don't worry too much either for I'm doing everything to keep safe.

Glasgow: There were very few American soldiers in this city. Those who were there stood along the main stem — Charing Cross — ogling girls. They looked very much like a Main Street in America, holding up the corners, smoking with cigarettes drooping from the corners of their mouths.

Pretty much like a tourist, I went around to see the town. Went out to Loch Lomand which, incidentally, is a great feudal estate which you enter through a gate with a huge crown above. It is a beautiful place in a menacing sort of way. I got an idea of the Morgan estate—you've seen no such thing in America. They run for miles. From here I went to the castle of Mary, Queen of Scots. Really, history and literature takes on new meanings by these experiences. Her castle—today in ruins—was situated on a great island in the Clyde River, about a mile out from Glasgow. You can very well understand her career, after seeing these ruins.

···

A Scotsman asked me about Maxine Sullivan—they all know her here.[25] "What does she mean, when singing Loch Lomand, 'I'll take the high road, and you'll take the low,' There's no high road!" I couldn't help him at all.

Lewis Gannett, Tribune correspondent, is still trying to get into France, which gives one an idea of how lucky I was in getting there so soon after arrival.

I must add this: I stayed at the Central Hotel—which is the Waldorf of Glasgow. The place is ornate in a mid-victorian way, all mahogany woodwork and marble bathrooms. After a pretty active day, General Davis and Major Roberts and I went into the cocktail lounge for drinks one night to witness a rather curious sight: There were refugees present. But the men, curiously enough, looked like Broadway sharpies with their drape suits, high collars and narrow waisted, tight fitting garments. The women were a little more modestly attired, used makeup heavily, which of course is a European custom. But talk about loud in the Coney Island sense, they were it. They took over the place with two quarts of Scotch on their table. There was much waving of the bottle—much like Negroes when they are high—and shouting to neighbors at adjoining tables.

I am told they're just waiting for the war to be over so they can rush back to Germany, Austria, France, etc. They seemed wealthy, though not the top layer of wealth. Perhaps, just enough money to have enabled them to get out of their various countries. They recently left London to duck the buzz bombs.

···

I also saw Elizabeth Welch, famous Negro singer. She was in the lobby with a girl friend. I felt her greeting rather chilly, though she asked me to

---

25. Maxine Sullivan (1911–1987) was an African American jazz singer who scored a popular hit with the Scottish folk ballad "Loch Lomond." Sullivan had a long career, winning a Tony Award in 1979 for her performance in the musical *My Old Friends*. See John S. Wilson, "Maxine Sullivan, 75, Dead; Jazz Singer Won Tony in '79," *New York Times*, April 9, 1987, http://www.nytimes.com/1987/04/09/obituaries/maxine-sullivan-75-is-dead-jazz-singer-won-tony-in-79.html?pagewanted=1?pagewanted=1. Also see "Whatever Happened to Maxine Sullivan?" *Ebony Magazine*, July 1974, 138.

the theater where she's playing. Perhaps it was just Negroes putting on the dog. She had just marched into the lobby with a poodle on a string, very swank and all that. Perhaps, I caught her with tiddies down!

August 17, 1944

As I write this I'm pretty worn out from a very exhausting day. I fear that I've been making too many appointments—much too much information to digest. Anyway, my first appointment was with Una Marston at B.B.C to broadcast to the West Indies. It went well—I was in good voice.

From there I went to see Brendon Bracken, Minister of Information by appointment.[26] He is a tall man with red wavy hair, and wears large glasses. His manner brisk, and to the point—much unlike most Englishmen. I used my visit to secure aid in escaping the restrictions of censorship on racial conflicts between Negro and American soldiers. The English seem as anxious as I am to get stories out of bad behavior of white Americans, so I suppose I'll be able to clear my stories. More important, though, was the fact that he promised to arrange an interview with Churchill for me.

From here I dashed over to the News Chronicle on Fleet Street to have lunch with the directors of this paper. They were suave and polished. The luncheon was excellent. They were vastly concerned with political developments in the States. They were a little worried lest the good attitude that Negroes here have for the English people may be translated into prejudice to England from the American white population. They were all for Roosevelt's election. They expressed admiration for Willkie. One of them asked me, had I ever "with my own eyes" seen a Negro who was married to a white woman! They all wondered if such relations were successful. My conversation with them made me late for a B.B.C. broadcast recording. Will do it tomorrow. Also broke an appointment with Van Mook—Dutch Minister of Colonies, because I am swiftly discovering it is a waste of time.

★ ★ ★

The Sunday before I went to Scotland, I visited a Dr. Clarke in a suburb of London called High Barnet.

He is an extremely successful physician. His patients are all white of

26. Brendan Bracken (1901–1958) was a leader in Britain's Conservative Party and a supporter of Winston Churchill's war policies. After serving as Churchill's propaganda minister during the war, he was briefly first lord of the Admiralty, losing the position after the Conservatives were swept from power. In the postwar years, he was known for bringing the modern version of London's *Financial Times* into existence. See Nicholas J. Cull, "Brendan Bracken," in Nicholas J. Cull, David Culbert, and David Welch, eds., *Propaganda and Mass Persuasion: A Historical Encyclopedia 1500 to the Present* (Santa Barbara, CA: ABC-CLIO, 2003), 46.

course. He is considered one of the outstanding diagnosticians in England. He is a charming, well-read man of about fifty, and looks like a person who has lived well.

He is married to a distinguished looking white woman. She is typically English in the best sense. She is tall, white-haired and cultured. They have a beautiful home, built fifteen years ago. It was peaceful and stable look-ing—the sort of place any one would enjoy. They have lived the good life together and seemed definitely in love—even at their age. He was born in Barbadoes and attended Oxford. He remained in England and married.

....

We talked about everything—especially the race "problem." The whole day was reminiscent of our evening sessions in Harlem. The same vigorous discussion held forth. In fact, if the scene had been transplanted, it could very well have been New York.

Early in the evening another Negro doctor came to visit and he too had a white wife. She looked Irish. He resembled Kenneth Bright on the slender side. They have quite a handsome son, with wonderful wavy hair and intel-ligent face. He was well-mannered. These two interracial couples had none of the self-consciousness of American couples. Nor did they feel they had a "mission." The fact is, at no time did they mention the fact that they were an interracial couple.

Interestingly enough, Dr. Clarke's mother-in-law was staying at their home. She was a dignified old lady who seemed quite fond of Dr. Clarke. He told me that she had been bombed out in London and he had insisted that she stay with him and her daughter. She helped serve supper. There were two or three other white men present, who seemed to be some sort of pals of Dr. Clarke. Everything was quite normal.

August 18, 1944

George Padmore was telling me today that when Walter White was in England he spoke before the West African Students Union, and the Afri-cans kept whispering to him, "Can we trust this white man?"[27] George says he assured them that "he was the blackest white man in America!"

....

27. Walter Francis White (1893–1955) was the chief secretary of the NAACP from 1929 to 1955. He was one of the leading spokespeople for African America in the first half of the twentieth century. White had a very light complexion, which accounts for the confusion of the African students. See Walter F. White, *A Man Called White: The Autobiography of Walter White* (Athens: University of Georgia Press, 1995); and Kenneth R. Janken, "Walter White (1893–1955)," *The New Georgia Encyclopedia,* http://www .georgiaencyclopedia.org/nge/Article.jsp?id=h-747 (accessed May 5, 2010).

Went to the Caribbean Club tonight. It is located in Piccadilly Circus. It is the rendezvous of Negroes and English—a sort of black-and-tan café. Everyone gravitates to this club. Curiously enough, its social patterns resemble those of night spots in America. It is one of the few places in London where Negroes feel at ease with whites. Though Negroes are admitted to most cafes, restaurants and night spots, they have a tendency to congregate here and at Frisco's club. Particularly this is true of the Africans and American Negro soldiers from the South. The place is frequented by as many whites as Negroes—but these whites are largely drawn from Bohemian elements of the upper class as well as swing addicts—for the orchestra here is quite good. Of course, a few "queens" (among the white boys) are always present. Physically the Caribbean is little different from a night club in Harlem—except that it occupies the second floor of a loft. It has the same small tables around the side walls, a bar, an orchestra, garishly decorated in gold and green, and is smoke-filled at all times. Even in a degree, the big doorman, who is constantly suspicious, is not missing.

August 19, 1944

PM has requested a story on Negro-white troop relations in England—which I intended to do anyway. So I'm off to Manchester as the first spot on a tour of principal English cities. Went by train—which was very comfortable and very dirty without water. Of course, there is no food to be had—so I got mighty hungry. The trip took six hours—though in normal times the ride only takes four. The French say "C'est la Guerre!" It was raining like hell. George Padmore gave me a contact in Manchester—Ato Makomen, a West African who runs a restaurant called the Cosmopolitan.

This restaurant, I discovered, cater[ed] exclusively to whites and is decorated with wall-paintings of distinguished Negroes! Ato was extremely cordial. Immediately upon arrival we sat down to a curry dinner which was quite good. Padmore is quite a guy with the Africans.

Later, I attended a meeting of Negroes to finance a home for foundlings discarded by British mothers. The fathers are Negroes and most of the mothers are married to British soldiers who have been away to the wars two and three years. A brown or black baby would prove quite embarrassing on their husbands' return. I understand there are six hundred such babies. These Negroes plan to open a home for them and appeal to the British Ministry of Labor to assume responsibility. The American authorities are discouraging American soldiers from admitting parentage.

August 20, 1944

Manchester—it turns out—is the most liberal city in England towards Negroes. It aggressively resists the attempts of American soldiers to import American Jim Crow patterns. I was introduced to a woman—wife of a local businessman—who was attacked brutally by American soldiers because she worked at a Red Cross club for Negroes.

I asked one of the Red Cross workers about the truth of there being 600 Negro foundlings which [have] been discarded by British mothers. She confirmed it. Moreover, she said, every day English women came to the club asking the officials what they should do when they became pregnant by Negro soldiers.

....

Tonight the Africans entertained the Negro nurses—just recently arrived and are billeted nearby. Plenty of food and drink—in true African style. A lot of fuss is being made over these girls—though none of them are glamour girls.

When they entered the Red Cross club tonight they created a sensation among the Negro soldiers present. Some of these boys haven't seen a Negro woman for two years! They immediately dropped all the British girls to talk with the American girls. The British girls, while admiring the Negro girls in their uniforms, became mighty jealous. Anyway, the little gathering at the African's restaurant later was the first all-Negro party I have attended since leaving the States. Negro Red Cross workers also present.

Tomorrow Liverpool!

August 21, 1944

Today I went to Liverpool. It is perhaps the dirtiest city in England. I understand that if there is a "race" problem in England—this is where it's keenest. It was from this city that centuries ago slaves were sent to America. I saw the slave market. One Negro with whom I talked remarked, "The blood of your ancestors has washed every cobblestone on these streets." Liverpool contains a large Negro, East Indian and Chinese population. Most of the men are seamen. This has produced racial tensions with the white Britisher. For the shipping companies employ colored seamen in preference to white because they can get them cheaper. This has also caused tension over women. Naturally the colored men have money and take all the women. The unemployed Britisher naturally resents this. In addition, there are very few colored women, so colored men marry white women.

....

Liverpool has a number of soap factories in the center of the city — there is no odor so suffocating and repulsive as soap in the process of being made. People here give directions by the odor. For example, they say, "You'll know you are on such and such a street when you smell the soap factories."

Met quite a handsome Negro chap named Banks. He was formerly an RAF flier. He made a number of bombing trips over Berlin. He was shot down over the Channel. Managed to remain afloat in a raft — but he got quite a ducking when he ba[i]led out — and thus got pneumonia. He now works for the Red Cross and is married to an American Negro girl.

August 22, 1944

Today I interview a Jewish woman, Fannie Flinder, and a Negro woman, Mrs. Frederick Johnson. They had both just been released from a Nazi camp, "Lichenau" — near Switzerland. The Jewish woman felt rather fiercely about the Nazis. She had been in Poland visiting her mother when the war started. She was promptly interned by the Germans. She told me a harrowing tale of her experiences. But somehow it differed little from those I have heard before, so it didn't make much of a story.

The Negro woman had two daughters, who spoke French and German fluently. They spoke English with an accent! Mrs. Johnson had no especial criticisms to make of the Nazis. She said that under the circumstances she was treated well. She implied that she had been quite attractive to the Nazi officers — and I guess she slept with them, which may explain the reason she was treated well.

....

Visited the Liverpool Red Cross Club for Negroes. The entire rank-and-file personnel is white. The director is a Negro. This seems to be the pattern in every club. The bulletin board had a number of pictures of pretty Negro girls — clipped from the Negro newspapers. But there are few Negro women in Liverpool. One sign on the board advertised a dance for the boys. White girls are the hostesses in all Red Cross clubs. I met a handful of Negro girls whose fathers remained in England after the last war and married British women.

Met Clarisse Brooks, Red Cross worker, and interviewed her regarding her experiences with white soldiers. She was nearly assaulted by them recently.

August 23, 1944

Back to Manchester today. Met a charming African named Jomo Ken-[y]atta.[28] He and his friends have decided to give me an African name, meaning "Philosopher." They refer in all conversations to all Negroes as "My Brother." I find they have a good deal of real warmth for each other. They band together to aid each other—for they still feel like strangers in a foreign land. One project they launched involved financing an African's medical practice. They gave 500 Pounds only upon his word and the promise to repay in five years! In England a doctor just can't hang up his shingle and start practicing. This would be considered very unethical. Instead you must buy the practice of a retiring or deceased doctor. If none is available—you just wait, or assist another doctor. The African had recently graduated and was assisting a doctor who had just died. The widow wanted 500 Pounds for her deceased husband's practice. Being without money, he appealed to other Africans and they promptly voted him the money. He, in turn, plans to bring his brother from Africa and finance his medical education. When the brother graduates the practice will be turned over to him and the elder brother will return to Africa. This practice is a property which the Africans plan to hand down to one other through the years. There also was much talk about financing native crafts, to help lift the living standards of the native African. Incidentally, I picked up a new word with which to describe white people, which rolls off the tongue nicely. The Africans call white people, "Mzungu."

August 23, 1944

Just returned from a trip to Liverpool and Manchester, England's great industrial centers. George Padmore, with whom I made the trip, observed the cobble-stones in Liverpool and said that the blood of Negro slaves had washed every foot of ground. The slave block is still here, a historic relic.

Liverpool has a large colored population composed of Africans, Indians and Chinese. This is the dirtiest city in the world, I believe. Not a modern building anywhere to lighten up the city's drab reddish buildings.

A bit of vital statistics—welfare workers in Manchester estimate that

---

28. Jomo Kenyatta (1894–1978) is considered the founding father of an independent Kenya, serving as prime minister of the nation from 1963 to 1964 and as president of Kenya from 1964 until his death in 1968. In the 1930s and early 1940s, Kenyatta studied social anthropology at the London School of Economics under the tutelage of Branislaw Malinowski. During these years, Kenyatta was an activist in the Pan-African political circles that Ottley tapped into during his stay in England. See Jomo Kenyatta, *Facing Mt. Kenya* (New York: Vintage Books, 1962), and Caroline Elkins, *Imperial Reckoning: The Untold Story of Britain's Gulag in Kenya* (New York: Owl Books, 2005).

at least 600 babies have been born to British girls. Negro soldiers are the fathers.

This has created quite an undercover problem—as officially the British say no British women have become pregnant as a result of relations with Negro soldiers. Anyway, I have seen a number of the children, for the British women are by and large abandoning them on the doorsteps of the American Red Cross Clubs.

The core of the problem seems to be this: The American Army is discouraging marriage between Negroes and white women here—not by fait [sic] however. The soldier is told that he will be sent abroad—or "somewhere," so why acknowledge parenthood. The problem of bringing his wife to the States after the war is also called to his attention—as the Army is making little effort to aid war brides—white or Negro—to get to America.

Perhaps, the most significant factor behind this business is that many of the women are married—and obviously with husbands away for two and three years it would be mighty difficult to present them with brown babies on their return.

Africans residing here are raising money to build a home for these foundlings. For no one acknowledges the existence of these wretched little ones. Yet, all this has not created any anti-Negro feeling in the city. The fact is, Negroes are plenty popular. I saw something at the Red Cross—where, incidentally, a dance was given to introduce me to Manchester folks—that was amusing. The dance was attended by five hundred G. I.'s and their girls. There were about five Negro girls present only, children of mixed marriages from the previous war! All the other girls were *white*. Practically all the soldiers were Negroes. They were dancing furious lindy hops all over the place—for Negroes have taught the British girls how to dance Savoy style. Who do you think was playing the music—10 white soldiers—Army musicians—and they were blowing their brains out, too.

One wag around here—meaning me—observed about the Negro birthrate in Manchester—that when the next war starts twenty years from now—Negro Red Cross workers needn't be imported to entertain the Negro troops—Negro soldiers are already providing them! Yeah, perhaps a little too corny.

What is happening in Manchester—a sort of test tube for me—is taking place all over England. Perhaps 20,000 births have already taken place. This doesn't include the production of the white soldiers—which is equally high. All in all, we're going to leave a sizeable American population in England. For the present—these facts are hush hush officially.

Four full-blooded Africans operate the most popular restaurant in

Manchester—Café Cosmopolitan. All the help is white. I spent a lot of time talking with the Africans—their names: Jomo Kenyatta, from East Africa; and Ato Makomen, from Nigeria. They told me of an interesting practice of all African tribes: It seems that because of the many tribal wars, the men-folks were away from their women a great deal. A situation developed—many centuries back—that resembled that Greek play, *Lysistrata*. Lesbianism developed like wildfire. To combat it, the Africans started a practice which today has religious honor. Every woman is circumcised! How? By shaving the clitoris. No African woman today can have an orgasm by massaging or playing with her clitoris—which, of course, outlaws completely lesbianism. Only through contact with a man can she have any sort of orgasm. Moreover, circumcision of women—like Jewish circumcision of men—is a religious rite. The women suffer no ill effects from this practice, I am told.

All men are circumcised as well. Jomo—who incidentally is a weird character—told me that Western peoples like the English and Americans—don't seem to understand that the customs of primitive peoples have validity because they arrive at a particular practice after centuries of trial and error.

One might say that they live a pragmatic life!

Back to Jomo for a minute. He wears a Van Dyke beard, has blood-shot eyes, and never combs his nappy hair. He wears loud pink shirts, sports coat and trousers, and sports a silver handled cane. He never wears a hat. Ato told me—when Jomo was caught indulging in homosexuality, he explained it away as part of his anthropological research. He told this story in Jomo's presence—and Jomo laughed heartily at the joke.

The Africans—all of them—embarrass me a little because they feel that I am quite distinguished. They are proud that I am a member of their race who has made the most of my contact with the white race.

I have talked to them a great deal about life in America—and given them some advice—off the top of my head—about the manner in which they should conduct their African affairs. I cannot recapture in words the wonderful childlike expressions on their faces as I related political, social, agitational affairs to them—a mixture of wonderment and admiration. Like, perhaps, a man who is explaining the workings of some new invention to children.

They call me a "philosopher" and "thinker" and have decided to give me an African name!—which, incidentally, will have practical worth in my journeys in Africa.

They had quite a contrary reaction to Walter White (N.A.A.C.P.) when he was here, I am told. They regarded him as "European." They have a racial bond with me, and feel that I am a member of a tribe that wandered off centuries ago.

....

While I feel a warmth for them—I do not think it is quite as racial as theirs. Mine, I believe, is my love for the underdog, of whatever color, race or nationality.

Yet, do not get the impression that these people are naïve—far from it—but they are wise in a different sort of practical way. For example, the manner in which they ended lesbianism among the tribes of Africa! Moreover, they do not have the fierce hatred for the white man that characterizes nationalist Negroes in America. The fact is, they admire the white man tremendously, and wish that they could peaceably work out a mutual relation of live and let live. But they do not go overboard in this either. They feel that African culture has much to give the Western world.

Africans here are not the slickers we know in America. Incidentally, some of the best food I have eaten here was prepared by Ato. With the meager ingredients he has cooked up some intriguing African dishes.

They always address me as "My brother."

Back from Manchester by train. I had to stand up the whole way. The roughing it here is knocking down that fat stomach of mine! If this keeps up I'll be streamlined by the time I return home.

August 24, 1944

Had dismally long trip back to London from Manchester. The train was so full with people I had to stand up the entire trip—seven hours! The British, though, are quite cheerful about these hardships.

....

Today I attended a showing of "The Negro Soldier" in company with Joe Louis.[29] I carefully watched his reactions. He was manifestly proud of the picture and the role of Negroes in it. He grunted, growled, and commented throughout its showing. Afterwards he said, "Anybody who says that ain't a good picture, is crazy." I was one of those who had said it wasn't a good picture.

In a walk to Talbay I discovered that all chairs in London parks are rented—you can't sit down without buying a ticket! By no means are the parks as well kept as those in New York—but this may be the result of a shortage of manpower.

29. See note 10.

August 25, 1944

Went to the American Embassy today — only to discover they had a copy of "New World A-Coming." They immediately asked me to autograph it. I've spent a lot of time in the Embassy library and have become fairly friendly with the girls who take care of the place. Today one of them asked me if I knew a girl named Edna Frazier. I said I did. She is a Negro girl attached to the staff of the O.W.I. [Office of War Information] and has just recently come over here. Anyway, the librarian told me that she has been looking for a "boy friend" for the Frazier girl. Now, there's nothing wrong with this Negro girl but I have never sought to build any friendship with her. The fact is, I've ducked doing this. But I thought it nervy of this girl to attempt to arrange a date — simply because we were *both Negroes!* I told her I was married — and that Edna Frazier knew my wife — and close[d] the matter there. The librarian seemed manifestly disappointed.

....

Had drinks with Ed Murrow (CBS) today — that is, this evening.[30] He seems like a swell guy and very liberal. He says he wishes he could do more along the racial front. He told me he is very distrustful of the British Government officials and is convinced they plan to do little in the post-war period to improve the condition of the Colonies — especially they will not let go of India.

August 27, 1944

One of the biggest shocks — of many — that I have had in this city of London was to discover that laundry costs $5 — just to do a few trunks, shirts and handkerchiefs, not including linen or towels! The shortage of gasoline has, of course, sent dry cleaning prices sky-high — one pair of trousers costs me two dollars. Any sort of sewing of buttons cost 50 cents apiece. Most merchants are doing a land-office business at expense of the Americans. Scotch whiskey costs 20 dollars a quart — and you can only get it if you beg the bootlegger. There is little to be had in the stores and then only by producing a ration card, which few American[s] possess. Since practically the whole town closes down at 11 P.M., Londoners have resorted to having "bottle parties" — a party in which whiskey is not sold but you bring

---

30. Edward R. Murrow (1908–1965) was one of America's most influential journalists, initially on radio and then, in the 1950s and 1960s, on television. During the war, his radio broadcasts were listened to by millions, and Murrow became an enormous celebrity. See Gerd Horton, *Radio Goes to War: The Cultural Politics of Propaganda during World War II* (Berkeley: University of California Press, 2002), 30–38; and Bob Edwards, *Edward R. Murrow and the Birth of Broadcast Journalism* (New York: John Wiley, 2004), 43–60.

your own. These are held in night clubs — resembling American speakeasies of Prohibition Days. Much peekhole looking, handshakes, graft, etc., to enter one of these places. The fanciest and most expensive is called the "Blue Lagoon." The house serves soft drinks for which you pay night club prices. Most of the bars charge $1.20 for one jigger of whiskey. So, before you have had three or four drinks, you've spent five dollars and more. Most the correspondents figure it costs them $100 a week to live in London.

August 28, 1944

There is much off-the-record talk about Jews in England — sometimes from the most unexplained sources. One Englishmen told me that he dare not invite Jews to his home — for his friends would politely leave. I first became conscious of a "Jewish problem" in England from two Jewish friends who I met in New York. They felt very strongly about it and told me of instances of discrimination. I have noticed a feeling of kinship of Jews for Negroes here, caused by their treatment in the Army. According to talk current here Jews prominent in England include Bevin, Beaverbrook, Hore Belisha, Montague Norman, head of the Bank of England, Lord Woolton, Minister of Food and prominent department store owner, and Sir Samuel Hoare, an M.P. and member of Churchill's cabinet. Jews are charged with operating the Black Market. Gossip has it that the Jews left London during the blitz — which, of course, is manifestly untrue. Churchill's two daughters are said to be married to Jews. One is the wife of Vic Oliver, England's most popular comedian. The fact that such information should be accumulated certainly indicates the existence of some sort of problem. As far as I can learn this anti-Semitism is an expression of the middle and upper-classes exclusively. On[e] never hears the rank-and-file talk about Jews. Southern Americans do a lot of talking about Jews. They blame lack of promotion and uninteresting assignments on the Jewish officers above them. Negroes do no talking about Jews here. The fact is they have no contact with Jews as such.

August 29, 1944

Today I interview M. Albert de Vlesschauwer, Belgian Minister of Colonies. He is a short man who strikingly resembles Leon Henderson. I had the feeling he was on the defensive about the Belgian colonial career in Africa which is one of the blackest pages of colonial history. When I mentioned the lack of education in the Congo, he replied by pointing to the startling illiteracy revealed in the American Army. He stoutly protested against the use of terms "black" and "white" for the populations in the Congo. He said they were "Blacks" and "Europeans" — and both "Congolese." The Minister is a member of the Catholic Party. He said that the Africans were not like me — for actually I was "European" in my thinking, education and deportment. He discussed the bad state of hygiene and ignorance among the natives. He illustrated this by saying the Colonial Administration had built a fine new, white hospital and the natives would not go there for treatment unless they were bribed with presents. He was convinced that at no for[e]-seeable time would the African be equipped for self-rule. The fact that the Belgian people have felt the heavy hand of Nazi oppression has not done anything to mellow the Belgian attitude toward the Congo people. He was frank enough to say that no universal education was planned. All that has been recorded was said "off the record." He refused to be quoted directly, except from a prepared statement which he is forwarding to me. The picture for the Congo seems quite black.

....

August 30, 1944

After much personal agitation I went to see Dr. H. J. Van Mook, the Dutch Minister of Colonies. I have become reluctant about seeing these men for they rarely say anything of importance "on the record." But I guess I must go to at least evaluate their mentality — the mentality governing and exploiting millions of black, brown and yellow peoples. As it turned out, I was right. Dr. Mook — a red-faced man, with rimless glasses, who looked like the stage Irishman — was amiable enough but said little of importance. His office was housed in an old office building on the fourth floor. Next door to his room was a neatly painted sign, "GENTS." It seems the Dutch have worked out a new pattern to get by the fact that "colonies are in disrepute." He spoke of integrating Indonesians into civil, economic, and diplomatic service, and doing away with the term "colony" all together. He was eminently pleased to note that Dutch people had little or no racial prejudice. This I presumed to have been a slap at white Americans. It was evident that Dutch colonial policy is still

[*Page missing in original manuscript. Date of subsequent entry unclear. From the internal evidence, this was a list of questions that Ottley prepared for his interview with the British secretary of state, Oliver Stanley.*]

… Political unity?

III. Under what conditions would you release Congress leaders now detained? In view of the fact that Gandhi, who speaks for Congress, has more or less repudiated [the August] "quit India" resolution, supports war, will not start civil disobedience movement—is this not a guarantee that Indian leaders could be trusted during wartime in a National Government?

IV. Do you think under present Constitution there cannot be a National Government with full powers even though Congress-League political unity is achieved? If so, then surely by an emergency Act of Parliament the present Constitution could be changed and a new one devised in order to facilitate functioning of a Provisional National Government?

V. People in India fear that Britain intends to repudiate her Sterling balances accumulated in Britain. How far is this statement true? How is Britain going to pay this debt—in cash or in goods exported from Britain? At Bretton Woods it was suggested that Britain and India could come to some sort of financial arrangement through a bilateral agreement. What sort of a bilateral agreement do you envisage and how will it affect the "Bombay Plan"—industrialization of post-war India.

VI. Is there a political censorship of messages leaving India? In spite of your repeated declarations to the contrary, Indian Press still clings to the fact that (1) there is Political Censorship, (2) Newspapers are suppressed for political reasons, (3) Editors fired and some imprisoned. How can you explain these paradoxes?

VII. What are Britain's conditions for the recognition of Indian Independence now or after the war?

VIII. It's felt in America both by whites and colored people that Britain wants to maintain her status quo in India. They argue like this: Churchill said he is not going to preside over the liquidation of the British Empire. And Britain without India means in political and economic terms the liquidation of the Empire. How can you explain this paradox?

IX. Do you agree howsoever benevolent an alien government may be, it cannot tackle social, political and economic matters with same zeal and enthusiasm as a people[']s government—Government of India as constituted today is an alien government. Famine, poverty, disease—and all social evils cannot be conquered by present alien India government. Therefore only a truly people[']s representative government can successfully tackle these problems. What do you think?

X. Is it not true that (1) Gandhi has more personal following than the combined leaders of the United Nations; (2) Gandhi living is a great force Indo-British rapprochement than Gandhi dead, which may mean final cutting off of Indo-British relationship; (3) Nehru is an anti-Fascist and wants free India to take part in the defeat of Japan and Germany; (4) That a Provisional National Government is better able to organize the resources of the country than the present unrepresentative character of the government.

XI. Supposing you were an Indian Nationalist—how would you have liked the British Government to settle the present deadlock?

XII. Do you agree that there cannot be peace in the world if 400 million people are a subject nation?

XIII. Senator Chandler accuses Britain for William Phillips recall to U.S.A., because Phillips pro-Indian sympathies. What do you say?

XIV. There are more colored peoples in the world than all whites put together. All colored peoples are under domination of the whites. If freedom is not given to them after the war, don't you think a major catastrophe will surely overwhelm the world?

August 31, 1944

Today I interviewed Colonel Oliver Stanley, British Secretary of State. I had a sinking feeling as the time approached for me to enter his office, as I felt it involved still another failure as to getting anything tangible regarding colonial plans for the future. Anyway, I tried my best to pin Stanley down, but every time I would establish a vital point he would squirm out by saying what he said was "off-the-record." The aggressive liberal policy of PM makes officials here extremely cautious. As a matter of fact, the Belgian at first refused to see me saying that he distrusted PM—and that it had misquoted him in the past. Stanley was equally cautious. I think he felt that I was somewhat awed that English officials were easier to see than American government officials—implying, I suppose, that I should feel honored at having successfully secured an interview. Well, the fact is, it was quite an accomplishment. The other correspondents mentioned this fact. In discussing the African situation, he said the Africans were not ready for self-rule. He said they were "savages," still eating each other! Well, this statement would have made a big story—but he cautioned me as soon as the statement came out of his mouth—that it was "of course, off-the-record." I learned later that he himself had only spent *three weeks* in Africa, although he was administering the destinies of millions of Africans!

★ ★ ★

[*This story was censored by the military*]

The noose of prejudice is slowly tightening around the necks of American Negro soldiers, and tending to cut off their recreation and associations with the British people. For—to be frank—relations between Negro and white troops have reached the proportions of grave concern. There are, of course, hopeful aspects.

This is my considered opinion after a careful survey, in which I interviewed British men and women in all walks of life, as well as white and Negro American officers and soldiers. To get an overall picture I visited the key cities of Glasgow, Belfast, Manchester, Liverpool, Bristol, and many small villages that do not appear on the average map.

Because the problem is of vital importance, not only to military morale, but also to Anglo-American amity, and to a peaceful transition from war to peace in America when the soldiers return, I feel the facts should be reported—not for inflammatory purposes, but in order to serve as a basis for a fruitful discussion of the issue. Moreover, the issue can no longer be ducked, for in one way or another it has touched the lives of every American soldier here. He will return with pretty concrete opinions which may have profound influence on the future of the nation.

The racial situation in England is a vast contrast to that in France, where I found few had the time or inclination for racial discrimination and insult. The reasons for its acuteness in England [are] complex. Much of it lies deep in the American way of life. But in essence, there are those here who are still fighting the Civil War—this time on British soil. To change the figure—one might say we are washing our dirty linen in public.

American observers who were here in 1942 when the first contingents arrived from America saw amicable and smooth relations develop between the Negro troops and their British hosts. Some were even lionized—so much so that certain white American soldiers became openly resentful. And they lost no time in attempting to discipline the British people. For—and this is perhaps the crucial issue—in back of the Southerner's mind here, is the belief that on his return the Negro will be mighty difficult to remold into the Jim Crow pattern.

....

Many thousands of American Negro troops are in Britain. They represent a larger Negro population than the British Isles has ever known—except perhaps during slave trading days. For most Britons it is the first time that they have seen Negroes in relatively large groups. For most of the Negroes it is the first time they have been away from their homes and communities.

But the people here have a racial tolerance which gives them a social lever. To begin with, the British attitude toward race is something quite different from that of the average American. They are inclined to accept a man for his personal worth. Thus the Negro has social equality here in more ways than theory. To put it in the language of a Negro soldier, "I'm treated so, a man don't know he's colored 'til he looks in the mirror."

The fact is, the British do draw racial distinctions, but not within the doors of the British Isles — at least not until the arrival of the white American soldiers. This is not to say that British are without racial prejudice. They do have it in a subtle form. But, in the main, it is confined to colonial and military officials in the colored colonies and derive from their incomes from them.

What contact the British people had with Negroes before the arrival of the American troops was on the whole very good. Paul Robeson, as well as many other Negro artists and entertainers, made quite an impression on the British.[31] In the ten years he resided in England, Robeson created a good opinion of the American Negro.

An aggressive pro-Nazi attitude developed in the Italian attack on Ethiopia. Negroes who lived here during those days, say that the average Englishmen was quite ashamed of the Baldwin-Chamberlain policies which gave open succor to Mussolini. Englishmen were known to have met Negroes on the streets and apologized.

By and large Negro troops have been billeted in the country sections of England, Scotland and Ireland. The British people in the country districts are naturally hospitable. They warmly greeted the Negro troops. Even sometimes giving them preferential treatment. It was not uncommon for a pub owner to save whiskey for Negro troops and refuse it to white soldiers. Soon Negroes were invited to British homes, churches, and trade union meetings. Easy and friendly associations developed between the races.

This was a great shock to many white Americans, particularly those from the deep South. At Highton in northern England — to illustrate — a Negro soldier had an appointment with an English girl to meet him in front of his camp. When he got outside she was engaged in conversation with two white American soldiers. The Negro soldier walked over and greeted the girl. "I've been waiting about fifteen minutes for you," she scolded cheerfully. They smiled and locked hands and walked down the road. One of the white soldiers snatched off his hat and flung it to the ground. He broke into tears and kept repeating over and over, "I'm from Georgia an' I jes can't take that!"

---

31. Internationally renowned singer, actor, and activist Paul Robeson (1898–1976) was a dominant figure in African American popular culture and a major player in anticolonialist, antifascist politics. He was prolabor and largely antiwar. His leftist politics eventually crippled his career, but in the 1930s and 1940s, he was at the height of his power and influence. See Martin Duberman, *Paul Robeson: A Biography* (New York: New Press, 2005).

It is just this sort of thing to which certain Americans are vigorously attempting to put a stop. There are those white commanders who when they arrive in an area with their units restrict passes to Negroes until after they have visited the nearest town or city. They choose the best cafes, restaurants, theaters and hotels for the white personnel and inform the proprietors that they are to bar Negro soldiers. If a startled English[man] protests, the officers retaliate be declaring his premises "Out of Bounds"—which of course means that neither white nor Negro soldiers can enter the poor man's place of business.

This has proved an effective strong-armed instrument for establishing the Jim Crow pattern in public places, and, incidentally, relegates Negroes to the worst sections on the outskirts of town or along the waterfront.

To reinforce these discriminations, Negroes are sharply restricted. I learned from soldiers stationed near Stratford-on-Avon—the birthplace of Shakespeare that this [place] has been declared "Off Limits" to Negro troops. There are camps with curfews for Negroes and not for white. Sometimes alternate days for white and Negro troops are fixed for visiting nearby towns and villages. Negroes in the neighborhood of Cardiff, Wales, were made particularly unhappy. For this city was also made out of bounds for Negroes—though it has the largest Negro population in the British Isles.

This capricious control over Negro soldiers, obviously cannot be exercised over the private lives of Britishers. This has produced a problem which certain Americans feel compelled to deal with. How?

Lynch law takes over in some cases:

A middle-aged woman, wife of a local businessman, became a volunteer Red Cross worker in Manchester. She was assigned to a club for Negro soldiers. One night a group of white American soldiers stopped her as she made her way home alone. They warned her to stay away from the club, or they would give her the "nigger cure"—whatever that means. Then they cuffed her about and remarked, "We string up women like you in Georgia!" The woman staggered back to the club bruised and hysterical.

....

Afterwards a Negro soldier remarked, "It's a damn shame men from the same country can't agree. But then these guys don't even respect women, so what can you expect."

The lash of prejudice is felt high and low. Brigadier General Benjamin O. Davis, highest ranking Negro in the U.S. Army, was refused service by a white private assigned to wait on him at the Officers' Mess. Even Sgt. Joe Louis has felt the sting. He was refused admission to a Shrewsbury Theater with the explanation that this discrimination had been insisted upon by the American command in the district.

Ironically enough, Joe Louis is on tour to improve the morale of soldiers. But one evening in Manchester he was to receive another jolt. He was having dinner with friends in a restaurant operated by Africans. A colonel—then military liaison officer for the North Region—entered and sought an interview for a woman reporter of the Sunday Chronicle.

Joe politely explained that he was off duty and out to have some fun with his friends, and, if the colonel didn't mind, would he arrange the interview for some other time. Anyway, he said, all his interviews with the press were arranged by the Army.

"That's the trouble with these niggers," the colonel snarled as he abruptly stalked out of the restaurant. "I'm just waitin' to get back home!"

Such people are apparently no respecters of American women either. A Negro Red Cross worker, J. Clarice Brooks, former New York social worker, was alone late one night at a Belfast Red Cross Club waiting for transportation home when in walked five white American soldiers. This is what transpired:

....

"There's the bitch that's runnin' the club for niggers," one shouted as they strode toward her.

"This is a Red Cross club for American soldiers if they behave themselves," she replied pluckily.

"What do you mean? Niggers is better behaved than we are?"

His companion interjected. "You gonna let her talk to you like that?"

"Let's beat her up," another said.

"Yeah, we know how to treat niggers!"

They were about to assault her when luckily a white officer happened along and intervened. Miss Brooks told me that although she attempted to press charges against them that was the last she heard of the affair.

Negro Red Cross workers in England have been known to go home nights with baseball bats to fight off prejudiced white soldiers. Yet the Red Cross officials have taken no position on this situation. The fact is, they have ignored it. The number of rank-and-file Negro workers with whom I have talked say there has not been a single instance where Red Cross has protested to the Army against the treatment of its Negro personnel.

In some areas, gangs have been formed by white soldiers to terrorize Negroes. When such groups arrive in a town, they immediately declare it "their" territory. Any Negro seen is run out of town on sight. This lawlessness produced a week of sporadic rioting in Manchester. The fights started when a white soldier struck a Negro soldier with a bottle because the Negro was in the company of a British girl. The MP [unit] was enlarged to meet the situation. But whereas the white MPs were armed with guns, the Negro MPs had only clubs.

There are many cities, towns, or villages that have witnessed race rioting. The most infamous of these clashes is called "The Battle of Bamber Bridge"—an area in Lancaster.[32] Negroes billeted here complained of unfair restrictions. They were burning with resentments. One night a white MP—regarded by Negroes as their mortal enemy—shot a Negro soldier in the back following a fracas. News of the killing soon reached camp. The Negro soldiers felt they had reached the limit of their endurance. So they broke into the arsenal, took arms, and barricaded themselves for battle.

When the first white officers approached, they were met by a volley of gun fire. Four of them went down. The other officers sought cover and summoned armored cars. A great tragedy was averted by Lt. Edmund Jones, a Negro popular with the troops. Well aware that these desperate Negroes were prepared to fight to the death, he persuaded his white commander to give him authority to end the affair without further bloodshed. He was made a Provost-General for three days and was successful in having the Negroes end the futile battle. He assured them, communicating by radio, that reforms would follow and in the future they would be dealt with fairly.

Listen to a Negro soldier who arrived in England two months ago. He is Corporal Harold Snell, a former union organizer in Chicago. "My experiences in England," he told me, "have been uniformly bitter as far as my relations with white American soldiers who blindly accept the Jim Crow policy of higher officers. I am still convinced that the average American is fundamentally decent, but some Army brass hats seem determined to maintain the racial situation only to be found in the deep South.

"Every effort is made to separate the races with the same shop-worn excuses being given for this policy that one encounters in the states. This separation here, as at home, inevitably results in inferior accommodations, rations, sanitary and recreational facilities.

32. The so-called battle of Bamber Bridge began on June 24, 1943, when two white military policemen (MPs) attempted to arrest a black GI who was out without a pass. Other black soldiers, British soldiers, and English citizens rose to the GI's defense. Tempers eventually spiraled out of control, shots were fired, and a number of servicemen were shot. The MPs surrounded the encampment of African American GIs with machine guns. The black troops armed themselves and prepared for battle. After a night of skirmishing, the conflict was defused. See Harold Pollins, "The Battle of Bamber Bridge," World War II People's War: An Archive of World War II Memories, February 17, 2005, http://www.bbc.co.uk/ww2peopleswar/stories/85/a3677385.shtml (accessed May 2, 2010).

"All of us soldiers are agreed that constant vocal opposition on the part of organized liberal groups at home offers the only possible solution for this, the one blind spot in Army pol[i]cy."

This distressing racial situation must be laid squarely on the doorstep of the white officers. Certainly if they wished to do something concrete about the problem, there are sufficient memorandum, directives, and orders to bolster them. Tons of such literature has been published. I have seen much of it. Most is forthright in explaining, and even insisting, upon mutual respect among soldiers. Many are masterpieces of clarity. The declared policy of the American Army in relation to the Negro soldier is absolutely clear:

"He is to receive the same treatment, wages, rations as the white troops. He is to have equal opportunities for recreation."

To use General Eisenhower's words: "Recreation and entertainment are necessary for soldiers in the European Theater of Operations. Commanders should try to make it possible to attend plays, movies and lectures, as well as to accept privately offered hospitality. Officers and men should have equal opportunity for recreation."

....

Unhappily, certain of the officers whose tasks it becomes to implement these instructions violate them where the Negro is concerned. Few of them even bother to read the instructions. They well know that in practice there is no penalty for any show of racial hostility. The fact is, there is ample evidence to prove that racial prejudice is encouraged by such officers, a group often dominated by Southerners.

An RAF flier told me of an indoctrination course he attended, conducted by an American Lt. His whole lecture was devoted to explaining to the British the reasons why they should not associate with Negro soldiers. He made no bones about the fact that not to conform with the American view of race, was to be the victim of actual physical violence.

These roughhouse tactics have, of course, been augmented by world-of-mouth propaganda. At every turn attempts are being made to discredit the Negro. The catalogue of lies and misinformation is well known in America. But new twists have been given old clichés. A Negro major told me of being surprised when he visited a British home by the total concern for his comfort. The mistress of the house had placed a number of soft pillows in his chair. Every so often she would anxiously look in his direction. Before the evening was over he learned the reason. His hosts had been told by American soldiers that Negroes have tails!

To an American this may sound like sheer nonsense. But such stories were actually believed in the northern areas of England and Scotland until

Negroes arrived. Children along the roads innocently asked to have a peek. Every Negro soldier here can give a new slant on this "animal angle"—as they call it—from his own experiences. A typical story concerns a Scottish woman who was asked for directions by a Negro soldier. After he spoke she was speechless for two minutes. Then she exclaimed in amazement, "Oh, but you can talk! The white Yanks told us that the blacks could only bark."

Perhaps much of the propaganda would stick, if many white American soldiers did not abuse the feelings of the British people. Some of them stride about the city streets with the look, "We came to save you dopes." The English people are actually sensitive to their dilemma after Dunkirk. But some Americans not only mention it, but are noisy about it, even boastful. Much of their behavior would never be countenanced in America. It has embarrassed many Americans—for bad manners are bad whether at home or abroad.

September 1, 1944

I heard a story today which illustrates something of the housing situation for mixed couples—Negro-White—in London: A girl I know—a member of an upper class family—fell in love with a Negro. She resided in her own place in the swank Mayfair section. Subsequently she married this boy and he moved into her apartment. She had a three-year lease. When it expired, the landlord refused to renew it, saying the apartment had already been rented to another family. Meanwhile, a lot of Americans had moved into the area and building. She attributes her being evicted to the protest of Americans in the house who objected to a Negro coming and going in the house.

Then she determined to get a place where the landlord would commit himself about Negroes living in the house beforehand. Subsequently she rented another apartment, informing the landlord that her husband was a Negro. He made no comment. She asked that the fact be acknowledged in the lease. He ignored the request twice. When she raised the question a third time, he said he didn't rent apartments to Negroes. Although he had rented an apartment to her, with her colored husband, the lease was made out in the name of a white person. This closed the matter as far as the landlord was concerned.

September 2, 1944

A Negro sailor told me a story tonight which illustrates how fantastic certain whites can be on the race problem: He was in Dakar in the early days of the North African invasion. He said there were few white women in the city, so the white G.I.s had colored girl friends—but violently objected to Negroes going out with colored girls!

★ ★ ★

[*This story was censored by the military*]

Two weeks of sporadic fighting took place between white and Negro American soldiers at Leicester in the Midlands. Four white soldiers and one MP were killed. Many whites were hospitalized. Numbers of Negroes were hurt and wounded. Following these incidents, signs appeared in public places with variations of the following theme:

"FOR BRITISH CIVILIANS AND

U.S.A. NEGRO FORCES ONLY"

I believe this is not uncommon in England today. I have covered a wide sweep of England and Ireland, visiting camps, talking with American officers and soldiers—both white and Negro, and interviewing public officials and Red Cross directors.

In frankness I must report that the American race problem is being transplanted to British soil—sometimes with a venom unknown in the United States. For certain white Americans cannot reconcile themselves to the warm reception the British people have accorded the Negro troops. What is more, the problem threatens Anglo-American understanding, as well as the morale of Negro soldiers.

To begin with, there are thousands of American Negro soldiers in England. They have been equipped for combat and combat-support duty. Before their arrival great sections of England had never seen a Negro in person. And for the most part Negroes have been billeted in the rural sections. Today, with the early awkwardness gone, they are known affectionately as the "Black Yanks."

There was apprehension in some areas at first. An elderly lady living in Glasgow was asked to billet an American soldier. To her dismay, two Negro soldiers showed up. Never having met Negroes before she was filled with dark forebodings. The first night she barred her bedroom door and spent the hours quite awake. Early next morning there was a knock at her door.

"Who's there?" she cried.

"Just a cup of tea ma'am," came the answer.

When she came down later the boys had cleaned up the kitchen and made her breakfast. Today they are the firmest of friends.

Today the British are aggressively resisting the prejudice which certain white American soldiers are intent upon imposing. This seems to have been the case when American soldiers boarded a bus in London and tried to eject two Negro soldiers from seats they already occupied.

["]You can't do that sort of thing here," a woman conductor protested. "We won't have it. Either you stand or off you go."

··

They stood. But the seeds of prejudice are easily scattered. Even some white troops who shared no feeling of prejudice in the United States have accepted the anti-Negro attitudes held by certain Americans. Inevitably, in their contact with the British some have sought to transfer these attitudes. This is the reason that one of England's best-known columnist[s], Swaffer, flatly declared: "Discrimination against blacks started at the request of certain American authorities."

What's true of the United States, seems equally true in England: The customer is always right. When the manager of a restaurant was questioned recently about refusing service to a Negro soldier, he had a ready answer: "White Americans say they will not patronize my place if Negroes were served." A Negro civilian, long a resident of London, told me that a pub owner, whose place he had frequented for more than seven years, pleaded with him not to visit the place any more. He said some Americans had warned him about serving Negroes and they threatened to break up his place.

Nevertheless, the Negro soldier has appealed to the British heart. He has won many friends. Brendan Bracken, Minister of Information, told me that the behavior of the Negro troops has been remarkably good. There is a reason: after negotiating the delicate business of living Jim Crow in America, these men feel amply prepared to live with any people. As one put it, "We have the passport to life."

The Negro's easy manner has fitted in nicely with the British. Not accustomed to asserting himself, a Negro is neither hurried nor pushy. And, of course, he is not a braggart here because he feels he has little to boast about. His peculiar status in the United States has equipped him for special relationships with the reserved English people — though some Britishers interpret the shyness of Southern Negroes as part of the race's acute awareness of the social amenities.

He has brought along his gifts. I was quite surprised to find British girls in Manchester, Liverpool, Glasgow, and London dancing the lindy hop. Every Monday morning newspapers are full with reports of Negro activity with the British — such as hikes and picnics. Negroes have enjoyed the simple pleasures of the British. They are seen at churches, groups of them taking over the choir loft on occasion.

The British are shocked by the bad manners of certain Americans, which is displayed in racial hostility to Negroes, and on many occasions to the British. I was talking to an attractive white girl in a Manchester Red Cross club about this very thing. She was enthusiastic in her praise of the Negro troops. She said they were always polite and appreciative. She had had a group of them to her home. While we talked three white soldiers were playing pool nearby. One of them—to make a difficult shot—backed his buttocks into her face without so much as a nod.

"That's what I mean," she said. "A Negro would never do that."

Actually, he might. But in England there is no doubt about it that Negroes—of whatever strata in civilian life from which they come—are on their very best behavior. They are fully aware of what is at stake. Their Negro officers and Negro Red Cross directors have done a splendid job of making them conscious that they are the guests of the British people, and as such they must prove themselves worthy of the warm hospitality.

Negro troops stationed near Manchester originated the idea of entertaining the local children to repay some of the hospitality which they had received in that city. I attended the second of a series of six weekly parties. About twenty Negro soldiers sung and danced. Then they distributed chewing gum and candy from their rations. Five [h]undred children attended the party given at the Red Cross club. The Lord Mayor was present.

The treatment of the Negro soldier by his fellow American has become a burning issue. When eighteen Negro soldiers, who entered a hotel lounge in Paighton and were refused service because of their color put up a fight, their trial was covered by every newspaper. The London Daily Mail headlined its story: "FINDINGS SECRET IN U.S. TRIAL FOR 'MUTINY.'"

Hardly a day passes that there is not newspaper comment about the race problem in England and the U.S. Here are a few heads chosen at random to illustrate the manner in which this topic is being handled:

LAW IS THE SAME FOR WHITE OR COLORED
— Gloucestershire Echo
BECAUSE THEIR SKINS ARE BROWN
— London News Chronicle
RECORDER HITS AT COLOR BAR
— London Daily Mirror
COLOR BAR IS 'SHAMEFUL'
— London Daily Mail

National attention was recently focused on a case which came before a Liverpool court. A West Indian Negro, George Alexander McGuire, charged that he was refused admission to a public dance because of his race. American instigation was clearly implied. The judge used this incident to strike out at American race prejudice in England. His opinion was reported widely and in much detail by the press. He said:

··

"I am told that the position of colored people in this country has somewhat changed since the nationals of another of our allies joined us in this country.

"When people come here to risk their lives they are entitled to think that they are coming to conditions of decency and order fit for a country that claims the title imperial in its best sense.

"I think it is impertinence for any country to accept the aid of colored people from any part of the world and then to say: 'Our laws don't enable us to deal with you on terms of complete equality.'"

Mounting opinion has not ended there. The newspapers have been deluged with letters-to-the-editor from British people protesting the imposition of American racial attitudes. A typical one appeared in the News Chronicle signed by a Rev. J. Giles. It said:

"The impression our Negro guests made on Nuneaton was one of natural and profound culture. Their courtesy, their politeness, their manly bearing, their frankness, and, above all, their unfailing cheerfulness and good humor quickly endeared them to the inhabitants.

"They brought with them next to no rowdiness or gross drunkenness, and on the very rare occasions when tempers rose there had been more than adequate provocation. We were sorry when they left us.

"Perhaps an unsolicited remark from a casually-met citizen to myself sums up what the town felt.

"'These Negro boys are good fellows and as straight as you like—they're certainly teaching the town manners.'"

··

The Tribune, a popular weekly, received a letter from a British soldier complaining that his detachment had been given a list of "suggestions" advising them to adopt an "attitude not unfriendly toward Negro troops but not too friendly." To members of A.T.S. [the British military's Auxiliary Territorial Service] it forbade associations with Negro soldiers. A bit bewildered he asked: "Why should comrades not be treated wholly as comrades? Can there be any question for segregation on the battlefront? Can the rule of the cocktail bar apply to the front? Aren't we fighting, among other things, for the abolition of class and color bars?"

The race issue has been the subject of discussion at citizen meetings, with many petitioning their leaders to raise the question with the government. Trade union groups, too, are stirred. But if labor's leaders cannot speak out because they are members of the government, and thus would embarrass Anglo-American relations, certainly the rank-and-file have not lost their tongues.

Three months ago two Negro soldiers were charged with rape and were sentenced to death by court-martial in Gloucestershire. A dispute arose as to whether these soldiers were guilty. Thirty three thousand people protested. Workers in a local factory immediately sent a protest to the American authorities and copies to the newspapers. They charged that the men were sentenced to death because of their color. The formal statement went on to say, "In England we have learned the meaning of equality and freedom and we are revolted by the unjustness of American laws concerning Negroes."

In another factory shop stewards were instructed by the rank-and-file to "take action to obtain commutation of the death sentence." "It is the almost unanimous opinion," the formal protest read, "that this severe sentence, when compared with sentences of imprisonment passed on white American soldiers for similar offenses, suggests a racial discrimination that will be deplored by all peoples fighting against this very thing in the war against Fascism and racial persecution."

The Negro soldiers feel keenly about the frequent show of racial animosity. Voicing a fairly typical attitude of troops who have recently arrived in England, Pfc. William B. Brown, Newark, N.J., told me how he felt:

"Since my arrival I've been constantly reminded that I'm a Negro. The pattern seems more pronounced here than in the deep South.

"The morale of Negro combat units certainly can't be any lower than that of the service units, if their experience is just partially like mine."

Sgt. Charles Brown, Indiana, expressed it in pithy language: "We feel misused."

Traveling between London and Manchester I met an intelligent soldier, who was on some sort of mission. He gave me a slant, which I've heard often enough to make me believe it can be chalked up as what every Negro soldier thinks:

"What I want to see is a real struggle to overcome this race question, which, as it stands today, threatens to make this war quite useless in relation to the great aims for which we are said to be fighting.

"I want to see some organization really trying to reach a solution."

The fact is, numbers of people are scrambling around for a solution. I talked quite extensively with British officials. They are frankly embarrassed and even alarmed by the race situation provoked by certain Americans. None will talk for the record. Lend-lease makes them keep their official mouths close[d], for they are well aware of the spitefulness of Southern politicians. Moreover, they feel that Americans are creating a vast amount of anti-white feeling throughout the world, which will make the dealings of the British with colored colonies pretty difficult. Many of them feel Americans presumptuous to talk of freedom for India in the face of the unresolved race problem in America.

Perhaps, no one here is more disturbed than Americans. But individuals cannot stand up alone. Friends, whom I knew in the United States, admit they are helpless. Yet white officers are daily sticking their necks out to make democracy vibrant and living within the Army. Such Army publications as "Yank" and "Stars and Stripes" are dramatizing the Negro soldier's vital role in the war. Several white American seamen signed a petition protesting the barring of Negroes from a ballroom they visited.

The one hopeful aspect of this situation, is the fact that the noose of prejudice has not closed. The reason may be found in the fact that many of the most rabid anti-Negro American soldiers are not so sure of their position. They do not have wide public support for any show of racial hostility. The great tragedy lies in the fact that such elements arrived in England with the presumption that wherever there were white people they had their heels on the necks of black people. Their ignorance is appalling, and indeed a little pathetic.

S. L. Solon, an American reporter working for a London paper, relates a conversation he overheard. It sums up the situation, tying it in a nice tight knot.

"Personally," a town councilor said, "I have no feeling of race prejudice. I've been led to believe, however, that our relations with American white troops will be better if we conform to what I understand to be American practices of discrimination."

··

The answer to that came from a white American officer. "Discrimination is not American," he said. "Even less so today, when we are fighting a war to preserve and extend democratic values in the world."

September 4, 1944

Today I made a most unusual contact—I had supper with a gal named Toby Frazier Lowell Holman. I met her through mutual friends sometime ago. She is married to a British officer who is a mining engineer. She is an

American. She is a flier, but was grounded because of two mash-ups. Now she edits the Red Cross paper in England.

It turns out that she is rabidly pro-Negro—though she is opposed to intermarriage because of off-spring. After supper we went by her flat in a hotel, where we had more drinks and talk. She lost her three-month baby in the buzz-bomb attack on London and doesn't seem to have gotten over it. While she was bathing I talked to her Irish maid. She told me that her Madame had a no-good husband as well as a no-good lover. It seems that both men are interested in her for her money only. In this kind of situation, the Englishman is a master. He apparently is unconcerned about her personal activities. What it turns out to be is "pimping" on a fancy scale.

Toby was shocked to discover, when I told her, how her money is used to exploit people. Before the war, she spent much time on the Riviera—where she has a place. Much that happened in the States escaped her. But she is very conscious of the Negro problem as everyone is here.

September 5, 1944

A reflection on my trip to Glasgow. One of the girls with whom I flew back to London works for the War Department and formerly was a World-Telegram reporter. I judged her age to be about 40, but she seems to have worn well. Well, anyway, she was quite affable on the plane, so much so that she discussed her sex life by saying she was a virgin. I believed it. The point about all this is, that this white woman once removed from her environment was a normal friendly human being. When we arrived in London, she immediately took on the frigidity of so many Americans toward Negroes. I met her today at the correspondents headquarters. She was a changed person. Here she was under the social pressure of white men, and perhaps didn't want them to presume anything from any show of friendliness toward me. I am coming to believe the race problem is a matter of public attitude and behavior. Few whites want to acknowledge friendship with Negroes. In some way they feel they lose status. I suppose. Others, however, are different. But the most democratic whites I have met in England are those whose status is fairly secure. Those who are trying to gain status are the most difficult ones—and most people are trying to gain status. The race issue today has nothing to do with color, that is, among people who are educated or traveled. It is merely a question of status. Negroes have little.

September 6, 1944

Today I went to the India Office to interview the Secretary for India, Mr. Amery.[33] He is a great mountain climber. His son is a Nazi, who broadcasts from Germany with Lord Haw Haw. I talked with the Secretary about India. He would only speak off the record. He declared that Gandhi was a "Fascist," that Americans were ignorant of India's problems, and that Senator Chandler is vicious and mischievous. He was anxious to know about affairs in America along racial lines. He felt Americans were presumptuous to criticize England's handling of [the] Indian problem in the face of America's own unsolved race problem. He placed rigid checks on what I might write by reminding me that I had to get permission to enter India. I will not do a story on this interview.

Supper with Toby. She brought along an American flyer who turned out to be quite a guy. We went to a French restaurant for supper and had a swell time and excellent food and drinks. He explained to me that they had had little contact with Negroes in the States for the simple reason that they had no way of meeting them socially. Toby drinks hard and often, though she doesn't get drunk.

September 7, 1944

Talked with Clarice Brooks today. Most people here call her "Jackie." She was pretty downcast because she was declared physically unfit to go to Paris with the Red Cross outfit. Heart trouble, they say. She has been drinking pretty hard, which may have raced her heart. She is being sent to a hospital for three weeks' treatment.

I saw Nancy Cunard—of Cunard Steamship Line—and she was nice enough to give me a list of her contacts to look up in North America and Paris.[34] What a fright that woman is!

....

Ernest Hemingway continues to distinguish himself as a character. I had supper at La Petit, where I ran into some fellows just back from France. They told me of Hemingway walking into a French town and taking over

33. Leo Amery (1873–1955) was a British Conservative Party politician. He served in the House of Commons, where he was an opponent of the appeasement movement. When the war began, Churchill made Amery his secretary for India. See David Faber, *Speaking for England: Leo, Julian, and John Amery—The Tragedy of a Political Family* (New York: Free Press, 2005).

34. Nancy Cunard (1896–1965) was an heir to the Cunard Shipping Lines fortune, and she used her wealth to establish herself as a patron of the arts and to fund innumerable political causes. She was also a working journalist who wrote passionately about the oppression of African Americans and trumpeted the looming threat of international fascism. The best biography of Cunard is Lois Gordon's *Nancy Cunard: Heiress, Muse, Political Idealist* (New York: Columbia University Press, 2007).

leadership of the Resistance Movement. He had the French people mine all the approaches to the city to prevent German invasion. But the German Army wasn't moving in that direction at all. Instead the mines held up the advance of American columns!

Incidentally, there was considerable talk about Richard Wright's attack in the Atlantic Monthly on Communists. It now turns out that he isn't as brilliant as every one supposed—instead he is an ignoramus. He will no doubt be ostracized.

September 8, 1944

Had dinner tonight with Peggy Cripps—who is the daughter of Sir Stafford Cripps.[35] We talked a lot about Russia, India and America. She is definitely on the liberal side—further left than her father. But she was sensitive to any criticism of him and his handling of the Indian situation. She felt the Americans generally are appallingly ignorant of the problems inherent in the Indian situation. She felt that the Indian leaders were wrong in fighting for—as she put it—"all or nothing." She felt they would make more concrete and swifter gains by accepting a little at a time. She was nice enough to agree to help me get an interview with her father. She works for the Soviet government! Peggy is a plain-looking girl with rather abrupt manners. But she is vitally interested in social problems. She introduced me to a Russian who was helpful about places I should visit when I get to the Soviet [Union].

One thing I am faced with here is the very curious situation of having to defend Negroes' advancement in America. Most people here—supposedly well informed—feel and think that most Negroes are almost slaves in the U.S. They believe that Negroes can't even walk on the same sidewalks with whites. So I've been put in the unenviable position of explaining the subtleties of Jim Crow.

35. Sir Stafford Cripps was a British Labour Party politician and socialist who served as chancellor of the Exchequer in Clement Attlee's government, from 1947 to 1950. In the early years of World War II, Cripps was ambassador to the Soviet Union. See Gabriel Gorodetsky, *Stafford Cripps Mission to Moscow, 1940–1942* (Cambridge: Cambridge University Press, 1984). His daughter, Peggy Cripps Appiah, shocked London society in 1953 when she married Ghanaian politician Joseph E. Appiah. Their first son is the Princeton University philosopher Kwame Anthony Appiah. Peggy Appiah was a prolific author of collections of Ghanaian folktales, poetry, novels, and children's books. See Nadine Brozan, "Peggy Appiah, 84, Who Bridged Two Cultures, Dies," *New York Times*, February 16, 2006, http://www.nytimes.com/2006/02/16/international/africa/16appiah.html (accessed May 2, 2010).

September 9, 1944

Nothing happens much in London on Saturdays, for the whole community seems to go to the country for the week-end. Anyway, it gives me a chance to catch up on my reading and research.

About five o'clock, I met Toby Holman at Frisco's. James E. Jackson, who is the accountant for the Red Cross in England, was along. He developed quite a crush on Toby. So, after the three of us had supper, he went off with her—I judge to spend the night. She seemed in the mood. Perhaps my long talks with her about the race problem have done something—but in what direction I don't know!

Lt. Edmund Jones and I went back to Frisco's and drank and talked the night away. Jones has a Negro girl friend who worked in Lew Leslie's "Blackbirds" when it played in London. It seems that Negro girls here can only get employment as entertainers—no one will even hire them for domestic work. This work is reserved for Irish girls who are imported. Most of the Negro girls must therefore turn to prostitution. The same seems to hold for Negro men of course.

September 10, 1944

Spent a mighty quiet Sunday. Awoke at noon. Had breakfast at the Liberty Club. Then did a story on Brendon Bracken, British Minister of Information, who warmly praised American Negro soldiers in an exclusive interview a few days previous.

Met Lt. Edmund Jones, who passed the day cursing about a race riot at Bamber Bridge. We went for a walk, after which we had dinner at his girl friend's, a Negro girl who used to work in Lew Leslie's "Blackbirds." Then the three of us went to see Bing Crosby in "Going My Way," which was sentimental but good for the mood we were in. Barry Fitzgerald sneaked off with the acting honors. From there we went to the Caribbean Club for drinks. The place is run by a Negro named "Rudy," who used to operate a night club in Paris. Actually, the club is a dump but has a rather nondescript group of patrons. From here home and to bed. On the way home I could not help observing that the Americans are making one great brothel out of England.

September 11, 1944

The Europeans I have met in London are greatly bewildered by the American race problem. The English feel that it is creating a vast amount of anti-white feeling throughout the world. They are, therefore, concerned because anti-white feeling makes their ruling of colored people that much more difficult. Every public official I've talked with has asked about them. Cadbury—one of the owners of the "News Chronicle"—wanted to know if the white Americans would develop an anti-British feeling because of the warm welcome given American Negro troops.

People from the Continent have no concept of the race problem—a man's a man to them. The whole business is sheer insanity. Much of the good will Americans could enjoy in Europe is destroyed by rabid anti-Negro feelings which many Americans never fail to express. The fact is, Americans can't conceive of a world where there isn't a white man with his heel on the neck of black men.

Yesterday I interviewed Sir Stafford Cripps. He is a tall, distinguished looking man with iron-gray hair. I was successful in persuading him to give me a statement on the Indian situation. We talked quite at length about India and, of course, about America. He seemed somewhat on the defensive about his role in the Indian situation and was glad to be able to state his side of the case.

★ ★ ★

Well, the time grows shorter when I'll be home. Yet I have plenty to do as yet. Tomorrow—all going well—I'll be in Paris. To all intents and purposes this concludes my trip to England, which I've found exceptionally profitable. I was lucky enough to interview everyone I've sought to see—with the notable exception of Churchill, who never seems to be in the country! I've interviewed Cripps, and the Belgian, Dutch and British Ministers of Colonies, in addition to the Secretary for India.

I've met a few characters as well. In a previous letter I told you about Toby Holman. Well, I introduced her to a fellow named James Jackson, a Negro who is an accountant for the Red Cross territory in England. He is quite a guy. He took her home the other night—which means something or other in the way in which I discussed the Negro question with her. No surprise, but it was interesting to see. Hoped she would react once she met a Negro she was romantically interested in.

Incidentally, talking of characters, I met Cripps' daughter Peggy. We've had lunch a number of times. She is the plainest looking gal in the world—even I think a bit of the wac. But she is bright and interesting company. She was nice enough to help me to arrange an interview with her father. Anyway, we talked a lot about Russia, India and America. She is definitely a liberal—much to the left of her father. But she was very sensitive about any criticism of him. She felt that his mission to India, to persuade Gandhi to accept the Government's proposition was good, but American liberals misinterpreted it. She works for the Soviet information service.

September 12, 1944

Rose at 6 A.M. today to catch plane to Paris. No taxis running. Luckily the underground just began operating. Arrived at Haymarket, the meeting place. Six Frenchmen were there also, apparently returning. While waiting for the bus to the airfield, a terrible crash sounded a half mile away—the Nazis are sending over V-2. The ground under us shook with the impact of the explosion.

The trip to Paris was by bomber. Took three hours because we went around the Cherbourg peninsula. Two newspaper men and a French officer were my companions. All very pleasant. One was Bill Stoneman.[36]

....

Paris! First impression: Not an automobile on the street. Helen Kirkpatrick of the Chicago Daily News was kind enough to drive me from the airport to my hotel—which is the swank Hotel Scribe. She was meeting another member of her paper at the airport. She told me enroute that a good French dinner cost 4000 francs or $80. She hadn't had a hot bath in three weeks. There is no coal in Paris or electricity. But there is an undeniable thrill to enter Paris along the famous Champs Elysee.

Spent the rest of the day getting set up—exchanging American money into French, securing room overlooking the Rue Scribe, and shopping for presents.

September 13, 1944

Ollie Stewart and Rudolph Dunbar are the only other Negro correspondents here. Rudolph seemed glad to see me. He took me on a short tour of the city and helped me buy presents. He lived in France before the war and speaks French fluently. Incidentally, he is the butt of much behind-the-back ridicule for his pompous manner. But, in one sense, it is a reflection of the resentments the white correspondents have to Negroes. They feel Negroes are invading some exclusive fraternity. Whereas, once they could speak learnedly of foreign and military affairs, Negroes are now in possession of the same knowledge and much of it is sheer hooey. This reminds me that Alex Uhl, foreign editor of PM, has been most uncooperative. He somewhat resents my presence, for he feels that in some way it lowers his

---

36. William H. Stoneman (1904–1987) was the longtime chief European correspondent for the *Chicago Daily News*. He had covered events in Rome, Moscow, and Paris before the war. After the war, Stoneman took a leave of absence to serve as a special adviser to the UN secretary general Trygve Lie. See "Obituary: William H. Stoneman, 83; Foreign Correspondent," *New York Times*, April 14, 1987, http://www.nytimes.com/1987/04/14/obituaries/william-stoneman-83-foreign-correspondent.html?pagewanted=1?pagewanted=1 (accessed May 4, 2010).

status among the other correspondents. He has given me no leads for stories, though he wanted to clarify what my exact status with PM was. He seemed relieved to know that PM was not paying all my expenses. His ego was given a decided lift. I could see. For after all, it was the same [as] his status. This is not to say that the white correspondents are not friendly — they are: Men like Charles Collingswood (CBS) and Bill Stoneman (Chicago Daily News) are the right sort even aggressively for Negroes and the underdog.

★ ★ ★

I walked the boulevards yesterday. One would never think this city was in the midst of war. Except of course the presence of soldiers, who, incidentally, walk about armed, for there are still Germans lodged about the place hiding.

I walked along Paris' famous shopping district, Rue Rivoli. American women would knock themselves out buying things. Certainly that was my feeling — so I did.

I'm staying at the Hotel Scribe — and such swank. The lobby has display windows right up to the staircase. It was one of the pre-war better places. The Germans used it as their headquarters. The only fly in the ointment is that it has no hot water — Paris has no coal. Besides providing us with rooms and bath — mine faces Rue de Scribe, which is opposite L'Opera, a famous Paris showplace.

Yesterday I spent a few hours seated at a street café, watching the passing show. One thing I've noticed, which I like, is that every woman from six to sixty is very much aware of being a woman. I haven't seen one pair of slacks on a woman yet — and I repeat, I like that. Much to everyone's surprise, the French women are still very well dressed. The Germans encouraged, apparently, the luxury trades in order to supply the German woman.

Today I visited Rene Maran, author of "Batoula."[37] He is quite a chap. He is quite a celebrity here. From him I am learning a lot about what happened in Paris during German occupation. His wife is a Frenchwoman who seems quite devoted.

Only two Negro correspondents are here at the moment — Ollie Stewart and myself. He is at the moment in Brest, seeing the fighting. I've seen enough for a lifetime, so I don't plan anymore front line stories right now.

37. Rene Maran (1887–1960) was born in Martinique and as a child lived in Africa and in France. His father was in the French Colonial Service. Maran became a poet and novelist. His 1921 novel, *Batoula: A True Black Novel*, won the prestigious Prix Goncourt in France, making Maran the first Black writer to win the award. See Keith Cameron, *Rene Maran* (Boston: Twayne Publishers, 1985).

Instead, I think I'll go on a tourist trip and see the historic things of Paris. There's no night life in Paris as yet, so everyone gets to bed by 10 o'clock.

September 14, 1944

Ed Toles, whom I like best of the Negro correspondents, arrived from Cherbourg today. I was as glad to see him as he was to see me. He was nearly hit by a shell in Brest, but he looks none the worse for the experience. He joined me at the Hotel Scribe, which, incidentally, is the swankiest hostelry in Paris. The Germans used it as a headquarters for the high command in Paris. The service is impeccable; beds soft, linen clean and changed regularly. The lobby is a promenade of show windows of items one might buy. Quite a few Americans stayed here before the war. A bar is open with all sorts of liquors. Some of the correspondents practically live there. The rooms here are the closest approach to rooms in the U.S. The floors are heavily carpeted. But the French do not seem to include closet space in their planning of buildings. Every room has a magnificent mahogany wardrobe in it — with plenty of full length mirrors. Even in homes this seems to be the rule. The beds are brass, but the mattresses are with inner springs. One experience you have here — you do not have in the States is the fear of air raids — I have been sleeping soundly — only to be startled by the sound of airplane motors. Often they are our own planes — or big trucks passing. But it does give you a scare. Paris, of course, has been attacked by the German robots — doing much damage in life and property.

September 15, 1944

Last night I heard a dismal story — told to me by a Cameroon Negro named Lucas — of how his wife is in prison as a collaborator and she is innocent. They have been married for sixteen years. They were dancers in better times. He says his neighbors were jealous and falsely charged his wife. He seemed so sincere and appealing that I decided to have a look. So this morning I went out to "Drancy" — on the outskirts of Paris. It is the most infamous prison in France. It contained 15,000 Jews before Paris was liberated. It was built originally by the French. Ironically enough, the Nazis used it to imprison Frenchmen! When I arrived 6,800 political prisoners were milling around an expansive courtyard. I wondered how in hell 15,000 Jews must have fared in the same space. To my surprise more than 100 Negroes were included among the prisoners. "Drancy" looks like a vast modern government-financed housing project in America — except that it is white relieved by a few patches of blue decorating the buildings. They all face a vast courtyard where once a day the prisoners go for exercise. After much palaver, I was directed to the official in charge. The place was heavily guarded by members of the FFI [the French Forces of the Interior—the French resistance], some of them mere boys. When I asked for Madame Lucas, no one could find any record of her. The records were in a shambles. People will be buried there for years before they are released. They promised to make a search. I said I would return tomorrow.

September 16, 1944

Today I returned to "Drancy" to investigate the case of Madame Maria Wodmenduga-Lucas, wife of my Cameroon friend. She was born in Serbia. When I arrived today the French officials were all smiles. They had found Madame Lucas and her record. She is a converted blonde with large false teeth in silver, which is pretty prevalent in France. She was not handsome, though. When they brought her into a room which very much resembled the N.Y. Department of Welfare offices in the early days of the depression, she looked quite bewildered. I was taken before a three-[man] board who read the charges against her, asked a few questions and then palavered among themselves. They finally told me she had been charged with being a "collaborationist." But they had investigated the case and found this to be untrue. I explained that I was merely interested in seeing how justice, as administered by the Resistance Movement, operates in Paris. I was told Madame Lucas would be "liberated" in two or three days after a superior council reviewed their findings. Madame Lucas was full of tears. As I made my way across the vast courtyard, prisoners sought to talk with me about their cases, as word apparently had gotten around that I had helped Madame Lucas.

September 17, 1944

Today a most unusual experience. While walking along Rue Pigalle with M. Lucas, a Cameroon Negro, a white soldier walked up to me and smartly saluted me as an officer. I had just completed greeting "Didi," a white musician's wife whom I had met. She was smartly dressed and blonde. I had visited her and her famous husband at their home where the "Hot Club of Paris" was reorganized. He showed me his gun tucked in his belt and attempted to intimidate me for talking with "Didi." Not in an obvious manner, but enough to indicate that the Southern "white folks" were present and were watching what I was doing—which, of course, was nothing.

What actually is taking place in Paris is of great bewilderment to white American troops. They do not know what to make of the complete freedom

Negroes have in Paris — or, for that matter, the complete lack of racial in-hibitions on the part of the French. And unhappily for them, they do not know how to speak French and so are unable to communicate their preju-dice to the French people. By and large the French people are extremely lib-eral in racial matters. But Negroes here complain that they are only giving lip-service to liberalism. Actually, Negroes contend, the Frenchman is anti-Negro. The French woman pro-Negro. I think, however, the French — like the English — stand on status.

September 18, 1944

Madame Lucas is back with her husband after six weeks in "Drancy," the prison camp that held 15,000 Jews during Nazi occupation. She is extremely happy for my efforts on her behalf. Had a splendid dinner and wine to cel-ebrate her release. All her friends were in to greet her.

••

I have been observing race relations in Paris: Visited Café Mon Jardin on Rue de la Bruxelles. Here a Negro and white band beat it out in Ameri-can style. Everyone seemed quite happy. The Germans frequented the place before the liberation of Paris. There were a number of white soldiers present. But they seemed not to care about Negroes dancing with French women — this, of course, included French Negroes. But I fear the reason is that they feel all French women are "whores." Actually they are unable to distinguish between good women and whores.

Women in Paris do not go through the ceremonies of pre-sexual con-nection that English and American women do. That is, they are very frank about whether they do or don't — without taking offense at the inquiry. Some French women — similar in cultural development and economic to those who frequent the Savoy in Harlem — only come to dance. They like to dance with Negroes. The white Americans do not seem to understand this. But they are trying hard to make an adjustment. I am at present with Arthur Briggs — most famous trumpet player in France — and his white wife.[38] He was born in America and is now a Canadian citizen. He was in-terned for three years by the Germans — and led the prison orchestra.

38. Arthur Briggs (1899–1991) was a trumpeter and bandleader who gained widespread renown in France and across Europe between the world wars. Briggs was imprisoned by the Nazis during the war. After liberation, he resumed playing in the jazz clubs of the Left Bank. In 1968, Arthur Briggs was inducted into the French Academy of Arts and Sciences. See William A. Shack, *Harlem in Montmartre: A Paris Jazz Story between the Great Wars* (Berkeley: University of California Press, 2001), 25–29, 85, 113–125, and Tyler Edward Stovall, *Paris Noir: African Americans in the City of Light* (New York: Mariner Books, 1998), 158. For those interested in hearing what Arthur Briggs sounded like, recordings of his orchestra are posted at http://www.archive.org/details/ArthurBriggsSavoySyncopatorsOrchestra-11–15.

September 19, 1944

A most exciting day today. Visited Madame Gustave Levy—upon the request of friends in New York—and found her none-too-well. She was very ill. Her doctor came to visit her when I was about to leave. She is a Jew and suffered keenly under Nazi occupation. Her sister, who was almost 85 years of age, was taken to a concentration camp two weeks before the liberation of Paris. She died one week later. Madame Levy's son died in the French Army. Around the eyes she shows the terrific emotional experiences of Nazi occupation—fear. She gave me the yellow "Star of David" she was compelled to wear while the Nazis were in Paris. I sought to give her money but she said the banks would reopen and she would again be able to support herself. She showed signs of having starved and admitted food was scarce. She was very appreciative of my visit and asked me to return soon. She is the aunt of Governor and Judge Lehman she told me.[39]

Tonight Ed Toles and I had dinner with Madame and M. Douchet. Wonderful! A real French dinner in spite of war rations—I suspect they buy in the Black Market. Met Madame and M. Dallot. Very charming people. Madame Douchet served a cheese that was terrific. Said it had been hidden for four years. For the first time I got a glimmer into French middle class life. We ate by candle light, since there is no electricity in Paris.

September 20, 1944

It looks as though I'll never get rid of M. Lucas. This morning when I came down he was in the lobby waiting to see me. He wanted to ask me to dinner again, and also to help a friend of his who has a son in "Drancy." I had to explain that I could not do anything because I was not a member of the military—a rather weak excuse. But I had to stop being, what Ed Toles called, "the Liberator."

I was scheduled to do a series of broadcasts for Columbia from Paris. But the line has broken down. No broadcasting from here. I am disappointed.

I saw a sign today saying that ordinary beets cost 750 francs or $16. Everything in Paris is extremely expensive. A drink of cognac in a café costs $1.20. The chambermaid in my hotel told me that she earns 600 francs a week. You wonder how these people manage to live. But she looks strong and healthy. A very big item is "chip"—or tipping. You tip everybody for everything. Yet the French women seem well-dressed. Incidentally, they

39. Madame Gustave Levy was the aunt of Herbert Lehman (1878–1973), the former governor of New York. Lehman served as governor from 1933 to 1942. He was later elected to the U.S. Senate and served from 1950 to 1957. See *Biographical Directory of the United States Congress*, http://bioguide .congress.gov/scripts/biodisplay.pl?index=L000224 (accessed May 6, 2010).

wear the most daring designs in hats, and they wear them well. The same hats on Fifth Avenue would be howled off the streets. Certainly the women wear daring colors, too. I like that. The women in America are inhibited about bright colors. Not here, though.

September 21, 1944

It just occurred to me to record the fact that Madame Levy's sister is dead—two weeks before the Allies arrived in France. The Gestapo came at 4 A.M. and took her to a concentration camp. She was 85 years old. She died of a broken heart two days later. Madame Levy is the sister of Irving and Governor Lehman's mother. Madame Levy's eyes embarrassed me—for they were filled with tears and thankfulness because of what Americans had done to free the Jews in France. My heart has never been moved by suffering like it was in visiting with this wizened old lady. She told me that Jews had been barred from cafes, public places of amusement, even from concerts. She told me of nights of terror—when footsteps and a knock on the door was thought to be the Gestapo. Yet, my mind couldn't help flashing back to the South where the same restrictions obtain for Negroes. No torture chamber could have been more dramatic in explaining the terror of Nazi occupation—as the still frightened look in Madame Levy's eyes. Every Jew who is anti-Negro and anti-anyone should see this little woman. She lives in an area that seemed to be the Bronx of Paris. It was certainly one of the better-class neighborhoods of Paris. She begged me to return to see her.

September 22, 1944

This evening Rene Maran gave a party for me. I met a number of very nice French people. One man had been a government official in Kenya. Though he talked fiercely about a free France, he was not so sure Africa should be free! They all expressed the view that Americans didn't understand the Germans. The French are all for revenge. They feel the Americans will let the Germans get away with a "soft peace." Everywhere I go in Paris I hear the same refrain—and I heard it expressed again at Rene's home: "What will America charge the French for her participation in the war—after all, she is not doing it for nothing." An interesting lad was seated next to me at the dinner table. He was fifteen, the son of a French physician who is now in Indo-China. He hasn't seen his parents for five years. He displayed a keen interest in the war and politics and plied me with questions about America. He spoke almost fluent English—which he was learning in school. Everyone seemed to have a real affection for Rene and

Madame Maran. When we started leaving, the Frenchmen kissed Rene on both cheeks—which, of course, is the French custom—but [I] couldn't help thinking of all the white people in America who wouldn't even shake a Negro's hand.

September 23, 1944

Today, by appointment, I interviewed M. Pleven, the French Minister of Colonies.[40] It was quite an experience. For he is the first diplomat I have met who was willing to discuss affairs frankly—on the record. I felt that some of his remarks were rather incautious for a man in his position. He is a tall, lanky bespectacled man, who looks like an American professor. He was very pointed on the race issue, saying that France would resist with her "strongest strength" any attempt by Americans to import prejudice. I gathered from his talk that French leaders are keenly aware of the low birthrate in France. They feel that 40 million Frenchmen cannot be a great nation in a world of power politics—so they need the blacks of their empire to supply the needed manpower. Thus, in the post-war period, intermarriage will be aggressively encouraged! Both in France and in Africa. There is nothing sentimental about this attitude. They realize that Negroes are a great reservoir of manpower and they must utilize it to survive as a world power. The implications are tremendous! It most certainly will be opposed by the white South Africans as well as the English. Certain Americans won't be pleased with the total collapse of racial barriers. If the De Gaullist government has its way—France will lead the world in the solution of the race problem by assimilation!

September 24, 1944

Paris has roughly about 10,000 Negroes—from Africa and the Western Hemisphere. They form a body of people who most certainly will put to the test the new racial policies planned by the government. I've been thinking about what M. Pleven said yesterday: His scheme is fraught with dangers for France. Because American leaders may oppose her. Anyway, the Negroes in Paris will provide a test tube of the government's sincerity on

40. Rene Pleven (1901–1993) was a supporter of Charles de Gaulle and the Free French during the war. He served in de Gaulle's National Committee as the commissioner of colonies. He also occupied multiple cabinet positions throughout his career and was prime minister twice. He retired in 1973. See Bruce Lambert, "Rene Pleven, 91, Prime Minister of France Twice in Early 1950s," *New York Times*, January 20, 1993, http://www.nytimes.com/1993/01/20/world/rene-pleven-91-prime-minister-of-france-twice-in-early-1950-s.html (accessed May 5, 2010).

the race issue. The soil is here — for the average Frenchman is not anti-Negro. Moreover, Negroes are very popular with the French people. Actually, though, Negroes in Paris complain about the lack of sincerity of the Frenchman in racial matters. But most of them have never been to the U.S. and do not know how "tough a white man can be." The chief cry is economic — jobs are not open to Negroes as readily as white Frenchmen. But a period of prosperity in France would overcome this one obstacle to his total integration. In all other matters, the Negro here gets equal treatment. For one thing there are no "Negro" cafes, theaters and the like. Though most Negroes here live in Montmartre, there is no residential segregation. This is largely economic, and perhaps gregarious on the part of black men. They feel a kinship to all black men. They are proud of the American Negro soldiers who visit Paris, and seek to talk to them.

September 25, 1944

This is in the form of a flashback concerning an experience I do not want to forget — though at the time I failed to make notes about it. Last Sunday I attended mass at Notre Dame not for worship, however, but because this cathedral is an historic monument and I wanted to visit it in all its Roman Catholic glory. Archbishop Spellman celebrated the mass to which 3,000 American soldiers attended as well as French people.[41] The magnificence of the ritual, the architecture of the building, and its whole history, was breath-taking. Spellman wore Irish green vestments — I suppose in sentimental gesture to the Irish-Americans in the Army. The French prelates wore scarlet, Catholic Army officers sat up front. Apparently the fabulous stained glass windows had not been removed like those in England. They sparkled in all their ancient glory. The center of the church was reserved for members of the American Army. Somehow the scene was a strange mixture of medieval pageantry with the new world simplicity of Americans. Not one Negro — except myself — was present at the mass. Outside Notre Dame is chipped with bullet holes and shrapnel caused by the German skirmishes with the Resistance Movement. I chatted with Archbishop Spellman afterwards. He told friends he had read my book and thought it good. He had immediately recognized me and asked photographers to take pictures of us together.

41. Francis Joseph Spellman (1889–1967) was the sixth archbishop of New York, from 1939 until 1967. He was made a cardinal in 1946. Spellman was an ardent anticommunist and a supporter of Senator Joseph McCarthy. He was frequently embroiled in political disputes throughout the 1950s and 1960s both in and outside the Catholic Church. See John Cooney, *The American Pope: The Life and Times of Cardinal Spellman* (New York: Dell Publishing, 1986).

September 26, 1944

At lunch in the Hotel Scribe I got to talking with other correspondents about the course of the war. We all agreed that it's probably going to last longer than most people in the States think, for our forces have been unable to budge the Germans for three weeks now. No one seems to recognize that the Nazis have very skillfully withdrawn their best troops behind the Siegfried Line and will probably make a determined winter stand. Most of the enemy troops captured to date have been "racial" Germans—as well as Russians, [M]ongolians, Poles and others captured in German campaigns.

Ed and I went for a long walk after dinner tonight, finally ending up in a café called "Mon Jardin." We had two glasses of wine—costing four dollars! The place was filled with French girls and American aviators out on a spree. The walls of the place were decorated with pictures of naked women. One girl—to excite an aviator—showed him her picture!

* * *

Paris is terrific. I have made copious notes. For instance, I went to see a Mrs. Gustave Levy (aunt of ex-Governor Lehman). She was quite a nice old lady who showed the wear and tear of Nazi occupation. She was extremely glad to see me—someone from America. Her wizened old face showed that she has been through hell.

The day I arrived she hadn't eaten! Food is very short in Paris at the moment. She told me that a week before the Americans arrived in Paris the Nazis invaded her home at 4 A.M. in the morning and took her 85-year sister off to a concentration camp. She died three days later.

The old lady's husband died in the last war and her son in this war, so she is quite alone. She gave me the yellow star identifying her as a Jew which she was forced to wear about the streets during Nazi occupation. Jews were barred from every café, theater, hotel, public places of amusement, even concerts which hurt her very much. She told me she hasn't been out of the house—except for an occasional walk for four years. Imagine!

She lives in the Bronx of Paris, in a very nice and typically French house. She has a housekeeper [who's] been with the family thirty years. She needed no money, for the banks have reopened. The Nazis had frozen her bank account so she couldn't draw any money. She had lived by selling her jewelry and silver.

A few days ago I visited "Drancy," the infamous prison for Jews just outside Paris. It held 15,000 Jews until Paris was liberated. It was the most dismal place—as all French prisons can be, for originally it had been a French prison. When I was there, there were 6,800 political prisoners—people accused of being collaborationists—who were packed jammed into the place. I wonder how 15,000 Jews could have survived there. They did though. When the Americans advanced on Paris and the Germans retreated, they did not free the Jews. One day the Jews just discovered there were no more guards. But for two days they feared to venture out of the prison for fear that it was a Nazi trick—and that they might be machine-gunned as they emerged outside the gates!

I saw the torture chambers—containing all sorts of implements for pulling out finger nails, gouging out eyes, etc. The Jews must have gone through a living hell in "Drancy." Whenever you mention the place in Paris, the French people practically shake with fright. There were almost 100 Negroes among the political prisoners at "Drancy."

I haven't seen a recognizable Jew in Paris yet—they have melted back into the population since their liberation. With all the Nazi attempts to create anti-Semitism, I have not found a wisp of it among the French people. No one even mentions the fact that he or she is a Jew. Nor, for that matter, is there any anti-Negro feeling apparent.

Immediately after the Nazis retreated, all Jim Crow restrictions against Jews and Negroes were relaxed for some unexplainable reason three days after the Nazis first arrival. As far as I can learn Negroes were able to survive—this may have been tied to the Nazi African ambitions. Anyway, I can say with complete confidence that the rank-and-file of Frenchmen are not anti-Semitic.

I attended mass at Notre Dame Sunday. What a spectacle! Archbishop Spellman celebrated the mass. I chatted with him afterwards. Notre Dame, incidentally, was originally built as a temple to an Egyptian goddess. The present structure was built right on top of the old one.

Naturally enough, Ed Toles and myself have taken in some of the night life. It is fabulously high. We had two drinks of wine and it cost $4. Imagine. All the post-card publicity about naked girls stuff just doesn't exist—except for the tourist. And I'm no tourist. But prostitution is carried on full blast, and with a blatancy that would make anyone blush. But to the Frenchmen, it is quite the ordinary way of things. I now understand Claude McKay's crack about J. A. Rogers in his book "Negro Metropolis." Nearly every unemployed Negro in Paris is a guide to the hot spots. He gets a commission of 10%, so you have no trouble making the acquaintance of Negroes here.

Montmartre, of course, is where this sordid business is all carried on. They do have some splendid looking night clubs though. The Café de La Venus, for example, has a glass dance floor through which lights shine through. All night clubs have a body of "hostesses"—who are in fact whores. It's interesting to see the white boys perform — those from Touga-loo, having their first fling. They go about it with such utter seriousness!

....

Paris is the most beautiful city in the world. I am sure no one tires of looking at it. The architecture is something magnificent. The shops are smart — and window displays are in such good taste that they make you want to buy every time you pass them.

Paris, from appearance, doesn't look like a city that has been through four years of Nazi occupation. The women are smartly dressed, shops full of things — only the absence of automobiles do you notice. I have spent a lot of time seeing the city, visiting the historic spots and centers.

There are 600,000 bicycles in the city!

September 27, 1944

I haven't been feeling so well lately — and this has slowed my writing down to a walk. I'm tired and lack ambition. Perhaps I'm just plain home-sick. Anyway, I haven't had the drive lately. I will leave Paris soon — maybe the change of scenery will perk me up. I slept practically all day — just taking time to make notes and eat. This is definitely unusual for me.

At lunch today a correspondent — returning to America — said he was going to cover the football games. He said these would be a lot more ex-citing than the stalemate on the front. Others are returning to cover the elections.

I'm getting awfully itchy! There is no hot water at the Hotel Scribe — though every other accommodation. Bathing and shaving with cold water every day is pretty difficult. I never feel clean. The white cor-respondents are having the time of their lives in the hotel, though. Every night they have women up in their rooms. Evenings when I come in there are always three or four French women in the lobby who will come to your room for a mere nod in their direction. I suspect, though, I'd make myself immensely unpopular if I was so inclined — and took one of these very good-looking women to my rooms. In a matter of hours I would be in-volved in a scandal. Moreover, the correspondents would band together to keep me from betting news breaks! Happily for me, I'm not bothered.

★ ★ ★

A few nights ago I was the guest of M. and Madame Paul Douchet, who are leading members of the Resistance Movement. I got a real chance to see how French life is lived outside of cafes. They had friends in and pre-pared a real French dinner which was, to say the least, delicious.

They are "advocates" or lawyers, trying the cases of collaborationists. I met them in the process of attempting to find out about the processes of resistance justice and how it operates.

Incidentally, one wine which Madame Douchet served during the meal was 50 years old and another 47. I haven't seen a drunken Frenchman yet. But when you have spent an evening eating, drinking aperitifs, wines, cognac in very small portions, by the end of the evening you are pretty gay.

Madame Douchet attended Swarthmore College in the States, so spoke English fluently. My French, of course, is terrible, though I am learning fast.

Last Sunday they took Ed Toles and me out to a little town outside Versailles where we had dinner and had quite a good time meeting their friends. The French are quite happy to see Americans, and, moreover, Negro Americans.

....

We here have been hearing a lot about people saying in the States that the war will be soon over. I hope people don't believe it. These Nazis are tough—though not unbeatable. I think the war correspondents in their anxiety to break good stories have allowed this impression to build up in the U.S.

Much of what is read about the war is so much hooey. Even the correspondents are sometimes kept in the dark as to the actual affairs.

It is my guess that we are about to enter a winter campaign with the Germans, which means the war in Europe will not be over before the summer of next year. We have, of course, penetrated the Siegfried Line, but not in sufficient strength as yet to make any difference.

Many of the correspondents are packing up and preparing to go home for the winter, convinced that the war will not be over this year. They are disgusted and weary. For being a war correspondent, as it turned out, is no picnic. Life is hard, primitive and dangerous. Life here at the Hotel Scribe has been a great relief for it approximates New York in its accommodations. It is in fact the top hotel of Paris, though I haven't had a hot bath in three weeks. There is no coal in Paris. Winter here is going to be mighty tough for those who remain.

The Resistance Movement in Paris, I learned, is quite a business. It is, of course, the moral strength of Paris, but it also contains much of the hustling element. For example, the first night club opened after the liberation of Paris is owned by a captain in the FFI—it was his graft—a la Tammany Hall. Youngsters, who would be considered delinquents in the States, have big cars at their disposal driving about Paris like mad. They are supposed to be on the look-out for collaborationists and Germans—for there is said to be something like 100,000 Germans undercover in Paris.

I was in a café one night when a boy of 18 stepped in and demanded 5,000 francs from the proprietor, or, as he said, he would denounce him as a "collaborationist." Luckily for the man, his friend—prominent in the Resistance Movement—was present in the café and they both threw the boy out into the street. People who never participate in politics always have a fear that they may be denounced as a collaborationist by a spiteful neighbor.

Now, the Resistance Movement is attempting to avoid false arrest with the proviso that if you denounce a person as a collaborationist and you are proved to be vicious and wrong, then you yourself must go to jail. This is bringing a noticeable decline in false denunciations.

September 28, 1944

Chatted at length today with Vladimir Rogoff, Tass London correspondent who is in Paris. He had heard I was on my way to Russia and offered to help. He gave me a few names of people on "Red Star" and of the Foreign Affairs Commissariat to contact. They are friends of his. He said PM was well thought of in Moscow and I would have no trouble in getting around and in getting information. He warned me against "speculation" as to Russian foreign policy. He said many American correspondents make the error of writing stories about Russian foreign policy from sources that are in no position to say what it is—or that are antagonistic to the Government. He assured me that I would get every cooperation from government officials. He was particularly concerned about reporting what Russia would do about the war against Japan. I gathered that American journalism is in bad standing with official Russia. Rogoff explained that "bureaucracy" in Russia is not the same as it is in Washington and London. If they believe you are honest and they can trust you, he said, the Russians will give you any information you wish. This is perhaps an overstatement of the case. But I guess if the Russians feel that you are not anti-Soviet they will be cooperative. I shall be guided by this advice until things turn out otherwise.

September 29, 1944

Carlton Moss arrived in Paris today. Ed Toles and I joined him at the Hotel Majestic, where he is staying. He had just returned from Italy, where, he said, nearly everyone was going barefoot. He had very dismal reports of life in North Africa. He appears to be showing the wear and tear of much travel. Says he is returning to America next week. Wish I was going!

Though I haven't finished my assignment. As a matter of fact, all the correspondents are leaving in droves. They are disappointed with the stalemate at the front—many had predicted the war would be over by September 15, 1944. Now it appears we are in for a winter campaign. Things are so quiet here that one correspondent, who was leaving for the States, said he was going to cover the football games for they would be much more exciting than the front this winter. Most are returning to cover the elections—which, of course, will sweep everything else off the American front pages. I made reservations to fly back to London—then Africa and Italy. Last night Allan Morrison joined Carlton, Ed Toles, Doc Kelker (a Red Cross worker) and myself and we all visited a few cafes.[42] We went to Café Salbouette—run by a girl named Frede. It looked like any Hollywood set—so magnificent in appearance. It is situated within a stone's throw of Notre Dame. The music was good, but the entertainment was terrible. As it turns out, one joint is like another!

September 30, 1944

There are practically no American Negro soldiers in Paris. The Negro correspondents agreed that this is by design. None can get passes to stay in Paris. The few that we have seen are all AWOL. Why this is so, no one seems to know. Our speculation is that they do not want them to associate with the French women. However, white soldiers too are barred from Paris. Only those who have business (military) can come in. Something is definitely wrong. Inflation has been suggested as a reason.

Today the Army declared all brothel and whorehouses "off limits." However, this was not done directly. Instead the Army had the French government inform all "houses" that they are to bar all men in uniform. This will work quite a hardship on those soldiers who are only in Paris for two and three hours and have no chance to build up contacts. The correspondents are agreed that the purpose of this order was:

1: to reduce the amount of venereal disease among American soldiers;
2: to reduce the number going AWOL;
3: to eventually establish better medical control over the houses.

42. Frank "Doc" Kelker (1913–2003) was born in Dover, Ohio, and was a graduate of Western Reserve University in Cleveland, where he was a star on both the football and basketball teams. After his wartime service, Kelker returned to the Cleveland area to teach at Central High School. He later accepted a position with the YMCA and was the executive director of the Cedar Avenue branch. See "Remembering 'Doc' Kelker," *Art/Sci: A Semi-annual Publication of the College of Arts and Sciences,* Case Western Reserve University 6 (Fall-Winter 2009), http://www.case.edu/artsci/artsci-fall-2009/kelker.html (accessed May 6, 2010).

But this will eventually bring about the American Jim Crow pattern—houses for whites and houses for blacks. The correspondents say that Paris won't be the same. Wherever Americans have a hand in affairs, all the joy is taken out of it. The ruling will not stop soldiers from picking up girls on the streets—which is vastly more dangerous. French houses are inspected. There is no control over streetwalkers.

October 1, 1944

Sunday—spent the day doing a piece for PM on Rene Maran which, I felt, was pretty good. He was approached on many occasions by the Nazis to be a collaborationist. He refused. But when faced with going to a concentration camp, he wrote an essay—requested by them—on American race problem, which turned out to be quite a positive piece. He hinged it on Langston Hughes' poem, "I, too, sing America." Took courage. He shows the strain of hard times.

After dinner Ed and I went to a nearby café—where we got into a conversation with the proprietor. He said the night before he had to eject high-ranking American officers because they brought along whores. He described the place as "First class," hence would not tolerate such goings-on. His place, he said, was one of those barred to Negroes and Jews during the Nazi occupation. He had much to say about Negroes and Americans generally. He was convinced that many Negroes in France were forced to work with Germans—or starve. For no employment was open to them until the Nazis found they were short of labor. He said the French are quite surprised by Americans, because of their open association with whores. They do not take the time to make friendships with decent French people. He said further that the reason everything is so high in Paris, is that it is all bought on the Black Market.

October 2, 1944

Ben Johnson—former Columbia track star and now a Lieutenant came to the hotel to see me. Had quite a chat lasting all morning. He is in the Quartermasters division—Red Ball Express, which received a commendation from Eisenhower recently. He was of the opinion that Negroes were not combat troops for the following reasons:

1. That the Negro would get too cocky.
2. The average white man still believes that the Negro is incapable of being made into a first-class soldier.

He was convinced that Southern Negroes were harder to command than Northern Negroes.

Our last night in Paris—we spent at M. Lucas' house talking and drinking cognac—Ollie Stewart, Ed Toles and myself. Then about 11 P.M. we started home—to the Hotel Scribe. We stopped off at the Café Mon Jardin—as we entered a rough-looking Negro was brandishing a gun, threatening to shoot up the place. Ed and I attempted to quiet him, but he felt the power of his gun and had everyone, including white soldiers, intimidated. He just wouldn't listen to reason. He felt the power of his gun. He claimed that someone had stolen a 1937 Ford car he had bought that afternoon for a thousand francs. The Frenchman who sold him the car had apparently stolen it—but the Negro could not be persuaded to be quiet. The MP's finally came and rounded up all the Negroes in the place—excepting Toles, Stewart and myself.

....

[*Page missing from the original manuscript*]

October 5, 1944

I received word today from Doc Kelker—a Red Cross Director—that certain Army officers attempted to establish Jim Crow drinking accommodations for the Negro troops in Cherbourg. Two bars were opened in that city for American troops—a bar for whites in the center of town and a bar for Negroes, serving beer, on the outskirts of town. Kelker sought to find out the reason from Army officials. None knew who had established this Jim Crow plan. Finally Kelker told the Negro troops to boycott the place. There are some 10,000 Negro soldiers in Cherbourg now and to a man they didn't visit the Jim Crow bar. After a week the barriers against Negroes visiting the bar in the center of town were lifted.

October 6, 1944

Today I went to the Army Dispensary for treatment—first since my arrival in Europe. I've been scratching for more than a month—in fact, since I left France in August. The ailment was diagnosed as "battle itch"—caused by the front line battle engagements and the excitement they produce. While here the Captain—a Northern man—got to talking about Negroes and the future. He was worried lest the English were "spoiling" Negroes and making it impossible for them to resume their old Jim Crow place in American life. Then he got to talking about the superiority of races. I said, "You know, as a doctor, that there is no such thing as congenitally superior or inferior people." He admitted this, but said he had been examining members of the Army for three years, and he discovered Negroes had larger penises than white men, two or three inches larger. It's odd how ordinary sociological discussions about Negroes always eventually drift into a sex discussion.

October 7, 1944

On our way to lunch today, Ed Toles and I were stopped on the street by an Englishwoman. She apparently had been following us for two blocks. Suddenly she broke into a run until she came abreast of us. She asked if we were war correspondents — when we replied that we were, she asked, "Do they trust you to report the news?" Ed said, "Sure — do you see all these Negro soldiers — they trust them to carry guns and lose their lives!" Then she said that as a white woman she knew more about what was going on than we as Negroes. She bade us goodbye and went her way. Ed remarked that it was typically British.

Tonight Len Hill — Red Cross Club London Director — and I went out to visit Dick and Vicky at their Cambridge home. Dick Bourne is a wealthy Jew married to an attractive Negro girl who puts on airs. But who is nevertheless quite a nice person. They say they are coming to the States for a visit after the war. Dick wanted to know whether the Hotel Theresa was a good place to stay! He guaranteed the rent for the Stage Door Canteen recently opened — but when he attempted to attend the opening with his wife, his British friends advised him against bringing her because there would be Southern generals present and it was believed they would object. However, they invited her to a dinner party they were having afterwards — because they were not inviting any Americans! Dick Bourne was quite disgusted with the whole business.

October 8, 1944

At dinner tonight I ran into a Negro Red Cross worker who just returned from Southampton where she was stationed. She says she is having a problem with officials of the Red Cross because her skin is so fair. And she is indeed fair — white with blond hair. She says she is constantly being mistaken for a white person much to the embarrassment of white people.

October 9, 1944

Today I was invited to the home of Lady Lindsay, who seems to be quite a gal. I was introduced to her friend, Baroness de Haviland, who also seems to be quite a gal. They are pals. Lady Lindsay's husband was recently killed in a flight over Germany. He was a RAF flier. She seems somewhat glad because—as she confesses—she never loved him anyway. Baroness de Haviland is also married. Her husband is in the British Navy. Nevertheless, she has for the last four years—during his time away—been going with a big bruising Negro wrestler. About a month ago she broke off with him—but he's raising hell about it. He threatens—I am told—to cut up her sable coat, cut her face and beat her on sight. She seems quite genuinely frightened. Spending an evening with these two women—twenty-two and twenty-three years of age respectively—has given me quite an insight into British upper class life. Both are violently anti-Semitic and agree with Hitler's treatment of the Jews—though they are opposed to Hitler's treatment on political and patriotic grounds. They admit to buying their clothes and food on the Black Market—which they say is run by the Jews. They have avoided war service by having themselves declared to have weak hearts. They really are two useless dames—but have good incomes from their families and husbands which entitles them to enjoy life in the midst of war.

October 10, 1944

Saw Toby Frazier today at a café. She was with one of the blackest Negroes I've ever seen. She seemed quite happy with him. He is a wrestler. Toby is going places fast. First time I'd seen her since I returned from Paris. She seemed glad to see me, and said friends in America had sent her my articles in PM on the race relations situation in England.

A new terror weapon has been unleashed by the Nazis—V-2, which is a rocket bomb. It seems impossible to stop it. The fact is, no one knows what time of day or night it will hit. For it comes over silently, even stealthily. It is even worse than the buzz bomb because it sneaks into London and no one seems to know where they are being launched from now that the Allies have the whole French Coast. It makes a bigger crater than the buzz bombs and a louder noise. Officially the correspondents cannot report its existence. The censors say this ruling is for security reasons—but certainly the Germans know what damage they are doing in London—actually they are raising havoc. Since they have been coming over, there have been no air raid alerts. You can only hope and pray that one doesn't have your name on it. There is no doubt about it, it is an ingenious weapon and suggests just how future wars will be fought.

October 14, 1944

I've been sort of marking time until I take-off for Africa. This has been the longest delay I've had in getting transportation. I hope I won't be placed in this position in the future legs of the trip.

I am just beginning to get some reaction here to the articles I did on race relations in England. Liberals have been applauding. Reactionaries are silent. But they can be very effective in making my trip difficult. I wondered for a short time whether or not it was the publication of these articles that suddenly brought me to an abrupt halt in getting transportation. Just as I was about to make an issue of it, I received my traveling orders.

Recently I was the guest of Lady Lindsay and Baroness de Haviland. These two young women are splendid lookers. The Baroness just recently broke off a relationship with a Negro wrestler here. The Lady Lindsay's husband was just killed. He was an RAF flier. They have, quite unwittingly, been giving me quite a slant on the British upper class. Both have avoided war service through having a doctor declare they have weak hearts.

They are fiercely anti-Semitic and say quite frankly they think Hitler was right in the way he treated Jews. My defense of Jews fell on deaf ears. They countered by saying that I ought to hear the way the Jews talk about Negroes. If I did I wouldn't defend them like I do. They also hate the working class. My status rests on the fact that I am an "officer" and war correspondent. But—on the other hand—they are fiercely pro-Negro.

They have an unrelaxing hatred of the white Americans, thinking them crude, ignorant and possessed of an inferiority complex. They admit quite frankly that they buy their clothes, food, etc. on the Black Market—operated, as they say, by "Jews!" Normally you would say they are the corrupt elements in British life, but I've run into so many cut from their cloth that you come to accept them as fairly typical. All this is not obvious, however. At first glance they appear quite charming, well-mannered and sophisticated.

I ran into quite a situation with Alex Uhl, PM foreign editor, when I was in Paris. It had a great effect on reducing my efficiency in that city. He frankly resented my presence. This was observed and mentioned by other correspondents. Somehow he felt my presence humiliated him in the eyes of the white correspondents. You see, being a war correspondent has become a sort of cult—like some swank upper class fraternity. Among some of the white correspondents, I am a crasher. Others—more liberal—are quite regular. They don't mind the Negro correspondents too much, because they do not feel they are competition since they are working for Negro papers. The women correspondents particularly are bitchy. They are a collection of the worst looking dames in the world.

Back to Uhl—he was very uncooperative. Since he was the senior correspondent from PM, he received all announcements, invitations, etc., but he never would keep me informed of what was happening. Very often I was working in the dark—except that Ed Morrow [sic] (CBS) and Liebling (New Yorker magazine) helped to keep me informed.[43] When I arrived he interrogated me rather sharply, I thought, about my status with PM. Instead of helping me to learn the ropes, he ignored me. Thought I spent a lot of time with the other correspondents—including a number of Southerners—not once did he invite me to have a drink. One would assume that since we were both working for the same paper there would be some getting together.

When we both covered De Gaulle's first public address at the Trocadero in Paris, I said to him that since he spoke French fluently, I would describe the "color" of the occasion—and it was something terrific—and he, I supposed, would write about the political aspects of the event. He told me to write nothing!

However, I managed quite well. You find liberals in the oddest places. Moreover, there are a lot of good guys among the correspondents and Army officers who aided me in getting material. Interestingly enough, it is the Jewish officers and correspondents who have stood on my side in all controversies, and even indeed a few white Southerners. This was the case when I broke the story about Cherbourg. It took me twelve hours to get the story cleared—after much battling against political censorship. When I asked Sonia Tomara, of the Tribune, to back me in the fight, she sniffed and declared the whole business unimportant. It was finally a Southern Naval officer and censor who stood on my side and helped me to get the story through.

The Negro correspondents are quite something. I think they resent a little that I'm working for a white publication—though we are on excellent terms. But by no means are they crusaders. Moreover, the kind of stories I am doing is beginning to embarrass them with their editors. They have received cables saying "If Ottley can get to see the top people, why can't you?" This, of course, has not helped my relations with them.

It was from them that I learned that certain white correspondents resented my presence—yet I do think there was a lot of yeast in their observations.

43. A. J. Liebling (1904–1963) wrote for the *New York World* and the *New York World-Telegram* between 1927 and 1935. In 1935, he accepted a position with the *New Yorker*, to which he contributed until his death. During the war, Liebling distinguished himself, earning the French Cross of the Legion d'Honneur for war reporting. See A. J. Liebling and David Reminck, *Just Enough Liebling: Classic Work by the Legendary New Yorker Writer* (New York: Farrar, Straus and Giroux, 2004).

Ed Toles made the observation—quite friendly, of course—that I was just the type of writer that Negro editors didn't want on their papers. He said, "They feel you think you know more than they do." One thing that completely disturbs them—according to their own admission—is the way in which I talk with and to the whites. They frankly say I would get more from them if I "Uncle Tomed" a little. Actually, I am getting more breaks than they.

Ollie Stewart, for example, will not eat at the Officers' Club. He says he don't go anywhere he isn't wanted. He seeks out the Negro Red Cross club. As far as I can see, no one resents Negro correspondents eating and drinking at the Officers' Club. I told them I didn't come abroad to hang out with Negroes only. I remembered Aiken Pope's remark about Negroes going abroad—missing everything the Old World has to offer—by hanging out at Negro clubs. Well, I'm the only Negro correspondent a member of the Overseas Club and the La Petit Club. Here I have an opportunity to meet people and find out what goes on. I took Ed Toles to dinner at La Petit, and he marveled. Actually, no one pays you any mind if you are not carrying a chip on your shoulder.

Yet the Negro correspondents are good guys and we have a lot of fun together. In essence, I am meeting here the same resistance by Negroes to my association with whites.

October 15, 1944

Tonight—which may be my last one in London—I went to the Caribbean Club in Piccadilly Circus. Somehow this place has an atmosphere not reproduced in America, though it is operated by a Negro for Negroes primarily. There is a curious mixture of Negroes of all types—those from Africa, the West Indies and American soldiers. Nevertheless they manage to get together and have a good time—which is something the American white soldier cannot do. He is usually fighting people, rather than trying to enjoy their company. Those whites who managed to find their way to the Caribbean seem to have a good time. Tonight two American white soldiers sat in the mixed band and played. They seemed to be having an immensely good time. The women—both Negro and white—also seem to have a wonderful time—though the place, like all in London—must close promptly at 10 P.M. As I made my way out the door I walked into the most vicious fight between a Negro British civilian and a gang of American white soldiers. They were beating this poor boy to death. I stepped in and dragged the boy away. Soon four MP's and four Bobbies came dashing up—instead of grabbing the white G.I.'s, they wanted to arrest the Negro.

I raised so much hell that they finally left the place. The four MP's gave me that cold, blue stare that only an American white seems to possess.

October 16, 1944

People have no idea how homesick one can get even in a place as lively as London. (The buzz bombs of course, are still sailing overhead, which is no help). Talked with Gannett last night. He's on his way back to France. He's like a school boy about being a war correspondent. He admitted that before he left the States he had all kinds of ailments. In fact, when we left New York he carried all sorts of bottles (medicines). Now, after a journey to the front, he says he no longer feels ill, or has any kind of ailments. Actually, one is so involved with self-preservation that you do not have time to think about minor ailments.

....

I met quite a charming chap in Paris named Rogoff—a Russian correspondent. He told me that PM is well thought of in Moscow, so I won't have any trouble getting good stories. He warned me against "speculating" about Russian foreign policy. He said it is simpler to go straight to the officials and get the true story. I noticed that there was little fraternizing between the Russian, British and American correspondents—each went his own way. I managed to fraternize with each individual. British correspondents—you might be interested to know—have almost a diplomatic status! They are a proud lot. They are the only correspondents who carry guns!

October 27, 1944

Talked with David Cohn, who is well-known ...

[*Page missing from original manuscript. Date of subsequent entry is unclear.*]

... often been surprised by the ease with which I've been able to move about, especially in Army circles. Negro reporters, by and large, have received the same treatment as white reporters for the Army public relations men. But since many good stories come as a result of social contacts, most of the Negroes have been excluded from them. Happily for me, I knew a lot of fellows, both in newspaper circles and Army circles, which made my movements much easier.

The principal resentments I have met, have come, curiously enough, from the newsmen. Most of them regard a war correspondent's occupation as something approaching an exclusive fraternity. Whereas they are liberal enough to welcome Negro reporters working for Negro newspapers, they are not as enthusiastic about a Negro representing a "White" publication. My appearance on the scene provoked considerable discussion. It must be said in truth, however, that they never manifested any open resentment—it was mainly subtle and unspoken in my presence. W. A. S. Douglas, who represents the "Chicago Sun" will illustrate one aspect. He has not spoken to me as yet—though we have been in Cherbourg, Paris, London and elsewhere together. His resentment has been openly spoken in the form of gossip. When I returned to London after the Normandy trip, he put out the story that I had been sent home by the Army. When I subsequently turned up in Paris he was quite embarrassed. I wasn't inclined to think his attitude too personal toward me, when I discovered he was giving Mecklin (Sun) hell behind his back.

Frederick Kuh, from the day of my arrival has been most helpful. But Alex Uhl—and this is perhaps a bit touchy—wasn't too friendly in Paris, though he did help me translate Pleven's interview. I think his was somewhat social pressure. I think it somewhat embarrassed him when I arrived with his colleagues from other papers. Again the business of exclusive fraternity—obviously a fraternity in American life that includes Negroes can't be too snooty! But after I had assured him—upon his inquiry—exactly what my status was with PM, he seemed relieved, and, I am sure, passed this information on to others. The fact that PM was not paying me a weekly wage, seemed to make his status more secure and respectable. After all, I am pretty much a freelance writer—and any paper, it could be explained, has all sorts of freelance writers. His annoyance, at first, was expressed this way: "What in hell has Lewis in mind, having two men in Paris." I explained that I had come of my own choice. Until I told him this, he said he was going to cable and ask that one of us be withdrawn. This attitude will explain why my stories from Paris seemed meager. As foreign editor of PM, he received all communications—I received none. Nor did he ever inform me as to what was happening. Two instances will illustrate this: I planned a trip to Antwerp, but when I discovered he was going I withdrew, somewhat in deference to him, as foreign editor. On another occasion, the French invited me to a De Gaulle function. When I arrived, I found him there. I said to him, that since he understood French better than I, perhaps it would be better that I cover the "color" of the occasion. He told me not to write anything, and so it went. With some planning, we both could have done a better job in Paris. After all, I do not think two men in Paris at such a moment were too many.

In Cherbourg I ran into another aspect of the problem: I was—and I say this quite innocently—first to discover that civil affairs was supporting anti-democratic and pro-Petain elements in Cherbourg. This all happened by accident. Most of the reporters had their social life with the Army officers, so most of their stories reflected the point of view which the Army desired. Maybe, some of them wrote their stories with no such idea in mind. But the net result was that they had little contact with the French people, and thus had no idea of what they were thinking. While I had one or two drinking parties with Army top dogs, I sough[t] contact with French people. Eventually, I got on chummy terms with the leader of the Resistance Movement. It was through him that I discovered that the democratic forces in Cherbourg were being suppressed. When I wrote the story, C. D. Jackson — Time-Life-Fortune executive — mangled it badly. It probably made no sense to you when it arrived in New York. To get the story through, I put up a fourteen hour battle. I sought to enlist the other correspondents in the fight. They took a hands-off policy, with Sonia Tomara (Tribune) who was partying with C. D. dismissing it as unimportant. The upshot was, that the Army public relations men retraced everyone of my steps and interviewed all the people I produced as documentation for my story. Everyone repeated their statements — except Howly — then civil affairs commissioner. When the implications of his interview with me were pointed out to him, he refused to let me quote him.

November 3, 1944

I don't dare write a story about something I haven't seen with my own eyes, though some of the boys here have written "eye-witness" accounts of battle engagements and surrenders when they were one hundred miles away. Perhaps it's okay to write such a story when colleagues are eye-witnesses — but the Army would promptly send me home, especially if any inaccuracies crept into the story. I do not mention this to carp — but rather to illustrate an attitude.

But I've been exactly 35 days trying to get transportation. Everyone here thinks I'm getting the run-around. Since those stories appeared on race relations, I've recognized a noticeable decline in Army cooperation. But — on the other hand — the British, French, Dutch, Belgian, etc. — give me excellent cooperation. And it's no trouble getting information from them. They do not have any racial reaction — the fact that I represent an American paper is enough to get their best.

The business of interviewing the various Ministers of Colonies was pretty simple. But came mainly as a result of social contacts made since my arrival here. For example, the Cripps interview came through Peggy Cripps, the daughter of the Minister. I took her to dinner and the theater twice and she arranged the interview, and, moreover, relaxed him sufficiently for him to talk fully—though hardly in line with PM—and my point of view. In this connection I must explain that I am not taken in by these boys—they mean to continue the status quo. I know it well.

....

✪ SELECTED JOURNALISM, 1942-1946

"A White Folks' War?"
Common Ground 2 (Spring 1942): 28–31

"This is war time," a letter to the editor of Harlem's Amsterdam-Star Newsran, "but I must remind our Negro leaders that they are making the same mistake now that they have made so often in the past—falling all over themselves to register loyalty to America in this crisis without finding out whether the black race is going to benefit it [the war] or not.

"That does not mean lineup with a foreign country, but it does mean, since we have been treated so badly after *all previous wars*, that we should be assured now that this condition will be remedied. It is all right to be loyal if it is encouraged. But I fail to see where America is doing anything to encourage the loyalty of black men …

"Remember that which you fail to get now you won't get after the war."

The issue of the paper that published this comment contained twenty articles by staff writers which dealt critically with the treatment of Negroes. On January 10, sixty prominent Negroes met in New York City in a conference called by the National Association for the Advancement of Colored People and the National Urban League to consider the Negro's part in the war effort. The group passed with only five dissenting votes a resolution introduced by Judge William H. Hastie, civilian aide to the Secretary of War, that "the colored people are not wholeheartedly and unreservedly all out in support of the present war effort." Walter White, executive secretary of the NAACP, attributed this countrywide apathy of Negroes to discrimination in the Army, Navy, and Air Corps, and especially in the defense industries.

This reflection of Negro thinking on the present crisis has its roots in the immediate past. When the First World War involved the United States, Negroes sought at once to participate as soldiers. With full consciousness of their duties as citizens and with the desire to act the roles of men, they gladly bore their share of the war effort. W.E.B. Du Bois, then the acknowledged leader of the Negro community, articulated the race's view toward the conflict with his now famous "Close Ranks" statement to the nation as well as to certain Negroes:

"We of the colored race have no ordinary interest in the outcome. That which the German power represents spells death to the aspirations of Negroes and all dark races for equality, freedom, and democracy. Let us, while this war lasts, *forget our special grievances* and close ranks shoulder to shoulder with our own white fellow-citizens and the allied nations who are fighting for democracy. We make no ordinary sacrifice, but we make it gladly and willingly with our eyes lifted to the hills."

This statement stirred Negroes in 1918. It would rally Negroes today—if there were only assurances. But a Negro leader would not dare call upon the race "to forget its special grievances" if he hoped ever to continue his influence. (There were Negroes even in 1918, like A. Philip Randolph, who rained criticisms on Du Bois for his statement.) For in the last war, in spite of the acknowledged bravery of the Negro troops, they suffered all forms of Jim Crow, humiliation, discrimination, and indeed slander—a pattern being followed today. And while this occurred with the A.E.F. abroad, the Negro civil population at home was the victim of the bloodiest race riots in American history. The most shocking were in East St. Louis, Illinois, disorders, in which white people drove thousands of Negroes from their homes and put to death more than two hundred by shooting, burning, and hanging. There were demonstrations all over the country; in New York fifteen thousand marched down Fifth Avenue in a "Silent Protest Parade."

Immediately after the close of the war, Administration leaders began a campaign to persuade Negroes that in spite of their full participation in the armed forces they could expect no great change in their traditional status in America. Newton D. Baker was particularly vocal on this point.

Thwarted and disillusioned, a wave of race-consciousness, which is still a compelling force, engulfed the Negro community. It began with the movement of the Universal Negro Improvement Association, which explored the fascinating abstraction of an African Utopia as a homeland for the black man. It was, in fact, a Back-to-Africa movement, led by Marcus Garvey, the first of the Harlem messiahs. Its slogan, "Africa for Africans," stirred two million Negroes in the country to wild enthusiasm. A cardinal tenet of the organization was unity with *all* darker peoples of the world—in Africa, India, China, South America, and Japan.

When the Back-to-Africa movement collapsed, it left a residue of fierce race- and color-consciousness which has propelled many a Negro movement since. Stimulated as they were many Negroes turned to Japan as the messianic race and the hope of the darker peoples of the world. They traveled in Japan on Japanese grants and subsidies; and others in Washington, Pittsburgh, and New York entertained Japanese. As late as 1941, debates were held in which the Chinese-Japanese war was the subject, with Japanese spokesmen presenting their side of the conflict.

When Japan declared war on the United States, Harlem's Nipponese visitors disappeared, but not altogether the effects of their propaganda in Negro life. To be sure, Negroes to a man are outraged by the treacherous assault upon their country—not having digested Japanese propaganda whole cloth—but the significant result of Japanese infiltration into the Negro community is that Negroes bear no *prejudice* against the Japanese people. And largely because the "yellow Aryans" drew no color line. But the unhappy leadership of their war lords is regarded in Negro circles as a betrayal of the darker peoples.

However, since the present war began, the utterances of the Negro press and pulpit have not reached the crescendo of denunciation that has characterized those of white circles. A survey of leading Negro newspapers throughout the country, since December 7th, reveals no letters-to-the-editor commenting on Japanese treachery, a fact that might suggest that many Negroes have been neutralized.

Little speculation is needed, however, to show that Negroes, while eschewing comment on Japanese aggression, are vitally concerned with the ultimate meanings of the war. Roy Wilkins, editor of The Crisis magazine, organ of the National Association for the Advancement of Colored People, for example, warns Negroes to watch the Anglo-Saxon and Union Now movements for the possible future cast of the world. He speaks of them as "sections of a larger concept." Less restrained in language is the Negro man-in-the-street. "Colored people in the United States," one comments, "should rise up as one man and smash this most damnable conspiracy [Union Now] against the darker races."

These attitudes are underscored by a grave suspicion. The very term "Anglo-Saxon" inspires little confidence in darker peoples. Many Negroes point out that Union Now, for instance, has not declared itself on minority groups as yet, particularly dark minorities. And they look with suspicion on Dorothy Thompson, one of the leading champions of a coalition of

Anglo-Saxon governments, for her vagueness on the black man's role in this hoped for social order; as well as Henry Luce, editor of Time, Fortune, and Life, who is regarded as the spokesman for the kind of world which will be created and ordered for American imperialism—"silk-gloved, perhaps, but imperialism."

"We must not be deflected," writes Wilkins, "from vigorous protest and action against the travesties on democracy now in vogue, by emotional and oratorical appeals to us to forget, forgive, and concentrate on larger issues." For, as he observes, the "larger issues" are inextricably bound up with (and are in fact) the detailed matters which concern the Negro daily.

Negroes see, but not with despair, the economic considerations involved in the present conflict as formidable bars to the extension of democracy. "It must be clearly recognized," writes Du Bois today, "that the main hindrance to such a [democratic world] movement is the more or less conscious feeling among white people of the world that other folk exist not for themselves but for their uses to Europe; that white Europe and America have the right to invade the territory of colored peoples, to force them to work, and to interfere at will with their cultural patterns, while demanding for whites themselves a preferred status."

To capital, he holds, colored labor means low wages, cheap raw materials, and high profits. "The strong motive of private profit," Du Bois argues, "is thus placed in the foreground of interracial relations, while the greater objects of cultural understanding and moral uplift lurk in the background." Here in the United States, and to a degree in England, curbs have been placed on industry limiting profits in the interests of the laboring masses. But in the colonies and quasi-colonial areas, according to Du Bois, the imperialist nations are tending to repeat and perpetuate the errors of the worst days of capitalist exploitation.

The maintenance of a capitalistic colonial economy, it is pointed out frequently by Negroes, frustrates and nullifies much of the reform effort within progressive countries which own or control colonies. Obviously acquisition of colonies by the United States will retard economic advancement of white labor as well as Negro. It will mean further debasement of subject peoples, by restricting their initiative, by ruining their culture and substituting no adequate cultural patterns.

As yet, no tangible plan has been advanced which will serve to evolve the best civilization for the largest number of human beings after the war. Hence many thinking Negroes are on the verge of developing a dangerous cynicism that will certainly trickle down to the Negro masses. Despite the high-minded talk of bringing the "four freedoms" to the world, Negroes often suspect there is a tacit understanding among the leaders of the white allied nations to limit democracy to white men only.

Observations of this character are suggested by such actions as the demand of the British Government that the United States send no American Negroes to work on the West Indian defense bases. And, what is more important, the fact that the Administration quietly acquiesced. Nor are feelings of this sort dispelled by revelations of wage differentials on defense projects. Recently Congressman Vito Marcantonio called attention specifically to the conditions existing at Borinquen Field in Puerto Rico, where skilled white workers receive $1.50 per hour and native skilled workers, 40 cents per hour; where white helpers receive 75 cents an hour and native helpers only 25 cents an hour. Similar discriminatory practices are reported in force in Jamaica, Trinidad, Bermuda, St. Lucia, Antigua, British Guiana, and the Bahamas.

Such reports are hardly reassuring to darker peoples, who, in spite of inadequate communication, are developing a broad unity because of common oppression by imperialist nations. Today the "vox pop" columns of the Negro press, faithful reflections of Negro mass thought, are brimful of anxious, some inflammatory, calls for unity among Negroes to meet the present crisis as it affects the darker peoples—excluding Japan of course. "As terrific as the war is in its impact upon America," a typical letter said, "it will not wipe out race prejudice nor alter greatly the American mind. . . . For the duration of the war, we beseech our people to suspend intra-racial bickering. This is the time for decisive action, but we cannot arrive at correct decisions nor can we formulate any effective action while there is strife among us."

And so today, Negroes are determined and will not be easily placated. For the black man, like all oppressed peoples, has a long memory. Certainly W.E.B. Du Bois' widely read autobiography, *Dusk of Dawn* (1940), will provide a constant reminder of the unhappy experiences of the First World War. "I am less sure now than then of the soundness of [my] war attitude," he confesses today. "I did not realize the full horror of war and its wide impotence as a method of social reform. . . . I doubt if the triumph of Germany in 1918 could have had worse results than the triumph of the Allies. Possibly passive resistance of my twelve millions to any war activity might have saved the world for black and white. . . . "

All that has been said here, of course, places the United States in a rather paradoxical position. But too long have its white people been apathetic to the clamoring for democracy of 13 million citizens, a group larger than entire nations involved in the present global conflict. Too few voices have been heard in protest against this undemocratic denial. Lillian Hellman, speaking through one of her Negro characters in the play, *The Little Foxes,* labels this tragic silence as a question of ethics:"There are people who eat the earth and eat all the people on it," she says. " . . . Then, there are people who stand around and watch them eat it. Sometimes I think it ain't right to stand and watch them do it."

"Roi Ottley Sees Negro Troops in Action in Normandy"
PM, July 31, 1944

Had American supply lines broken down in the first [words are missing from the torn article] the infiltration of paratroopers and strong armed attacks along the beachheads, in all likelihood the U.S. forces would have been thrown back into the Channel.

I have just completed a tour of the front. It is apparent now, though only admitted recently, that such a situation faced the American High Command. Today the sheer weight of supplies and men is breaking the back of German defenses and perhaps has staved off serious counterattacks.

The task of keeping an avalanche of food, ammunition and troops moving steadily toward the front is mainly the job of Negro troops. They would be the last to acknowledge the importance of their contribution. They insist others are doing more, but their officers warmly praise their heroic performance under enemy fire.

They are particularly proud of Negro Pvts. Bernard Henderson of New York City and Percy Cox of Peterburg, Va., who are slated for awards for valor.

SENT UP BALLOONS
While working at Cologne, they saw a German scouting party of 15 men creeping stealthily up a hill. Henderson and Cox sprang on them with their poised automatics. The Germans surrendered without firing a shot.

In the early days of the invasion Negro battalions moved on to the beachheads alongside the assault troops to send up balloon barrages. It was the success of this operation that kept the German planes at great heights and prevented them from dive-bombing and strafing our forces on the beachhead.

The American sector is subject to day and night attacks by air and shell fire. The men here say it is almost inaccurate to talk of front and rear under these conditions. Only tactically is there a front line. Once the American troops had landed, Negro amphibious craft units, the "ducks," brought in supplies and more men from ships anchored in the Channel, often within range of blasting German guns.

They rolled the supplies to dumps ashore. Many a life was lost when these ambivalent [*sic*] autos struck mines laid by the Germans. From these supply dumps on land, Negro motor transport units loaded their two-ton trucks and moved the supplies and men further toward the front.

Many Occupations

Traveling in their wake, the roar of bombs and guns, the swirls of blinding dust, the utter devastation, even the concern with self-preservation is apt to distract attention from the miracle of army organization being efficiently carried out by Negro units.

Significantly enough, Negro troops are engaged in a variety of occupations, many unknown to the average Negro in civilian life. Along the route to the front Negro Signal Corps men are seen astride telephone poles, easy targets for the German snipers. Nevertheless they are erecting and repairing communication lines destroyed by the retreating Germans.

The back-breaking, unsung jobs necessary to waging successful war are being done cheerfully by Negroes. They are repairing roads, constructing buildings, laying railroad tiers, salvaging, and even breaking stone in quarries for road building and repair. Two Negro units only are in actual combat. One is an anti-aircraft outfit and the other an artillery formation. Artillery is definitely one of the skilled jobs of war in which Negroes are making a creditable showing. Artillery played an important role in the successful offensive at St. Lo. I visited the Negro troops and officers at their bivouacs, some in apple orchards.

Spic and Span

The areas were spic and span, their tents neatly put up and covered with green parachute cloth, their foxholes dug deep and carefully boarded at the sides. Some had pinup girls on the rude walls. This was a luxury few had. The men took pride in their personal appearance and in their mess quarters. Cleanliness was easily evident everywhere I went.

I found the morale high. Officers corroborated this finding. The reason for this excellent morale, Negroes explained, is the noticeable change in the attitude of white officers toward Negro troops. A contributing factor is the exceptionally cordial welcome of the French people. No one here apparently can afford the luxury of Jim Crow, though the American Red Cross is now preparing to open quarters for Negro soldiers.

The Negro soldier feels appreciated by his white comrades. The white boys, one enlisted man told me, see us working hard and better understand our need to each other—that if we don't pull together we die.

There are about 30 Negro commissioned officers in France with the highest rank a major. Everywhere I went I asked the Negro troops what most they wanted the black folks back home to know. The answer was the same everywhere:

"We want to see the end of Jim Crow in America and equal treatment for everyone."

"Progressive Trend Seen in British Colonial Policy"
PM, September 12, 1944

The sweep of events seems to be pushing British colonial policy into the progressive stream—despite claims that the war is less and less ideological.

I gathered this feeling after talking with Secretary of State Col. Oliver Stanley who clearly indicated that his government envisioned a world in which all peoples will have an opportunity for development and self-expression.

He said: "I put education in the forefront of plans for the future. For we cannot have a successful modern society without education."

THE BRITISH MIND

I went to see him to get a glimmer, perhaps, of what postwar perspectives are on the mind of the British Government.

By appointment I went to Downing Street—that small one-way street of London where the empire is ruled. Following a brief palaver with two doubtful Bobbies, I was escorted to the Colonial Office.

The building was almost black with the soot of ages. England has been doing business at this stand for centuries. The drab hallways seemed to have an odor like the inside of a beer barrel.

I was ushered into an ante-room which resembled a country doctor's waiting room. A table was full of magazines. I picked up one. It was called "The Crown Colonist"—the unofficial mouthpiece of the Colonial Office. The title page carried a picture of a Madonna-like Negro mother and child. Down in one corner, a box contained this passage from Viscount Samuel:

"If the economic and cultural condition of these British Colonial territories as they now are, are compared with what they were fifty years ago . . . I am convinced that the contrast would furnish material for an illustrious chapter in the history of civilization."

50 YEARS AGO — AND NOW

I began to wonder whether the natives would agree. But about that moment a one-armed man came and led me to the Minister's ante-room. Three prim secretaries occupied this place. A blonde woman immediately swished toward me and shook my hand warmly.

Everyone's manners were impeccable. It is the same impeccable manner which characterizes British colonial administration—unhurried, polite and resilient. I had scarcely gotten settled when I was ushered through two more doors into the Minister's private office. As I entered the air raid siren sounded. For the first time since I've been in London, I felt safe and secure.

The room was a huge affair—with massive mahogany furniture which had the polite ornateness of English interiors. Tarnished gold frames held paintings [of] England's past colonial secretaries. The floor was covered with green carpeting frayed about the edges.

Looks Like Prof.

I walked into this room where a tall, spare figure stood opposite a tremendous desk. He walked to meet me and proffered his hand. He looked like a Professor at an American state college, with his black-rimmed glasses and dark sack suit. On a nearby table I saw his black Eden hate and umbrella.

I was face-to-face with the man who directs the policy of that vast chain of British colonies—involving upwards of six million lives.

This was the man who was recently criticized by Ben Riley, Laborite MP, for his administration of colonial affairs. Riley contended that the colonial office had only spent one million pounds during the last five years for the social welfare of fifty million Africans which according to his computation, averaged about one cent per African.

The British Secretary of State declared that the faults of British colonization in Africa had been those of omission rather than commission. He was sure that beneficial social changes would follow the war. He pointed to the recently adopted Jamaican constitution as a progressive illustration. This constitution gives suffrage to the island for a Congress for the first time in history. It allows for the election of representatives to the lower house, encourages political activity and gives the people political experience.

Hamstrung

Critics here say that the Governor's veto negates any act of the elected representatives. They point to the experiences of Ceylon. Further, the governor nominates half of the representatives in the upper house. And moreover, the governor's executive council—a sort of cabinet—is hamstrung because only half are elected by the lower house.

The Secretary of State refused to comment directly on the Soviet regime having raised the non-Russian peoples—who before the revolution were to all intent and purposes backward colonial peoples—to the same political, economic, and social status as the dominant Russian peoples.

He suggested that the achievements of Russia were not accomplished by government alone, but by full participation of every one of its citizens.

The role of colored peoples in the war received his unreserved enthusiasm. He recalled that it was West and East African units which were landed successfully behind Japanese lines in Burma.

"I wish," he said, "military security did not prevent me from speaking of the numbers of colored peoples in the Allied armies. But they have done extraordinarily well."

"Cripps Gives Official View on India Issue"
PM, September 13, 1944

To clarify American opinion, Sir Stafford Cripps, Minister of Aircraft Production, the other day set forth the official position of the British Government on the vexing India problem in an exclusive interview.

His statement was at once a defense of the Minister's failure in 1942 as well as to take sharp issue with the discussions now taking place between Gandhi and Mohammed Ali Janneh, President of the All-India Moslem League — discussions which are fraught with profound possibilities.

Observers here are convinced that the India issue will also come up for discussion in the Roosevelt-Churchill meeting.

CONSIDERATIONS

I talked with Sir Stafford at some length. He held that there were certain fundamental considerations which were necessary for any true appreciation of the Indian situation. These he saw as follows:

¶The offer made to the Indian people by the British Government in 1942 is still open. This offer was for a new constitution to be framed by the Indian people themselves as soon as hostilities are over.

There were no reservations as to India's freedom. The new Indian Government, under the new constitution, could elect to leave the British Commonwealth of Nations if it is desired. Certain suggestions were made as to the best way of framing that new constitution, but it was stipulated that if the leaders of the principal parties of India agreed upon any other method, the British Government would fall in with their desires.

VARIETY OF PEOPLES

¶ There are in India a great variety of races and religions. These are represented by different political groups, such as the Congress Party, which is mainly Hindu; the Moslem League, which is entirely Moslem; the Hindu Mahasabha, which is wholly Hindu; the depressed classes organization, which represents the low caste Hindus; the Sikhs, who constitute a large minority in the Punjab — an otherwise predominantly Moslem province — and who are in sympathy with the Hindus; the Indian Christians, who are widely distributed in the separate provinces, and many smaller groups.

¶ If a new constitution is to be worked out, there must be a measure of agreement between these different sections of the Indian people as to the method of arriving at that constitution in the first place.

¶ The main difficulty which stands in the way of this agreement is the minority problem. The various sections of the community are afraid of being placed in the position of permanent minorities without any outside protection. Hitherto this protection has been given by the British Government.

¶ It is important to bear in mind the fact that racial and religious minorities are in a very different position in a democracy from political minorities. The latter can always hope to become by propaganda and persuasion a majority and so control the government. A religious or racial minority is permanently relegated to a position of inferiority, in which it can be oppressed by the majority race or religion.

¶ Hence, in so complex a society as that in India, it is a matter of great importance for the future constitution of the country that there be agreement between the different races and religions. This is well illustrated by the recent demonstrations by the Hindu Mahasabha and the Sikhs against any agreement between Gandhi for the Congress Party and Jinnah for the Moslem League, which would compromise the unity of India.

¶ The Congress Party and the Moslem League, as the two largest parties representing respectively the Hindus and the Moslems, must come to an agreement upon the means by which progress can be made before any further steps can be taken. No outside authority can force agreement upon them. When these two major parties have come to some agreement, there will still be the necessity of convincing the larger outstanding minorities that they will be given adequate protection in the new constitution.

British Anxious

¶ The British Government is anxious for an agreement so that orderly and speedy progress can be made toward the working out of the new constitution.

¶ It was part of the British Government's offer in 1942 that while this new constitution was being thought out and developed, the principal Indian parties should share in the government under the existing constitution. This part of the offer, too, is still open, but it is not possible to change the existing constitution, which would require a new act of Parliament. Pending the final working out of the new constitution, a new Constitution Act for India is a difficult and complicated matter, which cannot be undertaken in wartime. It is for this reason, amongst others, that any temporary arrangement for participation by the Indian parties in the government must be under the existing constitution.

¶ The provincial governments are fully representative, upon a democratic basis, and are responsible to their legislatures elected by the Indian people. Certain of these governments are not at present functioning, since the Congress Party withdrew their members and refused any longer to take part in the government. This made it impossible to constitute other governments, since the Congress Party was in the majority. There is no reason why, if the Indian parties can come to an agreement, these provincial governments should not again take up their functions.

"Belgium to Rule Congo without Major Changes"
PM, September 14, 1944

Brussels is liberated. There is overwhelming elation in Belgian circles here. Plans are speedily being polished up for the triumphal re-entry into Belgium. But no one apparently is talking about a new deal for the Congo—Belgium's rich colony and brightest jewel in King Leopold's crown.

To find out what's on the agenda for the African native in the Congo, I went to see M. Vleeschauwer, the Belgian Colonial Minister. This chunky, wavy-haired man, who formerly was a university professor, expressed considerable doubt about any major social changes. He was sure the African lacked capacity for self-rule within any foreseeable time.

11,000,000 NATIVES

He was convinced, though, that the Belgians were eminently qualified to continue their "trusteeship." Yet the Congo is crippled by sleeping sickness, malaria, inadequate transport, enormous distances from world markets, insufficient capital and large public debt—which, incidentally caused the Belgians to resort to a colonial lottery in an attempt to cover the financial deficit, as well as to tax the natives heavily.

The Congo is 80 times the size of Belgium. There are 11 million natives and about 30,000 whites. Only one out of every 10 Africans has a rudimentary education. Schools are chiefly run by missionaries. The Africans are trained to be carpenters, furniture makers, blacksmiths, plumbers, mechanics, printers, tailors and shoemakers.

M. Vleeschauewer was quick to say that native interests were of paramount importance. But private Belgian companies reap the harvest. About 200 private companies operate in the Congo. Of these 75 per cent of the capital is controlled by four financial groups. The biggest is the *Societe Generale*. The Government is a shareholder. Copper and diamonds head the list of exports.

SAW NO CLASH

Belgium's unashamed exploitation of resources, both human and natural, is one of the blackest pages of colonial history. Until the outbreak of war, there was considerable native ferment. What does the Belgium Government—which itself has felt the whiphand of the Nazi oppressor—plan to do about it. M. Vleeschauwer explains:

"The Belgian Government has committed itself to favor the emancipation of the Congolese people. This program is to be fulfilled in three principal ways: a. by instructing the bulk of the population; b. by raising the standard of life of the people; and c. by associating the African people with its own government through employment in the administrative services."

Though metropolitan Belgium lives largely by the raw materials produced in the Congo, the Minister saw no clash in fundamental interests between the native and the Belgian.

Yet reliable authorities here say that the territory's railways, which were necessary to develop the mineral resources were built with compulsory labor. The morality is said to have been high. Compulsion is also used for the growing of specified crops. In particular, M. Vleeschauwer bemoaned the considerable persuasion it took to get the African to grow coffee—an item which of course is not essential to the native's diet.

With the outbreak of war, a native army was recruited to defend the colony. Many of these troops were used in the East African campaign. The Minister was full of praise for their loyalty:

"The Belgian Government, like everybody in the world, knows and greets the war effort of colored peoples. As regards specially our African population, it is clear that without the courage and tenaciousness of the Congo's people, our war effort would never have been as thorough as it really was."

LAUDS RUSSIA

I asked the Minister if he cared to comment upon the Soviet regime's having raised the non-Russian peoples of Central Asia—who before the revolution were to all intent and purposes backward colonial peoples—to the same political, economic and social status as the dominant Russian people. He replied:

"Everyone knows the extraordinary progresses accomplished by Soviet Russia in technical and cultural matters. It is obvious that the geographical, ethnical, linguistic, political and social conditions are completely different in Russia and in Central Africa.

"However," he added, "it may be said that the Belgian administration by instructing and raising the Congo people tries to spread the civilization and to improve the standard of life like Russia did and is still doing for her own people."

ANY PLANS?

Belgium has been attempting to spread civilization since 1883 when King Leopold took over the "development" of the new territory.

Today the application of the Atlantic Charter to Africa is not even within the realm of Belgian thinking. When asked recently what steps the Belgian Government in London was taking to extend self-government to the Congo, Pierre Ryckmans, Governor General of the Congo, told correspondents that the Africans needed "white trusteeship."

In answer to a question put to him by a Negro correspondent, M. Ryckmans said that the Africans were until 40 years ago not only fighting among themselves, but also cannibals. This is apparently the mentality of the men who are administering affairs in the Congo.

What worries liberal thought here today is what's going to happen after this war. Belgium got the Ruanda-Urundi territory from Germany, following the last war for its participation. This territory brought 3 million natives and excellent cattle-raising country under Belgian control.

"Dixie Invades Britain"
Negro Digest: A Magazine of Negro Comment
3 (November 1944): 3–8 (condensed from *PM*)

The noose of prejudice is slowly tightening around the necks of American Negro soldiers, and tending to cut off their recreation and associations with the British people.

For—to be frank—relations between Negro and white troops have reached grave proportions.

The reasons for its acuteness is complex. Much of it lies deep in the American way of life. For in essence, there are those here who are still fighting the Civil War—this time on British soil.

American observers who were here in 1942 when the first contingents arrived from America saw amicable and smooth relations develop between the Negro troops and their British hosts.

Some were even lionized—so much so that certain white American soldiers became openly resentful. And they lost no time in attempting to discipline the British people. For—and this is perhaps the crucial issue—in back of the Southerner's mind here is the belief that on his return the Negro will be mighty difficult to remold into the Jim Crow pattern.

Many thousands of Negro troops are in Britain. They represent a larger Negro population than the British Isles has ever known. For most Britons it is the first time that they have seen Negroes in relatively large groups. For most of the Negroes it is the first time they have been away from their homes and communities.

But the people here have a racial tolerance which gives them a social lever. They are inclined to accept a man for his personal worth. Thus the Negro has social equality here in more ways than theory.

To put it in the language of a Negro soldier, "I'm treated so a man don't know he's colored until he looks in the mirror."

The fact is, the British do draw racial distinctions, but not within the doors of the British Isles—at least not until the arrival of the white American soldiers.

This is not to say the British are without racial prejudice. They do have it in a subtle form. But in the main, it is confined to colonial and military officials who have spent their lives administering affairs in the colored colonies and derive their incomes from them.

What contact the British people had with Negroes before the arrival of the American troops was on the whole very good.

Paul Robeson and many other Negro artists and entertainers made quite an impression on the British. In the ten years he resided in England Robeson created a good opinion of the American Negro.

By and large Negro troops have been billeted in the country sections of England, Scotland and Ireland. The British people in the country are naturally hospitable. They warmly greeted the Negro troops. Soon Negroes were invited to British homes, churches, and trade union meetings. Easy and friendly associations developed between the races.

This was a great shock to many white Americans, particularly those from the deep South.

At Highton in Northern England—to illustrate—a Negro soldier had an appointment with a British girl to meet him in front of his camp. When he got outside she was engaged in conversation with two white American soldiers.

The Negro soldier walked over and greeted the girl. "I've been waiting about 15 minutes for you," she scolded cheerfully. The smiled, locked hands, and walked down the road.

One of the white soldiers snatched off his hat and flung it to the ground. He broke into tears and kept repeating over and over, "I'm from Georgia and I just can't take that!"

There are white commanders who when they arrive in an area with their unit, restrict passes to Negroes until after inspection has been made of the nearest town or city. The best cafes, restaurants, theaters and hotels are chosen for white personnel and the proprietors are informed that they are to bar Negro soldiers.

This has proved an effective strong-armed instrument for establishing the Jim Crow pattern in public places, and, incidentally, relegates Negroes to the worst sections on the outskirts of town or along the waterfront.

A Negro Red Cross worker, J. Clarice Brooks, former New York social worker, was alone late one night at a Belfast Red Cross club waiting for transportation home when in walked five white American soldiers. This is what transpired:

"There's the bitch that's runnin' the club for niggers," one shouted as they strode toward her.

"This is a Red Cross club for American soldiers if they behave themselves," she replied.

"What do you mean? Niggers are better behaved than we are?"

His companion interjected, "You going to let her talk to you like that?"

"Let's beat her up," another said.

"Yeah, we know how to treat niggers!"

They were about to assault her when luckily a white officer happened along and intervened. Miss Brooks told me that although she attempted to press charges against them, that was the last she heard of the affair.

Negro Red Cross workers in England have been known to go home nights armed with baseball bats to fight off prejudiced white soldiers.

In some areas, "gangs" have been formed by white soldiers to terrorize Negroes. When such groups arrive in a town, they immediately declare it "their" territory. Any Negro seen is run out.

There are many cities, towns or villages that witnessed race rioting. The most infamous of these clashes is called "The Battle of Bamber Bridge"—an area in Lancaster.

Negroes billeted here complained of unfair restrictions. They were burning with resentments.

One night a white MP regarded by Negroes as their mortal enemy shot a Negro soldier in the back following a fracas. News of the killing soon reached the camp.

The Negro soldiers felt they had reached the limit of their endurance. So they broke into the arsenal, took arms, and barricaded themselves for battle.

When the first white officers approached, they were met by a volley of gun fire. Four of them went down. The other officers sought cover and called for armored cars. A great tragedy was averted by Lt. Edmund Jones, a Negro popular with the troops.

Well aware that these desperate Negroes were prepared to fight to the death, he persuaded his white commander to give him authority to end the affair without further bloodshed. He was made a provost-general for three days and was successful in having the Negroes end the futile battle. He assured them by radio that reforms would follow and in the future they would be dealt with fairly.

This distressing racial situation must be laid squarely on the doorstep of the white officers. Certainly, if they wished to do something concrete about the problem, there are sufficient memorandums, directives and orders to bolster them.

Tons of such literature had been published. I have seen much of it. Most is forthright in explaining, and even insisting, on mutual respect among soldiers. Many are masterpieces of clarity. The declared policy of the American Army in relation to the Negro soldier is absolutely clear:

"He is to receive the same treatment, wages, rations as the white troops. He is to have equal opportunity for recreation."

Unhappily, certain of the officers whose tasks it becomes to implement these instructions violate them where the Negro is concerned. Few of them even bother to read the instructions.

They well know that in practice there is no penalty for any show of racial hostility. The fact is, there is ample evidence to prove that racial prejudice is encouraged by such officers, a group often dominated by Southerners.

An RAF flyer told me of an indoctrination course he attended, conducted by an American lieutenant. His whole lecture was devoted to explaining to the British the reasons why they should not associate with Negro soldiers. He made no bones about the fact that not to conform with the American view of race was to be the victim of actual physical violence.

These roughhouse tactics have, of course, been augmented by word-of-mouth propaganda. At every turn attempts are being made to discredit the Negro. The catalogue of lies and misinformation is well known in America.

But new twists have been given old clichés. A Negro major told me of being surprised when he visited a British home by the concern for his comfort. The mistress of the house had placed a number of soft pillows in his chair. Every so often she would anxiously look in his direction.

Before the evening was over he learned the reason: His hosts had been told by American soldiers that Negroes have tails!

The British are aggressively resisting the prejudice which certain white soldiers are intent upon imposing. This seems to have been the case when U.S. soldiers boarded a bus for London and tried to eject two Negro soldiers from seats they already occupied.

"You can't do that sort of thing here," a woman conductor protested. "We won't have it. Either you stand or off you go."

They stood. But the seeds of prejudice are easily scattered. Even some white troops who shared no feeling of prejudice in the United States have accepted the anti-Negro attitudes held by certain Americans. Inevitably, in their contact with the British some have sought to transfer these attitudes.

What's true of the United States seems equally true in England: The customer is always right. When the manager of a restaurant was questioned recently about refusing service to a Negro soldier, he had a ready answer: "White Americans say they will not patronize my place if Negroes were served."

Nevertheless, the Negro soldier has appealed to the British heart.

The Negro has brought along his gifts. I was quite surprised to find British girls in Manchester, Liverpool, Glasgow and London dancing the lindy hop.

Every Monday morning the news papers are filled with reports of Negro activity with the British—such as hikes and picnics. Negroes are seen at churches, groups of them even taking over the choir loft on occasion.

In England Negroes are on their very best behavior. They are fully aware of what is at stake. Their Negro officers and Negro Red Cross directors have done a splendid job of making them conscious that they are the guests of the British people, and as such they must prove themselves worthy of their hospitality.

Negro troops stationed near Manchester originated the idea of entertaining the local children to repay some of the hospitality which they had received in that city. I attended the second of a series of six weekly parties. About 20 Negro soldiers sang and danced. Then they distributed chewing gum and candy from their rations. Five hundred children attended the party given at the Red Cross club. The Lord Mayor was present.

The Negro soldiers feel keenly about the frequent show of racial animosity. Voicing a fairly typical attitude of troops who have recently arrived in England, Pfc. William B. Brown, Newark, N.J., told me how he felt:

"Since my arrival I've been constantly reminded that I'm a Negro. The pattern seems more pronounced here than in the deep South."

The fact is, numbers of people are scrambling around for a solution. I talked quite extensively with British officials. They are frankly embarrassed and even alarmed by the race situation provoked by certain Americans.

None will talk for the record. Lend-lease makes them keep their official mouths closed, for they are well aware of the spitefulness of some Southern politicians.

Moreover, they feel that Americans are creating a vast amount of antiwhite feeling throughout the world, which will make the dealings of the British with colored colonials pretty difficult.

Many of them feel Americans presumptuous to talk of freedom for India in the face of the unsolved race problem in America.

Perhaps no one here is more disturbed than Americans. But individuals cannot stand up alone. Friends whom I knew in the U.S.A. admit they are helpless.

Yet white officers are daily sticking their necks out to make democracy vibrant and living within the Army. Such Army publications as *Yank* and *Stars and Stripes* are dramatizing the Negro soldier's vital role in the war. Several white American seamen signed a petition protesting the barring of Negroes from a ballroom they visited.

The one hopeful aspect of this situation is the fact that the noose of prejudice has not closed. The reason may be found in the fact that many of the most rabid anti-Negro American soldiers are now not so sure of their positions. They do not have wide public support for any show of racial hostility.

S. L. Solon, an American reporter working for a London paper, relates a conversation which he overheard. It sums up the situation, tying it in a nice tight knot.

"Personally," a town councillor said, "I have no feeling of race prejudice. I've been led to believe, however, that our relations with American white troops will be better if we conform to what I understand to be American practices of discrimination."

The answer to that came from a white American officer. "Discrimination is not American," he said. "Even less so today, when we are fighting a war to preserve and extend democratic values in the world."

"Famed French Writer Took Nazis for a Ride"
PM, October 3, 1944

Rene Maran, a Negro and one of the most distinguished writers in France, declared today in an interview that the Vichy government—as a catspaw for the Nazis—tried to establish a new slavery for people of color in France.

Maran, a tall, erect, energetic man with a decidedly dark complexion, is the author of *Batouala,* widely read in [America] in the 1920s. He won the Goncourt Prize awarded by the French Academy in 1921.

In a gesture of resistance to the Nazis in 1942, the French Academy awarded the Negro author the grand prize for his *Bete de la Brousse.* This book, circulated in Paris during Nazi occupation, was a subtle political attack on the Nazis through the use of animal characters.

Although his royalties were stopped during the Nazi occupation, he did not capitulate as so many other French writers had done. He showed the strain of straitened circumstances.

"Negroes felt keenly the lash of Nazi rule," Maran said.

"Some 10,000 Negroes live in Paris. Negroes—like Jews—were barred from all theaters, hotels, cafes, and public places of amusement.

"To a French Negro this is slavery. Few black men were employed by the Nazis. But after the first few months, the Nazis relaxed the social restrictions against Negroes—but not so with the Jews.

"When America entered the war all American Negroes, mostly entertainers, were gathered up and dispatched to concentration camps. A few starving Negroes apparently did work for the Nazis."

To flip the other side of the coin, Negro members of the resistance movement were among those who courageously fought off German tanks and machine gun attacks on the Hotel de Ville.

RESISTED NAZIS

Maran, too, resisted the Nazis. Soon after the Nazi occupation of Paris, a deputy commandant visited Maran and informed him that he had been selected to write an anti-American tract, which to be built around the quote "brutal treatment" of Negroes in the U.S.A. Maran flatly refused.

"Sir," he said, "your fuehrer has described me as half ape. I am declared incapable of thinking or writing. I beg to be excused."

But the Nazis delivered an ultimatum—write or go to a concentration camp.

Maran wrote.

I have a copy of the original 5000-word essay which Maran gave to a friend for safekeeping. He asked that it be published after the war should anything happen to him, or should he be declared to be a supporter of the Nazi regime.

This document is one of the finest statements on the Negroes' hopes and aspirations and accomplishments in America. It details his story from his arrival as a slave in America to the present.

He related the achievements of distinguished Negroes including Booker T. Washington, Paul Robeson, Marian Anderson, George Washington Carver, [W. E. B.] Dubois and Walter White as evidence of the Negroes place in the future of the U.S.A. Its whole character is positive and written upon the theme of Langston Hughes' *I, Too, Sing America.*

NEGRO'S ADVANCES

He mentions the definitive advances made by Negroes under Roosevelt's administration. He concludes with these passages which he describes as the "very truth":

¶ "The American Negro is proud to be an American. He will never do anything that would jeopardize his country's standing in the eyes of foreign nations.

¶ "He has the liberalism of France. He has succeeded in using it, not only to improve his own position but also to improve the position of all people in America."

Maran is full of hope for the future period, but he was recently bewildered by the behavior of certain American liberators of Paris. Down the street from his home is a café he has frequented for a number of years. A few days ago, in French fashion, he took his French wife to the café for wine and talk with his French cronies.

When he sat down, five white American soldiers walked over and jostled him out of his chair. Then they rained insult and abuse on his wife for being in the company of a Negro.

Maran is bewildered because this never happened during the Nazi occupation. His wife remarked to me that she never before had received an unkind word because of her husband's color.

"France Plans Sweeping Reforms for Colonies"
PM, October 9, 1944

If the French leaders have their way, daring and historic reforms will take place within the French empire which may cause repercussions in the colonial-minded capitals of the world as [well] as with imperialist-minded Frenchmen.

Details of a 20-year plan soon to be launched, envisioning a form of French federation, was disclosed to me in an exclusive interview with M. Rene Pleven, French Minister of Colonies. This lanky, bespectacled diplomat, strongly for de Gaullist, [*sic*] discussed the plan with a frankness uncommon among government leaders.

It is apparent that France has no intention of turning loose her colonial possessions. He reminded me that his government was the only one in the world to discuss candidly future colonial policy during wartime. But he was quick to say that he was no dreamer.

"This plan is not utopian, but actually very realistic. For I see what has happened to the mind of the colonial people," he said.

NEED MORE PEOPLE

French colonial policy is erected on a very realistic foundation — but for more reasons than those enumerated by Pleven. French leaders here are fearful that 40,000,000 Frenchmen cannot survive as a powerful nation in a world of power politics. Moreover, modern wars cannot be fought with backward peoples.

There is a desperate need for an increased birthrate and a healthy and literate reservoir of citizens. It is for this reason that the Negroes of Africa, the Arabs of North Africa, and the Chinese and Eurasians of Indo-China — always provided, of course, that France succeeds in keeping her empire intact — are to be lifted to equal status with the white Frenchmen of metropolitan France.

Pleven indicated that any interference would be strongly resisted. He added:

"Gen. de Gaulle is most firm on this point. Any French official guilty of racial discrimination or prejudice will immediately be discharged from the service of the government."

"French policy has never ceased to reject racial distinctions. The detestable episode of Vichy does not contradict this truth. We can even say that it confirms it. For it was during the only period in the history of France, when the Government came under foreign ideas and control, that our country abandoned, in appearance, her traditional philosophy."

I found documentation for this last point. During Nazi occupation, Jews as well as Negroes were barred from cafes, theaters, hotels and restaurants. These restrictions were relaxed immediately when Paris fell under Allied arms. Today, from all appearances, Nazi occupation has not injured the Frenchmen's traditional liberalism with regard to race and color.

Pleven said the trend of French racial policy was indicated by the reappointment by de Gaulle of the late Felix Eboue as Governor-General of French Equatorial Africa, a federation of territories five times the size of France. M. Eboue was a full-blooded Negro—a fact which appalled white South Africa but not the French.

"We are determined," Pleven said, "to place at the disposal of the Africans the moral, intellectual and material means which will enable them to rise gradually to the level of French civilization, and thus become more and more French, fraternally a part of the French community."

I asked him how did the French Government plan to implement this to have it become reality.

Has Answers

Pleven was not lost for words:

"It is necessary, first of all, that the African have a high standard of health. No African ought to be without medical care."

He said this would be made possible through a 20-year plan, in which 1500 French doctors would be sent to Africa. Thousands of French nurses would be sent to operate health centers. A medical school for which plans already are formulated, would be opened for young Africans. Each year would produce new teams of Negro doctors who would assume the care of the population.

To elevate the masses, is the basis of the education plan about to be launched. Every village will have a school. As Pleven put it: "No African, boy or girl, should remain illiterate or incapable of taking care of himself in a modern life." He declared that there would be an elementary school for every 50 African children. High school, college and professional training, "naturally will follow," he said.

The educational plan involves the sending of French professors and teachers—both men and women—to Africa to establish schools and develop native teachers, who in turn, will assume the task of village schooling and eventually complete direction of African education.

20 to 30 Years

Pleven's enthusiasm caused me to ask how long he thought it would take. His estimate was significant because few imperialist nations dare fix a time for the assumption of native responsibility of any kind.

"According to our calculations," he replied, "this will take from 20 to 30 years, depending on the territory involved."

Once the African receives this training, I asked, what opportunities will he have for using it.

"Education is not an end in itself," he declared. "Those who possess it will be given the opportunity to attain positions of dignity and responsibility. It is not enough simply to say that employment will be opened. Any African fit to hold a public or private position will be admitted to such employment on equal terms with the European, for the entire program is designed to equip the African to assume his place in the affairs of French Africa and of France."

2 Aims Politically

Politically, Pleven disclosed, the program has two aims:

¶ To associate the native populations with the responsibilities of the development of their territories.

¶ To strengthen the fraternal and spiritual link of these territories with France.

To use Pleven's language: "We seek to have territories regard metropolitan France as the elder sister of the family."

Striking at old imperialist conceptions of exploiting colonies, he declared that the plan involved the development of modern agriculture and the creation of native industries.

"The riches thus created," he said, "will give the territories a sound prosperity, and will free them from that old conception, according to which certain countries are made to produced and others consume."

"Moreover," the minister continued, "political liberty will go hand-in-hand with economic liberty. The peoples of Africa will debate the budget and public affairs. Already future African assemblies are in the preparatory stage. Election by universal suffrage will come but not [be] immediately adopted because of the present lack of sufficient education among the masses. But every appropriate measure will be taken to assure a sincere expression of the interest and aspirations of the masses."

Own Assemblies

Each territory will elect its own constituent assembly. These individual assemblies will form a federation adapted to the principles of French political philosophy. This federal assembly will meet in Paris.

According to Pleven, "it will express the fundamental unity of both metropolitan and colonial France, always respectful of the rights, wishes, and character of each."

Pleven was vague on what policies would be followed with regard to trade unions. He said a recent decree extended freedom of trade unionism to all the territories, but it was a factor not too important at the moment because of the lack of large industry and lack of education. However, he was optimistic about the future of trade unionism. He pointed to the successful federation of Dakar unions as one encouraging sign.

He clearly indicated that the future of trade unionism rested on the successful creation of industry and the modernization of agriculture.

"French System of Justice Works Despite Confusion"
PM, October 15, 1944

A red-eyed, weeping man grabbed me by the lapel in the lobby of the Hotel Scribe and poured out a story involving his wife.

He said that the night before she had been thrown into Drancy, the center for political prisoners. She was charged with having been a "collaborationist." He said she was innocent and moreover a patriot and would I do something.

"I've been married to that woman for 16 years," he said, "and I should know her better than anyone."

He seemed so sincere that I told him I would go to Drancy and inquire about her. The next morning I started out for Drancy, which is about seven miles outside Paris.

WPA RECALLED

The place was heavily guarded by members of the FFI, most them mere boys. I was directed to a small, white-washed room, where officials walked on top of officials. The office looked like those during the early WPA—planks across wooden horses formed desks. Boxes were turned into chairs. The same excitement and bustle, characteristic of WPA, was apparent here—somewhat pointed up by the animated French speech.

I asked a girl for information. She turned me over to an official, who in turn, handed me over to another official. This all occurred within six paces. I asked to see Madame L— , my friend's wife.

Everyone was excessively polite and anxious to please the American. But no one could find a record of her. The records were examined before me. They were in a mess. They were a dog-eared collection of papers, pencil notes, and typed cards, which showed they had been gathered in great haste. Innocent people will no doubt be buried here for months before they are finally released.

ONLY SHRUGS

A word-of-mouth investigation started. Inquiries were made of the guards, but they only shrugged ignorance. A clerk again shuffled through papers. A courier was sent to inquire in a certain cell block. He returned without any information.

No one knew. There were bewildered shrugs. They promised to make a careful search. If I would return the next day. I said I would.

Next morning everyone was all smiles. Yes, they had found Madame

L— . A courier was dispatched. He returned promptly with a tall blonde woman, who appeared to be in her early thirties. Her eyes were red from crying but she smiled wanly showing a large false tooth of silver. She wore a shabby, wrinkled tan sportscoat. Apparently she had been sleeping in her clothes. When I was introduced, her first question was:

"Is my husband alive? I heard there was shooting in Paris."

I assured her he was. She brightened immediately.

Along with Madame L— , I was led into a large room that resembled the reception rooms of New York's Welfare Dept. In the four corners of the room, three-man boards were hearing cases. About 40 worried people, holding blue slips of identification, awaited their turns.

All cases were heard openly, even a bit noisily. One man screamed then fainted when he was declared to be a collaborationist. Those awaiting their turn for a hearing, wet their lips, blinked, and shuffled uneasily.

A clerk called out the name of Madame L— and beckoned to me. He handed the three-man board two sheets of paper — the dossier of Madame L— . As it turned out, this was no star chamber proceeding. The charge against her was simply read. Madame L— declared she was not guilty.

The dossier, though brief, was pretty comprehensive. I learned that she had been born in Serbia. She and her husband had been dancers. They appeared at the Casino de Paris before the war. Her husband had been in the French Army. They had traveled much. She spoke eight languages and her husband 12.

SPOKE GERMAN

It was this background which had gotten her into trouble. A neighbor had heard her speak German to her husband and had turned her name in to the FFI.

The three men, after a few polite questions, talked together in low voices for about a minute. Their spokesmen turned to me and explained that her case had been investigated. It was found that the charge was sheer nonsense. He said many innocent people had been so injured, but they could take no chances. In the future, he said, persons making false accusations will themselves have to serve time in prison.

He turned to Madame L— and said:

"You'll be liberated in two or three days."

He explained that a superior council had to review the case and confirm the findings of the trial board, but this was only a matter of routine.

Madame L— was full of tears. She stumbled from the room dazed, still a bit bewildered. But she was "liberated."

"There's No Race Problem in the Foxholes"
PM, January 1, 1945

*Last June PM sent Roi Ottley, distinguished Negro journalist and author of
New World A-Coming, overseas on a roving assignment with special emphasis
on the vital problem of the war and peace role of colored peoples everywhere. He
has just come home after covering 30,000 miles on a tour during which he talked to
numberless GIs, both Negro and white, on the fighting fronts in Italy and the West.
He also got exclusive interviews with important Allied political leaders, including
colonial ministers of Britain, France, Belgium and the Netherlands. His able dis-
patches from abroad told PM readers part of his story. Today he begins the first of
a series summing up his trip and the lessons it had taught him.*

Everywhere I traveled in France, England, Italy and North Africa, the
soldier was saying: "I'm going to get some of that Freedom they are talking
about when I get home."

If he is rebuffed, what then?

Whether bloody race conflict will ensue will depend largely on GI attitudes, both white and Negro — attitudes now being forged in the crucible
of titanic warfare.

Future race relations are of profound concern to every American abroad.

But the crucial issue in the mind of certain Southern GIs abroad is,
"How are Negroes going to be remolded into the Jim Crow pattern?"

Wherever I went I asked the Negro troops what most they wanted the
folks back home to know. The answer was the same everywhere:

"Tell them we want to see the end of ole Jim Crow in America and equal
treatment for everyone."

The crying tragedy behind all this is that there are certain Southern
white GIs who, if they were told the meanings and implications of the war
against fascism in terms of race, they would frankly be bewildered. But no
one, to be sure, dares tell them.

Yet such an element is distinctly an infinitesimal minority. Actually the
average GI has grown up. Both in his political and racial attitudes he has
become an adult. And this has occurred, curiously enough, without conscious effort by his officers. It is the consequence of daily contact with Negroes in a common effort as well as the results of frequent contacts with
politically-minded Europeans.

By the very logic of his present occupation, the average GI is a pragma-
tist. He learns well from his experiences.

Thus, what essentially will be his future attitude toward the Negro de-
pends almost wholly upon what front he is fighting on today.

This fact I discovered after visiting both the Western and Italian fronts and talking with GIs, both Negro and white.

On the Italian front the Negro soldier is in actual physical contact with the enemy. The 92nd Division, a Negro outfit which holds down one wing of the front, has been in combat since October, 1942. The group, commanded by Maj. General Edward M. Almond, is part of the American 5th Army. They have successfully held a large sector which is tough mountainous country.

When Gen. Almond was assigned to command the division, all the officers were white. Today two-thirds of the officers are Negroes, including three lieutenant colonels, two of whom command all-Negro field artillery battalions—the third is a division chaplain. All the enlisted personnel are Negroes, coming from all sections of the country.

Not alone do white and Negro officers eat together, but they do this without awkwardness or strain. The division headquarters mess is perhaps more than normally ample, so two division dance bands, including some well-known Negro musicians of the country, play music in the evenings.

This pattern is followed in the officers' rest camp. I visited the Hotel Excelsior in Rome, where the men stay during furloughs. The place resembles the Waldorf-Astoria in its appointments and sweeping marble stairways.

No Discrimination

Here again I saw Negro and white, this time from different divisions, eating together in the main dining room. There was much helloing across the tables. Rooms, too, were assigned on a first-come-first-served basis. Both the bar and dancing in the main ballroom were open without distinction as to Negro or white.

All this happened normally and naturally. Moreover, there was a friendship and camaraderie unknown in civilian life. The 92nd Division has gained a reputation as tough and stubborn fighters. Their casualties have been heavy.

The white soldiers respected them, displaying this in every little act. In some way they seemed to sense that equality of peril deserves equality of treatment and recreation. This feeling has been translated into a fraternizing between the races which will certainly carry over into civilian life.

I heard more than one white Southerner say he hoped, when the war was over, that Negroes would enjoy the social benefits that they were fighting to preserve and extend.

Enviable Record

The Air Force has perhaps achieved the greatest amount of mutual respect and admiration among its personnel.

Negro aviators have been overseas in combat more than 19 months. They have seen more action from Munich to Vienna, from Salerno to Budapest, and from North Africa to Sicily.

They have won commendation from Gen. Montgomery for their dive-bombing and strafing of enemy positions both in Italian and North African campaigns. In the desperate Anzio beachhead assaults, they shot down 17 enemy fighters and bombers in one day in providing cover for our ground forces.

This sort of performance is difficult to refute with nonsense about "inferiority" of the Negro. For the facts stand out dramatically and must of necessity make deep inroads into the thinking of every white GI in the Italian theatre.

This is not to say that there is not an occasional racial incident but what is taking place does indicate progressive trends and indeed point to eventual understanding between the races. For both white and black on the fighting fronts have seen each other in their strengths and weaknesses and have concluded that after all "we" are only guys—that is, mere human beings—doing a job.

The situation, unhappily, is vastly different on the Western Front. Here the Negro soldier is doing little more than service work, with the exception of one tank destroyer unit and two artillery units. But the Negro GIs have the backbreaking task of keeping an avalanche of food, ammunition and troops moving steadily to the front. They are repairing roads, washing clothes, constructing buildings, laying railroad ties, salvaging equipment, driving trucks, and even breaking stones in quarries for road building and repair.

These are obviously the unglamourous jobs of modern warfare. Such activity, as important as it is, gets no headlines. Nor do the correspondents swoop down on them to report their contribution. The job lacks "color," in the view of most newspapers.

This has placed the Negro GI in a dilemma not of his own making. The almost exclusive use of Negroes as service and quartermaster troops has naturally caused resentment among Negroes. Moreover, few people back home know of their contribution to the total effort.

But what is equally important is that it has caused tempers to mount among the white troops—but for vastly contrary reasons.

Fore example, the European edition of *Stars and Stripes* has been receiving letters from white GIs complaining that Negroes in France were "goldbricking." They contended that Negroes are behind the lines and therefore not exposed to danger.

The fact is they are exposed to danger from enemy strafing and bombing. But when Gen. Eisenhower praised the Red Ball Express, the supply line which contains more than 70 percent Negro personnel, as contributing as much to the rapid advance of Allied forces in France, *Stars and Stripes* received many letters protesting that Negroes were being "overplayed."

Even before they left this country, Negro soldiers anticipated this attitude from certain white GIs. Now they feel that on their return home this will be hurled in their faces and reduce their chances in ultimately sharing the social benefits to come with victory. For they feel there will be a body of veterans vociferously opposing them.

The combat soldier has an undeniable prestige, both at home and abroad. He feels strongly about his part in the struggle. His participation is indelibly impressed on his mind. He is proud of a job well done thus far. He has gained poise and self-confidence and will make no bones about voicing his opinions.

But it must be made clear that his [resentment] against those who have not physically grappled with the enemy is not alone against Negro GIs, but also extends to those white members of the armed forces who hold desk jobs away from the roar of battle.

His resentments against the non-combatant Negro GI, only [add] further documentation in his view to the reasons why he should dislike the Negro.

This is a grave situation which those in authority might well ponder—if they hope for a peaceful postwar America. For the chances of postwar race conflict will largely depend upon what understanding can be achieved between Negro and white GIs.

"Facists Used Jim Crow against Allies"
PM, January 4, 1945

Europe is greatly bewildered, even agitated, by American patterns of prejudice.

It makes no sense to a Frenchmen—to illustrate—for America to send Negroes abroad as members of a liberating army, and then to open Jim Crow accommodations for them and to withhold from them the dignity and respect due a warrior.

One British Government official wanted to know whether the warm welcome the British people had given Negro troops would have repercussions in America, and create rabid anti-British feeling.

There is no doubt that much of the goodwill Americans could create and enjoy overseas is kicked over by shows of rabid anti-Negro feeling. If all Americans were anti-Negro the situation for Europeans would be simple. But since this is not a fact, the average European is bewildered.

One irony of my travels as a Negro correspondent was constantly being compelled to explain, often defend, America in race relations matters—I, who, before going abroad, criticized the failure of American democracy.

While crossing the Atlantic aboard a convoyed troop transport, I met a Russian engineer and a Czech diplomat. Hardly had we become acquainted when the Russian expressed amazement at the separation of the Negro and white troops aboard ship.

"What does this mean?" he asked.

LOVE AMERICA
The Czech, who had had an assignment in Washington, tried to explain. But the Russian was not appeased.

"You know," he said, "all peoples in the Soviet Union are equal."

I said I had heard the report.

"Tell me," he continued, "why, in the face of such inequalities, do Negroes still love America?"

I said that Negroes loved America for the same reasons that the Russian peasant loved Russia during the Czarist regime.

"It is my opinion," the Czech observed, "that the Negro problem in the United States is increasingly being recognized as a fundamental issue of democracy by a growing number of white Americans."

The Russian interrupted to say, "It seems difficult to understand; Americans are fighting for democracy and at the same time not treating Negro citizens in a democratic way. I don't see how an Allied nation can do this in a total war against fascism!"

"Negroes," I said, "obviously hate the unfair treatment the race receives from certain elements in the country, but for 300 years Negroes have put blood, sweat and tears into the building of the Nation, so they have the love one has for a personal possession."

Actually, I felt at a disadvantage in trying to explain the American race problem to one without any background in the subject—and, moreover, without even the concept of race.

The implications and subtleties are so unique and the problem so vast that I found myself almost speechless. I was really trying to explain insanity—which, after all, is the sum and substance of the problem.

If the American race problem is bewildering to the average European, it certainly is crystal clear to the fascist elements. They have lost no time in utilizing the race phobias of certain Americans to whip up anti-Negro GI feeling, hoping thereby to disrupt our military operations against Germany.

I saw a clear demonstration of this fact in Italy.

Today no one in Italy admits to having been a fascist—it was the neighbors, they say. But there are certain elements who seem to have knowledge of the fascist propaganda line, often attempting to pass it off as profound truth.

The Fascist leaders, during the rape and pillaging of Ethiopia, attempted to create anti-Negro feeling among the Italian people.

Anti-Negro Leaflets

This feeling quickly dissolved. Today the Italian people are wonderful in their hospitality to the Negro troops, inviting them to their homes, churches and social affairs. Negroes, on their parts, have learned the language well and have established firm friendships with the people.

But like termites, the Fascists went to work to destroy this foundation of goodwill. Exploiting the acute feelings of some Americans concerning the fact of Negro troop associations with the Italian girls, they surreptitiously printed and distributed anti-Negro leaflets.

I first discovered this leaflet in Naples. It reappeared in other Italian cities in spite of American military attempts to suppress it. At night they were plastered on the buildings. Eventually they found their way into the hands of American GIs, causing some tempers to mount.

The leaflet was palmed off as the product of the "ITALIAN-AMERICAN

COMMITTEE FOR THE PRESERVATION OF THE ITALIAN RACE," and was signed by a "J. A. Jacono."

At first glance, the impression one gained was that it was a spontaneous protest emanating from a section of the white American troops, perhaps the Italian-Americans.

Actually, I was assured by the Psychological Warfare Branch of the U.S. Army, the whole business was a fraud. No such organization existed among the troops. And moreover, it was an old technique of the Fascist to divide the Americans.

Here is the text:

"We, Italo-Americans, most with deep regret take notice that a group of women of Naples, dragging themselves in the gutter, dare to go out on the streets with Negroes, even dare invite them to their homes.

"Only the lowest type of people lower themselves thus; and the Italian people, already beaten and humiliated, should not allow that more mud be thrown on the land.

"When will you see the reality? When will your honor and your pride for being white and Italian incite you justly to spurn the Negroes?

"Awaken!!!"

And more of the same.

This sort of propaganda, from Fascist sources, often hits America in its Achilles heel. We are vulnerable where race relations are concerned. But the average GI took this nonsense in stride. The fact is, it backfired on the Fascists, for the American soldiers got a glimmer of the manner in which the Fascists operate to utilize their possible prejudice to disrupt American military operations.

"Eyewitness Report on Reign of Terror in Greece: Men and Women Anti-Fascists Jailed, Tortured by the Thousands"
PM, July 15, 1945

A state of terror exists in Greece today, instigated by pro-monarchist elements which control the government and a recently recruited National Guard which is carrying out a studied program of eliminating democratic elements from Greek political life.

More than 25,000 anti-fascists, former guerilla fighters, are in prison, with little hope of being released within any foreseeable time. In Athens alone, I saw 4000 crowded into museums, office buildings and school houses, which had been converted into virtual concentration camps. These were surrounded by the Guardsmen.

The democratic groups charge the pro-monarchists with imprisoning 28,000 but UNRRA (United Nations Relief and Rehabilitation) officials say unofficially that the actual figure in concentration camps throughout Greece is nearer 33,000. This estimate is based on eyewitness reports by UNRRA field workers.

Nearly all have been in prison from two to six months beginning with the December events. None of the prisoners has been charged formally with any crime.

These are not ordinary criminals, but only people who disagree with the current policies of the pro-monarchist leaders. They were picked up arbitrarily off the streets on one pretext or another and jailed.

POLITICS

Political observers here are convinced they are being held until the pro-monarchists, aided by the British, can get a firm grip on the country. A complete seizure of power by these elements is expected momentarily.

Delegations of citizens have asked the authorities repeatedly why these people are being held and why they have not been brought to trial. They have been met only with rebuff.

I asked various public officials when charges would be made, and the only answer was: "We don't have enough judges to try them."

I visited three prisons in Athens. There are more. I found thousands of anti-fascists thrown in among thieves, cutthroats and fascists. Their condition was desperate, yet they maintained high morale which was buoyed up by the belief: "We are sure the democratic powers will not let us rot here. We helped to defeat the fascists. We are anti-fascists."

Didn't Cry

They were decidedly of the low income group—bank clerks, street car conductors, waiters, farmers, shepherds, and mountain folk. They were well-disciplined. They did not cringe or cry. They were content to have their situation explained through a chosen leader.

I was able to hear their stories quite frankly as I had been admitted under the pretext of [*portion of the radiogram garbled at this point*—Ed.]

The most abysmal treatment seems to have been reserved for the women for they were quartered in a converted office building without adequate toilets and no bathing facilities. I counted 40 beds for 600 women. The rest slept on the floors. They cooked their meals on makeshift stoves.

Everyone I talked with in Athens said that until recently the most horrible screams came from this building at night. American UNRRA officials testified to the truth of this statement. A British officer's wife told me that up to a week before I arrived, the treatment of these women became such a scandal that the British were forced to take steps to halt the torture.

Public Unaware

The public is largely unaware of it, but the torture continues today. At the headquarters of the National Guard, the woman manager explained that twice a week the National Guard sends for a group of girls and grills them for information about the ELAS (the now-outlawed fighting forces of the EAM, Greek Committee of Liberation).

They returned with broken toes, their hair shaved and their bodies bloody. This was no idle charge, for the women showed me.

I saw freshly-marked holes where nails had been driven into their backs and breasts. One girl lay in a corner whimpering. I found that her back had been broken. Another had her toenails pulled out, one by one. One girl was hysterical. I was told that she had been beaten on the head with the butt of a gun. Quite a few of them had fits and vomiting spells.

The women ranged in age from 14 to 60, all strong-faced, sun-burned guerilla fighters, bewildered by the turn of events which today makes them torture-victims.

Hope

They are not cynical enough to understand the diplomatic machinations which [cause] them to be herded into these prisons, but they have hope, as only a literal-minded folk can have hope. For they believe that when the big powers spoke of freedom, they meant it.

The grim joke of one prison is a very short man, a mountain fighter who had been condemned to death 42 times by the Nazis. Each time he escaped. This time the National Guard charges him with the killing of a fascist, his friends say.

Yet, he is convinced that he will escape the noose again, for he says that the democratic elements in the world will come to the rescue of his friends and himself.

"Nuernberg Trials Mold Pattern of 'Collective Guilt' Principle"
Pittsburgh Courier, October 19, 1946

The Nurenberg trials have established a fundamental principle in the world—the "concept of collective guilt." That is to say, that a nation is responsible for the acts of the individuals of that nation, especially their leaders.

To put this in American terms—the Nurenberg trials mean that today the North is responsible for the lynchings in the South. Moreover, it means that no white person in America can reject responsibility for Tennessee or Georgia.

Many white Americans in the North, and even in the South, are shocked when the details of Southern treatment of the Negro is revealed to them. So too were many Germans amazed and shocked when German witnesses told of an SS request for a high allotment of uniform material, such as gold teeth of concentration camp victims and the clothes of those executed in the gas chambers.

NORTHERNERS SHOCKED

White people living in New York have told me that they were shocked, for example, that there was jim-crow in the South. Perhaps some were lying. But the statement did indicate a wish to believe that these things did not happen, and, more important, that they were not responsible for conditions of the South.

The Germans were loath to admit there were discriminations against Jews and atrocities against them as well. And to be sure, no German wanted to admit personal responsibility. With the notable exception of Goering, not one of the defendants in the Nuernberg trial admitted personal responsibility for the acts they admitted had taken place. They pushed the responsibility upon Himmler or Hitler. Thereby, they tried to absolve themselves.

I remember visiting the Dachau Concentration Camp, outside Munich. I spent some days interviewing and talking with people within a stone's throw of the camp. Nearly everyone I talked with said they did not know what was going on in the camp, even though the odor of burning flesh could be smelled a mile away.

When I finally pinned them down they conceded that atrocities did happen at Dachau Concentration Camp, but they explained that these were not the acts of "good Germans." They said that only criminals and

Communists were the men in charge at the concentration camp, and it is they who should be judged for the atrocities.

White Americans, both abroad and in the United States, seem shocked that the Germans do not want to accept the principle of collective guilt. To be sure, there even still remains a large body of Germans who have withdrawn into themselves and ignore the acts of the Nazis as their responsibility.

Today, however, the allies are pounding into German heads the fact that they are responsible. But it must be noted that the creation of the concept of collective guilt, is a Russian contribution essentially to the trials. Before the Nuernberg affair, there existed no law to try war criminals upon. The Russians introduced one, called "Crimes Against Humanity."

The principle that moral standards apply to public as well as private life has been brought forward dramatically at Nuernberg. The Allies believe that this thought will permeate the thought processes of the German people.

Should Apply in U.S.

The Nuernberg trials should have tremendous meaning to Negroes in the U.S. because the establishment of the principle of collective guilt can now be applied to the American scene. The President of the United States cannot take a hands-off position in crimes against innocent minorities. Nor can public officials. The principle indeed extends to each white person in the U.S.

There was one great loophole in the Nuernberg trial:

The tribunal refused to decide that crimes against humanity, even the whole panorama of atrocities committed by Nazis, were punishable except in connection with aggressive war.

This means that the German Nazis cannot be tried for the atrocities against Jews before the war! The reasons that the U.S. and England took this position is obvious. (The Russians were opposed.) But U.S. and England could be themselves held accountable for their treatment of blacks around the world.

U.S., Britain Guilty

If the concept had held to crimes before aggressive war, then England could have been put on the block for her treatment of the Africans, Indians and Chinese; the U.S. would then be forced to answer for her acts against South Americans, Negroes, Jews and Orientals.

The judges were too wise to condemn their own nations by implication, even indeed if it meant allowing thousands of Nazis to escape punishment for their treatment of Poles and Jews before the war.

There is indeed great hypocrisy in the Nuernberg trials. The judgments must necessarily bring suspicion to the world.

Bibliography

Archival Sources

Richard Wright Papers, Beinecke Rare Book and Manuscript Library, Yale University, New Haven, CT.

Roi Ottley Collection, St. Bonaventure University Archives, Friedsam Library, St. Bonaventure University, Olean, NY.

Works Cited

Arnesen, Eric. "Reconsidering the Long Civil Rights Movement." *Historically Speaking: The Bulletin of the Historical Society* 10 (April 2009): 31–34.

Baldwin, James. "The Negro at Home and Abroad." *Reporter,* November 27, 1951, 36–37.

Bardolph, Richard. *The Negro Vanguard.* New York: Rinehart, 1959.

Bates, Beth Tompkins. *Pullman Porters and the Rise of Protest Politics in Black America, 1925–1945.* Chapel Hill: University of North Carolina Press, 2001.

Biondi, Martha. *To Stand and Fight: The Struggle for Civil Rights in Postwar New York City.* Cambridge, MA: Harvard University Press, 2003.

Borstelmann, Thomas. *The Cold War and the Color Line: American Race Relations in the Global Arena.* Cambridge, MA: Harvard University Press, 2003.

Clarke, John Henrik. *Marcus Garvey and the Vision of Africa.* New York: Vintage Books, 1974.

Cooke, Marvel. *"No Green Pastures* Is No Favor to Negroes." *New York Daily Compass,* November 16, 1951.

Delozier, Alan Bernard. "An Examination of Racial Relations in Great Britain and the United States, 1942–1945, by Black American Journalist Roi Ottley." Master's thesis, Villanova University, 1998.

DuBois, W. E. B. "The African Roots of War." *Atlantic Monthly* 115 (May 1915): 707–714.

Dudziak, Mary L. *Cold War Civil Rights: Race and the Image of American Democracy.* Princeton, NJ: Princeton University Press, 2000.

Ellison, Ralph. "New World A-Coming." *Tomorrow* 4 (September 4, 1943): 67–68.

Finkle, Lee. "The Conservative Aims of Militant Rhetoric: Black Protest during World War II." *Journal of American History* 60 (December 1973): 692–713.

———. *Forum for Protest: The Black Press during World War II.* Rutherford, NJ: Fairleigh Dickinson University Press, 1975.

Franklin, John Hope. *Mirror to America: The Autobiography of John Hope Franklin.* New York: Farrar, Straus & Giroux, 2005.

Gilbert, Jenifer W. "Vincent Lushington Ottley." In *American National Biography,* ed. John A. Garraty and Mark C. Carnes, 16:844–845. New York: Oxford University Press, 1999.

Gilmore, Glenda Elizabeth. *Defying Dixie: The Radical Roots of Civil Rights, 1919–1950.* New York: W. W. Norton, 2008.

Greenberg, Cheryl Lynn. *"Or Does It Explode?" Black Harlem in the Great Depression.* New York: Oxford University Press, 1991.

Hall, Jacqueline Dowd. "The Long Civil Rights Movement and the Political Uses of the Past." *Journal of American History* 91 (March 2005): 1233–1263.

Haygood, Wil. *The King of the Cats: The Life and Times of Adam Clayton Powell, Jr.* New York: Amistad, 2006.

Hill, Robert A., ed. *The FBI's RACON: Racial Conditions in the United States during World War II.* Boston: Northeastern University Press, 1995.

Hirsch, Jerrold. *Portrait of America: A Cultural History of the Federal Writers' Project.* Chapel Hill: University of North Carolina Press, 2006.

Hughes, Langston. *The Big Sea: An Autobiography.* New York: Hill & Wang, 1993.

Jackson, Lawrence. *Ralph Ellison: Emergence of Genius.* New York: John Wiley & Sons, 2002.

Jackson, Luther P., Jr. "Roi Ottley." In *Dictionary of American Biography,* suppl. 6, 1950–1960, ed. Luther P. Jackson, Jr., and John A. Garraty, 489–491. New York: Charles Scribner's Sons, 1980.

James, Winston. *Holding Aloft the Banner of Ethiopia: Caribbean Radicalism in Early Twentieth Century America.* London: Verso, 1998.

Kelley, Robin D. G. *Race Rebels: Culture, Politics, and the Black Working Class.* New York: Free Press, 1994.

Kirby, John B. *Black Americans in the Roosevelt Era: Liberalism and Race.* Knoxville: University of Tennessee Press, 1980.

Korstad, Robert. *Civil Rights Unionism: Tobacco Workers and the Struggle for Democracy in the Mid-Twentieth Century South.* Chapel Hill: University of North Carolina Press, 2004.

Korstad, Robert, and Nelson Lichtenstein. "Opportunities Found and Lost: Labor, Radicals, and the Early Civil Rights Movement." *Journal of American History* 75 (December 1988): 786–811.

Lawson, Steven F. *Running for Freedom: Civil Rights and Black Politics in America since 1941.* New York: Wiley-Blackwell, 2008.

Lewis, David Levering. *W. E. B. Du Bois: Biography of a Race.* New York: Henry Holt, 1993.

———. *W. E. B. Du Bois: The Fight for Equality and the American Century, 1919–1963.* New York: Henry Holt & Sons, 2000.

———. *When Harlem Was in Vogue.* New York: Penguin Books, 1997.

Marable, Manning. *Race, Reform, and Rebellion: The Second Black Reconstruction and beyond in Black America, 1945–2006.* 3rd ed. Jackson: University Press of Mississippi, 2007.

Meriwether, James H. *Proudly We Can Be Africans: Black Americans and Africa, 1935–1961.* Chapel Hill: University of North Carolina Press, 2002.

Milkman, Paul. *"PM": A New Deal in Journalism, 1940–1948.* New Brunswick, NJ: Rutgers University Press, 1997.

Naison, Mark. *Communists in Harlem during the Depression.* Urbana: University of Illinois Press, 1983.

Osofsky, Gilbert. *Harlem: The Making of a Ghetto—Negro New York, 1890–1930.* 2nd ed. New York: Harper Torchbooks, 1971.

Ottley, Roi. *Black Odyssey: The Story of the Negro in America.* New York: Charles Scribner's Sons, 1948.

———. *New World A-Coming: Inside Black America.* Boston: Houghton Mifflin, 1943.

———. *No Green Pastures.* New York: Charles Scribner's Sons, 1951.

———. *The White Marble Lady.* New York: Farrar, Straus & Giroux, 1965.

Ottley, Roi, and William Weatherby, eds. *The Negro in New York: An Informal Social History.* New York: New York Public Library, 1967.

Plummer, Brenda Gayle. *Rising Wind: Black Americans and US Foreign Policy, 1936–1960.* Chapel Hill: University of North Carolina Press, 1996.

Powell, Adam Clayton, III. *Adam by Adam: The Autobiography of Adam Clayton Powell, Jr.* New York: Kensington Publishing, 1994.

Rampersad, Arnold. *Ralph Ellison: A Biography.* New York: Alfred A. Knopf, 2007.

"Roi Ottley Dies; Wrote on Negro." *New York Times,* October 2, 1960, 80.

"Roi (Vincent) Ottley." In *Current Biography 1943,* 566–567. New York: H. W. Wilson, 1944.

Scott, William R. "Black Nationalism and the Italo-Ethiopian Conflict, 1934–1936." *Journal of Negro History* 63 (April 1978): 118–134.

———. *The Sons of Sheba's Race: African-Americans and the Italo-Ethiopian War, 1935–1941.* Bloomington: Indiana University Press, 1992.

Self, Robert O. *American Babylon: Race and the Struggle for Postwar Oakland.* Princeton, NJ: Princeton University Press, 2005.

Sitkoff, Harvard. *A New Deal for Blacks: The Emergence of Civil Rights as a National Issue: The Depression Decade.* New York: Oxford University Press, 1978.

———. "Racial Militancy and Interracial Violence in the Second World War." *Journal of American History* 58 (December 1971): 661–681.

Solomon, Mark. *The Cry Was Unity: Communists and African Americans.* Jackson: University Press of Mississippi, 1998.

Stevens, John D. "From the Back of the Foxhole: Black Correspondents in World War II." *Journalism Monographs,* no. 27 (February 1973).

Teed, Dexter. "Ottley Sees New World A-Coming." *New York Post Daily Magazine,* April 7, 1944, 1.

Von Eschen, Penny. *Race against Empire: Black Americans and Anticolonialism, 1937–1957.* Ithaca, NY: Cornell University Press, 1997.

Washburn, Patrick S. *A Question of Sedition: The Federal Government's Investigation of the Black Press during World War II.* New York: Oxford University Press, 1986.

Watkins-Owens, Irma. *Blood Relations: Caribbean Immigrants and the Harlem Community, 1900–1930.* Bloomington: Indiana University Press, 1996.

"What Became of Roi Ottley?" *Sepia,* September 1960, 60.

Wilkins, Roy. "Lot of the Negro in Europe." *New York Herald-Tribune,* November 4, 1951.

Wolters, Raymond. *Negroes and the Great Depression: The Problem of Economic Recovery.* Westport, CT: Greenwood Publishing, 1970.

Woods, Jeff. *Black Struggle, Red Scare: Segregation and Anti-communism in the South.* Baton Rouge: Louisiana State University Press, 2003.

Index